Ellen Glasgow's American Dream

ELLEN GLASGOW'S
AMERICAN
by
DREAM
Joan Foster Santas

THE UNIVERSITY PRESS OF VIRGINIA   CHARLOTTESVILLE

ACKNOWLEDGMENTS

To Professors Robert H. Elias and William M. Sale, Jr., of Cornell University I am deeply grateful for sustained help and encouragement in preparing this book. Professors Francis E. Mineka and Walter J. Slatoff of Cornell and Luther Y. Gore of the University of Virginia also provided valuable suggestions and assistance during various stages of the manuscript. Miss Bette White of Waltham, Massachusetts, gave invaluable secretarial and research assistance. In particular, I wish to acknowledge the generosity of the Radcliffe Institute for Independent Study, whose scholarship grants for the academic years 1964–66 made possible both the time and the baby-sitting assistance I needed to prepare the manuscript. My deepest debt, of course, is to my longest-suffering supporter and all-around assistant, my husband.

J. F. S.

Wellesley Hills, Massachusetts
September 1965

TABLE OF CONTENTS

Ellen Glasgow's American Dream

INTRODUCTION

WE FIND IN A CERTAIN MEASURE, WHAT WE HAVE TO GIVE, IF NOT
WHAT WE SEEK, BOTH IN THE EXTERNAL WORLD ABOUT US AND IN
THE MORE SOLITARY LIFE OF THE MIND. — ELLEN GLASGOW

Ellen Glasgow devoted nearly half a century of novel writing to
exploring, through the changing values and dying traditions of the
South, the quality of our civilization. While centering her emphasis
on the shifting patterns of existence that confronted the Southerner
and, specifically, the Virginian, from 1850 to the threshold of
World War II, she strove always to illuminate what she believed
universal and enduring in human experience. The code of values she
affirmed may be traced as it emerges from her twenty volumes, at
first awkwardly, suffering the growing pains of youthful romantic
rebellion against "romance," and then sharply with the firm irony
characteristic of her best work.

From the earliest days of her literary career she deplored with
spirit the elegiac and provincial tones of Southern literature. She
says of the cultural climate which had surrounded her from childhood: "Our innocence may have been as real as our gentility; but
our sentimentality was so close to the skin that it would drip if it
were touched. Years later, when an interviewer asked me what I
thought the South needed most, I replied instantly, 'Blood and
irony.' "[1] Young Ellen Glasgow acknowledged her share of Southern innocence; she clung to her heritage of gentility even into
literary maturity, so strongly that Alfred Kazin felt justified in
asserting flatly, "She wrote like a dowager."[2] And not long after she

[1] Ellen Glasgow, *The Woman Within* (New York, 1954), p. 104.
[2] Alfred Kazin, *On Native Grounds* (New York, 1956), p. 191.

began what seemed to her a solitary revolt against the false, affected, and pretentious in Southern writing, she recognized that although she might be sickened by the "superficial picturesqueness" of local color artistry, whatever she achieved as a delineator of timeless character and lasting reality must arise from her understanding of and sympathy for the Southern heritage she criticized:

All America had dropped back into adolescence in fiction; but in the South there was not only adolescence to outgrow, there was an insidious sentimental tradition to live down. I had been brought up in the midst of it; I was a part of it, or it was a part of me: I had been born with an intimate feeling for the spirit of the past and the lingering poetry of time and place. Underneath my revolt there was, I believe, an uprising of that old hatred of inhumanity. I revolted from sentimentality, less because it was false than because it was cruel. An evasive idealism made people insensitive; it made people blind to what happened.[3]

Ellen Glasgow thought she knew the literary ingredients required to face up to both our past and our present. She was persuaded, she said, that nothing "unless it is a recovered faith in Santa Claus, could confer greater happiness on a liberated world than the miraculous resurrection of a sense of duty. In a sultry age, when we need the tonic of a bracing literature, character has become a lost quantity in fiction, and we miss the full, clear, commanding note of the disciplined mind."[4] A sense of duty, character, the commanding note of the disciplined mind—surely these were sententious phrases resurrected from the Victorian twilight sleep. If these dingy formulas were all that the diminutive Richmond spinster could offer as tonic to a terrorized world, little wonder her work might come to seem outmoded, preserved only in the sticky sweetness of lost regrets. But it is unjust to imagine that Ellen Glasgow would so misrepresent the modern need. The prescriptions are those of a woman who could point an accusing finger at dripping sentimentality and formalized illusions before she left

[3] *Woman Within*, p. 104.
[4] Ellen Glasgow, "Heroes and Monsters," *Saturday Review of Literature*, XII (May 4, 1935), 3.

her teens; this fiery advocate of blood and irony had more than dusty certainties in mind. If she thought that contemporary societies might profit from a few well-placed inhibitions, she also emphasized that "the world could do very well with fewer and better beliefs, and that a reasonable doubt is the safety valve of civilization."[5] She distrusted "not only rhetoric, but the heart of the world,"[6] and asserted stoutly, "Faith has its victories, but skepticism remains the only permanent basis of tolerance."[7]

What promise, then, did her literary creed hold for a world she viewed through the sardonic eyes of Henry Adams as a place no "sensitive and timid natures could regard without a shudder";[8] an existence in which the essential questions were always: "How can an oversensitive nature defend itself against the malice of life? How can one learn to endure the unendurable? Not the cruelty of civilization alone, but the cold, implacable inhumanity of the universe?"[9]

In the face of such bleak if genuine despair, the point of view she adopted in her novels sometimes appeared to offer very little that might be called positive. As Henry Seidel Canby noted:

The tragedy which stirs Miss Glasgow's imagination is not eccentric, nor entirely unhappy. It is the tragedy of frustration—the waste of life through maladjustment of man to his environment, and environment to its men. It is the poignant tragedy of nobility cramped by prejudice, or of beauty gone wrong through inability to adjust to the real, or of a good philosophy without premises in existing experience.[10]

These were, truly enough, Ellen Glasgow's reechoing themes. But real tragedies, if not entirely unhappy, are grounded in the

[5] Ellen Glasgow, "What I Believe," *Nation*, CXXXVI (April 12, 1933), 404.
[6] "Ellen Glasgow," in *I Believe: The Personal Philosophies of Certain Eminent Men and Women of Our Time,* ed. Clifton Fadiman (New York: Copyright 1938, 1939, by Simon and Schuster) p. 105.
[7] *Ibid.,* p. 110.
[8] Ellen Glasgow, "One Way to Write Novels," *Saturday Review of Literature,* XI (December 8, 1934), 350.
[9] *Woman Within,* p. 168.
[10] Henry Seidel Canby, "Ellen Glasgow: Ironic Tragedian," *Saturday Review of Literature,* XVIII (September 10, 1938), 14.

unalterable, in the stern realms where fate is final and nothing might have been otherwise or may still remain to be done. Character, a sense of duty, and a disciplined mind avail in such atmospheres only to provide a graceful stance in the face of defeat and death. Was it only this forbidding if gallant grace that Ellen Glasgow proffered to her protagonists that they might "endure the unendurable," confront the "cold, implacable inhumanity of the universe"? This contention, shared by several critics, is affirmed strongly by Maxwell Geismar, who comments on *Barren Ground* (1925), the most celebrated of Ellen Glasgow's novels:

It was a chill, bleak moral universe of Glasgow's now, puritanical, austere, in the soft and festive country of the Virginia cavaliers, and this ground was almost too barren. The denial of human affection, however uncertain; the retreat into a compulsive design of work and achievement; the final goal of security with no personal commitments—this was a 'victory over life' that involved a repudiation of living. It was at best the cold triumph of the will, the compassion of the grave, a sterile compromise with pain that had become an end in itself. To include neither the heart's warmth nor the pleasure and comfort of the flesh—that may be the most durable form of existence, but then, is it, in the end, merely a matter of existing?[11]

Miss Glasgow herself insisted that her viewpoint never permitted a way of life that was "merely a matter of existing": "To me, the noblest passage in modern literature occurs in Santayana's *Winds of Doctrine:* 'Nothing can be meaner than the anxiety to live on, to live on anyhow and in any shape; a spirit with any honor is not willing to live except in its own way, and a spirit with any wisdom is not overeager to live at all.' "[12] Despite the sour note sung to wise spirits, Ellen Glasgow thought she perceived hope for the independent spirits of honor in the "slow and reluctant widening of the humane consciousness of mankind."[13] Something of worth, moreover, al-

[11] Maxwell Geismar, *Rebels and Ancestors* (Cambridge, Mass.: Houghton Mifflin Company, 1953), p. 260.
[12] *Woman Within,* p. 180.   [13] *A Certain Measure* (New York, 1943), p. 119.

ways remained to the individual consciousness as the foundation upon which modern man might make his stand.

I believe, as well, that on this long journey upward from lower forms man has collected a few sublime virtues, or, more accurately perhaps, a few ideas of sublime virtues, which he has called truth, justice, courage, loyalty, compassion. These ideas, and these ideas alone, seem to me to justify that blood-stained pilgrimage from the first cannibal feast, past the auto-de-fe of too much believing, to the moral and industrial crisis of the twentieth century.[14]

A handful of enduring ideas, then, elevated by common consent, formed for Ellen Glasgow a "moral order . . . not imposed by supernatural decree, but throughout the ages slowly evolving from the mind of man"[15] To these virtues as they were variously sustained in the minds and hearts of her protagonists, she devoted her novels, for she sought ever the approach to a "fairer order" and a "civilized world" which must lie "not without but within," since "the only way to make a civilized world is to begin and end with the civilizing of man."[16]

Certainly her goals and her creed were in one sense distinguished only by obvious dedication to the commonplace; moralistic platitudes, however unavoidable, cannot be caroled unaccompanied by the hollow ring of all clichés. Yet the controlling illumination of Miss Glasgow's central commitment shed a curious light on these convictions and lifted her work to a unique sphere. "I believe," she declared, "not in the Good alone, but in the good life which Spinoza called blessedness."[17] And, " 'Blessedness,' Spinoza has said in one of my favorite passages, 'is not the reward of virtue, but virtue itself.' "[18] That is what she said. What she meant was that she believed very literally in the possibility of and the necessity for a society of blessed individuals, a blessed community led by those who understand that blessedness is based on what they know to be

---

[14] "What I Believe," p. 406.   [15] Fadiman, p. 107.   [16] *Ibid.*, pp. 107–08.
[17] *Ibid.*, p. 110.   [18] *Ibid.*, p. 108.

virtue. This ideal which Ellen Glasgow pursues throughout her novels owes more to her interpretation of the enduring values of the Southern dream than it does to her understanding of Spinoza.

It is easy to see how the paramount importance of order, design, and a fixed concept of virtue in Spinoza's ethics appealed to her. Be that as it may, Miss Glasgow's ideas of human perfectibility derive from what has been called the mind of the South rather than from Spinoza's "mind of God." Indeed, with a novelist of Ellen Glasgow's somewhat strained sensibilities, the notion that her ideal emerged from intellectual rather than emotional convictions seems the area to be defended. Nonetheless, only a tough and critical core at the heart of her undeniably supersensitive reactions to cruelty and suffering could account for Ellen Glasgow's desire to seek out "hard truth" and "intellectual fortitude." For her emotional nature was strong, often not only feminine but purely female; the sympathy she insisted upon extending to all animate creatures, unfortunately within as well as without her creative work, made her sound at times like an incensed benefactress of the SPCA, which indeed she was. But chiefly she demanded an Absolute known of the reason; Pascal's God known of the heart was not sufficient. She placed her final faith in ideas, and she struggled always "to condense the results of experience and insight into a settled philosophy"—a paramount necessity since, "to the imaginative artist, emotions, and even ideas, may be inconsistent in relation to art, but the truths of philosophy must, in a certain measure, be confirmed by the intellect."[19]

Insistent as she was on a permanent "philosophy" that would stand close intellectual scrutiny, she intended that this philosophy should serve only as a frame for her view of human experience. It was to remain implicit in her novels—never to emerge as a series of formidable intonations hanging above the heads of her heroes, hopelessly detached from her narrative structure. Both her sense of craftsmanship and her temperament demanded this, for as she said

[19] *Certain Measure*, p. 153.

of Spinoza, "He may have been blessed, but he was not human."[20] The strength and shallowness of human beings, their foibles and atrocities as well as their triumphs of courage and virtue, must be her subject. Too much an artist every to rely on the ultimate rationality of individuals, she delighted in stinging with irony and stabbing with satire their most unlovely and ludicrous stances; she knew better than to expect from them the best behavior in any crisis. Still, laughter was always left, eternal laughter, the "ayrie spirit." "One could still laugh after one had finished with love."[21]

One preferred, of course, to love and honor the rare instances of genuine individual integrity one might find. Laughter was at best a negative, if useful, goad; at worst, a graceful admission of helplessness amid chaos. And so Ellen Glasgow came to adapt Spinoza's concept of blessedness as a guide to measure the lives of her protagonists—the blessedness that was never a reward of virtue, but virtue itself. Her adaptation was as complete as it was gradual, dominated always by her temperament and her heritage. Her devotion, however, to the ideal of blessedness was conscious and calculated from the beginning of her career. Indeed, dangerously so, for like many visionaries, her desire to propagate her faith exposed her to the temptation of the pulpit manner, a style she did not always avoid successfully. But from the beginning, with characteristic honesty and thoroughness, she attempted to apply her developing theories first to herself and her approach to her craft:

In seeking alike the known and the unknowable, I was trying to discover the laws of my own being, and to establish my own inner harmony. This, for a novelist of reality, remains, I think, the source of all indispensable knowledge: to order one's internal sphere, until the conflict of outward forms with the substance of personality may deepen the tone without impairing the design and proportion of a world the imagination reflects. . . . It is well, no doubt, that an artist should hold by a rational code; but it is even better, I believe, that he should have charted the obscure seas of his own consciousness, and that he should perceive clearly the distance

[20] *Woman Within*, p. 173.   [21] *Ibid.*, p. 177.

that divides the subject within from the nearer objects as well as
from the far perspective of the external world.[22]

These words were intended chiefly as a warning to herself against
excessive optimism about the "subject within." Ironically, she has
been accused of thoroughgoing skepticism combined with total
acceptance of the way things are, a position thought to deserve
criticism because her writing is always permeated with the terminology of conventional morality.[23] Yet throughout most of her career
she had to concentrate on giving the devil his due. For instinctively
she saw the realization of her blessed, orderly, well-designed paradise on earth as just out of reach—to be attained with relative ease if
one followed a few clear precepts. What she always had to guard
against was excessive irritation with, intolerance for, the deviations
and deviationists from her vision. This irritation, according to James
Branch Cabell, her lifelong friend and Richmond contemporary,
extended to include what she "esteemed to be the outrageous
unfairness of heaven in heaven's traffic with Ellen Glasgow"—a
temperamental reaction that might well account for the air of
unhappiness that broods over her autobiography, *The Woman
Within* (1954). Cabell, however, insists on disregarding this volume
altogether as a valid guide to interpreting either Ellen Glasgow's
temperament or her life: "I say merely that it is a book wherein
many matters in which I had a share, or about which I happened to
know personally, have been—whether in the behalf of kindliness or
of art or of pathos—so very freely recolored that I distrust the entire
book throughout as a factual record. I elect to applaud it rather as a
work of genius and as a volume well worthy of its writer."[24]

In any case her acceptance of actuality had its limits, limits all too

[22] Fadiman, p. 103.

[23] I have deliberately avoided conventional labels in alluding to both Miss
Glasgow's personal "philosophy" and her theory and practice of fiction because
both become distorted in any attempt to squeeze them into recognized categories.
For a reasonable discussion of the extent to which Miss Glasgow's art can be
classified according to any "ism" or related to the work of fellow novelists see
Frederick P. W. McDowell, *Ellen Glasgow and the Ironic Art of Fiction* (Madison,
Wis., 1960), pp. 19-24.

[24] James Branch Cabell, *As I Remember It* (New York, 1955), pp. 233, 217-18.

clear in her condemnation of the "monstrous creations" of writers like Faulkner and Hemingway. But fortunately she grew up in Virginia, where even her optimism could not fail to observe the tenacity of disorderly reality, to say nothing of formalized fantasy.

Our difficulty with Miss Glasgow's work arises almost always from her vision. Dangling in front of her protagonists, it is like the carrot enticing the donkey only in that, like the carrot, it is intended to keep the devotee moving. Otherwise the vision is disturbingly unlike any vegetable. That it is a cloudy symbol, external and almost alien to the sensibilities it directs, is bad enough, but there is also the problem of the source of the vision and its continued strength and meaning. Sensible reasons in plenty have been advanced to explain the origin and adhesive quality of the Southern legend—some of these even boast a factual basis. But despite the appeal of these reasons to Ellen Glasgow, her chief concern has always been with the legendary basis of the myth. What Miss Glasgow has tried to do throughout her novels is to show why this legend, in spite of its striking imperfections and malfunctions in practice, offers the best and most enduring vision and blueprint for human fulfillment that she knows. Above all, she lets us see why it is that, against the strongest odds, the misty vagaries of the American dream, Southern brand, continue to command loyalty. For we have known at least two other versions of the American dream: the New England or Puritan vision and the Western tycoon or Horatio Alger myth. Each of these dreams came equipped with its own distinctive morality and methodology. Only the Southern version was without a fatal flaw.

The main defect of the Puritan heaven speaks for itself; the heaven was not to be found in New England or anywhere on the continent; it was reserved for another place, deferred to another time—a non-American heaven where those who got in had to wait a lifetime for their pleasure. Besides, it was exclusive in principle, not merely in practice as the Southern and Western heavens turned out to be. And it was plagued with the doubly irritating notions of individual responsibility for imperfection and inability to overcome that imperfection. A freeborn American may stand for the notion that Adam sinned, that human beings are prone to sin, even that he is capable of sinning himself; he may accept the idea that he is born imperfect, though not the theory that he is born already a sinner; he will not agree that he cannot improve on Adam's mistakes. Admittedly, by the middle of the nineteenth century New England had eradicated most of these defects in its regional paradise with transcendental reforms. But while the transcendentalists reformed, they refused to conform—to agree on the community practices necessary for heaven. The Puritans had always insisted on individual salvation as heavily as they demanded individual sinners, but the community sat in judgment on the degree of sin or salvation. The heavenly communities of the transcendentalists never got off the ground because each man was allowed to decide not only the principles but even the daily diet necessary for salvation.

The Western tycoon or Horatio Alger vision is usually accepted as *the* American dream, probably because it has been seen in more areas and has persisted for a longer time than other visions. But it has always been a mirage for the majority. Founded like all American versions on religion or morality, its tenets were a mixture of Sunday school maxims and admonitions from Mother. These tenets stood up as long as they worked, but too often they did not. Either the young men who had abided by all of them failed to find fortune descending, which was decided betrayal, or those who got their reward found that, sooner or later in the process, they did something Mother would never have approved. The former cases were, of course, the most common, but the latter have always been the most discouraging. Apparently "good boys" never give up hope that fortune may still appear, but the lot of wealthy bad boys has always been a long and lonely lament for the faithful to sing; Christmas turkeys to the poor and private pensions to disabled retainers have always seemed inadequate to tidy up capitalist heavens; now even these individual redemptive gestures are out of fashion.

As it emerges from Ellen Glasgow's work the Southern dream

promises and provides more than either of its counterparts. Its goal of heaven on earth is far more pleasant and appealing than either the Puritanical eternity among the angels or the precarious temporal paradise of industrial power, perhaps the more so since it does not necessarily exclude either of the others. Its continually revised code of procedure demands possibly more careful and constant attention to more varieties of duty and responsibility than either of the other codes ever contemplated, but if it is more fixed, it is more encompassing and more free. Both of the other codes were developed for "classless" but limited societies; one had to be among the believers to be given space; unbelievers were fair game for hounding and banishment. The Southern code, of course, arose from the only approximation of an orthodox class structure of any proportion or permanence we have ever had. But the lagging pain of its revision indicates rather an overoptimistic belief in the endurance of the social structure than any abandonment of the dream. And even the strongest imperfections of the original code suggest overzealous attention to providing a space and sphere for every member of the society; a too rigid morality rather than neglect of morality.

Yet if it is comparatively easy to see how the code suffers from excessive ambition to fix and encompass its subjects, it is not so easy to see how it can be called free. Perhaps it cannot, for the freedom provided by the code is essentially negative, a freedom from exile by the society and deprivation of the dream. However popular this usage, it strains the meaning of freedom. But the negative freedom remains important as a distinctive Southern freedom: it is meant to take care of the failures and the sinners. For there are individual sinners in the would-be blessed communities Miss Glasgow depicts. What seems to be missing is individual sin and the individual blame that attends it. Individual actions may be labeled good or evil, but always the individuals themselves are seen merely as weak or strong. And it is up to the strong in the family or community to absorb and rectify the sins of the weak.

Perhaps because the sins of the weak seemed manifold to Ellen Glasgow, her conception of the ideal blessed community of her dreams took shape slowly in her novels. Her earliest works were "steeped in the mood of revolt." *The Descendant* (1897) and *Phases of an Inferior Planet* (1898), are amateur and adolescent novels of social protest cast in the "unfamiliar surroundings" of New York because the young author demanded rebels against her contemporary society, and she knew of no Virginian rebels. Still, her rebellion even in these early efforts was designed to point toward improving rather than abandoning the social order she knew best. With her third novel, *The Voice of the People* (1900), Ellen Glasgow "returned" to Virginia to initiate a long concentration on what was for her at the turn of the century a newly discovered "social revolution in the moment of triumph." It seemed the beginning of a way to recapture, to make viable once more the code of her ancestors. Recovery of the Southern dream became her central preoccupation. Through the career of Nicholas Burr, poor white and "civilized offspring" of his primitive predecessors in her first two novels, she sought to "render a permanent way in the flux and reflux of material disintegration."[25] Simultaneous with her awakening vision of a series of novels projecting a social history of Virginia dawned her first crude impressions of the power of individual character over social chaos.

Ellen Glasgow's mature formulation of her major theme did not appear until *Barren Ground* (1925). In almost a dozen novels, however, written during the quarter of a century between *The Voice of the People* and *Barren Ground*, she developed her concept of the vital principle needed for the survival of the dream—the hereditary "vein of iron" in individual character. She discovered hopeful signs both in her theory of the force of character and in its converse: the idea that in the disintegration of character lies "the beginning not the end of defeat." For decay discerned in a "weakening moral fibre . . . first revealed in the quick or slow decline of human relationships, and in the abrupt conversion to a trium-

---

[25] *Certain Measure*, p. 61. The remainder of the quotations in the Introduction are taken from *A Certain Measure*; page references to these quotations are given in parentheses within the text.

phant materialism" (252) meant to her a decay that might still be thwarted.

To rediscover the means of thwarting the plentiful signs of decay corrupting the contemporary Southern scene, she reached back to the first and most dramatic test of the Southern dream—the Civil War epoch. In *The Battle-Ground* (1902) she tried to uncover the distinctive and enduring elements of the Southern heritage. Tested and refined in battle, the South's vision of a blessed community on earth was to be perpetuated by the strongest devotees of that vision: those who had emerged from the chaos of the battleground with a new wisdom and a new courage.

Of her next novel, *The Deliverance* (1904), which dealt with the fate of the visionaries in the postwar era, she wrote: "In the character of Christopher Blake, I was trying to test the strength of hereditary fibre when it has been long subjected to the power of malignant circumstances" (34). Hereditary fibre proved strong and durable under Miss Glasgow's test, but hereditary illusions endured equally well. Laura Wilde in *The Wheel of Life* (1906) is made to reject these illusions by turning away from those who preserve them. Surrounded by disinherited Southerners drifting in aimless circles in the whirlpool existence of New York City, she awakens to the futility of attempting to hold unchanged the code of a vanished past. Refusing to surrender to the mockery the dispossessed make of their heritage, she strikes out on her own to work among the slum poor, hoping to perpetuate the genuine values of her heritage by serving those even more wholly dispossessed than her contemporary Southern expatriates. In *The Ancient Law* (1908) Miss Glasgow reinforces Laura Wilde's stand through the experience of Daniel Ordway, banker of good family who served a prison term for mishandling funds only to emerge from the prison house of his days with a renewed sense of responsibility cutting him off from the perverted traditions of his fellow aristocrats.

Yet increasingly, along with the strength conferred by adherence to the ideals of the true Southern heritage, Ellen Glasgow found herself forced to emphasize the obstacles to realizing their visions her heroes and heroines encountered in the Southern legend itself. Young aristocrats as dedicated to their ideals as Laura Wilde and Daniel Ordway appeared again in her works, but now they found allied against them the forces of contemporary chaos and past illusions. Indeed, David Blackburn of *The Builders* (1919), Virginia aristocrat whose political horizons and hopes are international, experiences a more final defeat through the insidious, perfect-mannered hypocrisy of his wife than he encounters amid the social confusions attendant on World War I. And young Stephen Culpepper, would-be champion of the needs of man in *One Man in His Time* (1922), finds the inherited illusions of his class more difficult to surmount than modern social dilemmas. Even the most nostalgic of Miss Glasgow's earlier novels, *Virginia* (1913), is dedicated to illuminating the inevitable defeat of the South's most lovingly cultivated illusions in a society governed by change.

But if she felt it necessary to deal a death blow to Southern fantasy, she found it even more imperative to shed light and hope on Southern glory—the genuine values behind the legendary vision guiding her South. In her most optimistic mood she created a counterpart for the defeated heroine of *Virginia*. Gabriella Carr of *Life and Gabriella* (1916) was a young woman of native energy and independence who had the good fortune to "discover her hidden strength and reach her true level of circumstances" (99). An incarnated spirit of the new South triumphantly wedded to the modern world, Gabriella, despite her creator's aspirations, appeared to make a forced marriage. And, even in that, her behavior was markedly exceptional.

Miss Glasgow grew slowly aware that her beloved "good families," the finest of "old stock," were helpless to recreate their vision unassisted. Too many lacked the will, and even when, as with Gabriella, the will survived, traditional ways could not. She turned more and more to the "good people" of the yeoman class and rising representatives of the "common man" to infuse new energy into her vision. New and old leaders of men were confronted with one another in Ellen Glasgow's transitional novels. The new leaders were, hopefully, to absorb from the old those elements of the tradition worth preserving. Occasionally they did, as in Ben Starr's chronicle, *The Romance of a Plain Man* (1909). But as novel succeeded novel, her treatment of the surviving remnants of Southern aristocracy in the modern world grew steadily more harsh.

All of those to the manner born in *The Miller of Old Church* (1911) preserved only the manner and, for the most part, relinquished even the pretense of noblesse oblige. Totally enervated and ineffectual, these aristocrats were set in sharp contrast to such new heroes as Abel Revercomb, who stood firm and invulnerable as one of Ellen Glasgow's noblest creations of the yeoman "good people" who rose to rebuild an honorable life out of the ruins of the South. Even the best of the old aristocracy who appeared in these novels semed helpless to act on their sense of responsibility for the affairs of their community. Characters such as Stephen Culpepper and his cousin, Corinna Page, of *One Man in His Time* (1922) could do no more than nurture their carefully cultivated instincts in private and lend powerless approval to the principles of rising new reformers like Virginia's Governor, Gideon Vetch—man of the people. And even Vetch, the last of Ellen Glasgow's political leaders, is, like her first public hero Nicholas Burr, a man of the people only in his origins. Like Burr he is devoted to ideals which please no faction, and like Burr he is murdered while interceding in factional strife. Clearly Ellen Glasgow had come to realize that neither the old aristocrats nor the new masses could be relied upon for recovery of the South's visionary Eden. Regretfully she concluded her search for public leaders as she had begun it—with the death of her hero at the hands of a mob and the death of her hopes that political leadership might recover the lost glory of her Virginians. In her future novels the Southern design for living was to be marked out by private citizens whose devotion to ideals was meant to enfold the community.

By the time Ellen Glasgow was ready to write *Barren Ground*, the first of her major creative efforts, the cluster of values she wished to emphasize, "the universal human chords beneath regional variations of character" (152–53), rose clear and sharp in her imagination. These values, as she conceived them, could conquer only through "the vital principle of survival" which "enabled races and individuals to withstand the destructive forces of nature and civilization" (169). She had labeled this vital principle the "vein of iron" in the individual consciousness. Possession of a vein of iron was to illuminate the character of Dorinda Oakley, heroine of *Barren Ground,* to show that a Dorinda Oakley exists "wherever the spirit of fortitude has triumphed over the sense of futility" (154). But the "implicit philosophy" of *Barren Ground* for Miss Glasgow remained to be summed up in a forbidding phrase: "one may learn to live, one may even learn to live gallantly, without delight" (155). The achievement sounds all too like one appealing only to a nihilist; the goal, if not a negation, a denial of life, is certainly repugnant at first sight. Who, after all, wants to live however gallantly without delight?

Regardless of these objections Ellen Glasgow insisted that Dorinda's was a triumphant victory over life; her vein of iron, emerging from "that deep instinct for survival," had "ceased to be a negative quality and had strengthened into a dynamic force." Hardened by adversity she might be; hard things were slow to decay. "And she would never lose her inner fidelity, that vital affirmation of life, I think, I feel, I am" (160). But this is a cryptic analysis, not altogether satisfactory as an affirmation of anything. Dorinda Oakley's character and achievement demand careful examination before either can be understood or judged clearly in the light of Ellen Glasgow's American dream.

The vital principle of survival—the "vein of iron"—also mystifies and confuses. It is clear that the phrase fascinated Miss Glasgow; she used it over and over, finally selecting it as the title of one of her books. Her protagonists stand or fall before life in the measure that they possess a vein of iron, for "character is fate," victory over circumstances is all, and to those in whom the vein of iron is lacking, there remains only the pity accorded the weak. How then do the select few in Miss Glasgow's novels come by a vein of iron in the first place and by what means, fair or foul, does it fail to appear or atrophy in so many of her characters? Apparently, to have or not to have a vein of iron is chiefly a matter of heritage.

"These people," she wrote of her Virginians, "were the remote shadows of a stalwart breed; they were direct descendants of the Scotch-Irish and the English conquerors of the wilderness" (156). Among most members of the aristocracy the native spirit of adventure had disintegrated into a "philosophy of heroic defeat"; among the "more backward rural group" the spirit of fortitude had degenerated into "moral inertia." But originally this culture had sprung from the oldest and strongest roots in the American soil. The ancestors of the present puny breed of men were intrepid pioneers, the lone hunters, the long fighters, battling ceaselessly against hostile circumstances with their only weapon—"some deep instinct for survival." This instinct was "the Virginian strain, the American fibre," presumably the mother lode of the vein of iron. Erosion, decay, a thick coating of mildewed illusions formed over a social structure as worn and barren as the Southern soil after the Civil War corroded that vein of iron until it rotted and crumbled to ineffectual dust in the consciousness of the modern majority. Their "vital energy" wasted away; "sterility, like an untamed evil, had sapped their power of renewal" (158).

Yet in a handful of men and women there survived a living germ of fortitude, which if strenuously nurtured through adversity, provided immunity from "the fatal germ of resignation," promised victory for the vein of iron. From among this handful, then, Ellen Glasgow selected her most staunch and stalwart heroes and heroines—those who carried the vein of iron triumphant into the future. From among the majority she chose many individuals to pity and few to censure. For if their weakness arose from a defective heritage, it was for her useless to condemn them. She saw the many as victims of confused emotions and overwhelming circumstances, pathetically unstable and unreasonable in their human bondage. She preferred the few who struggled toward blessedness and human freedom, and she never stopped hoping that they might take the many with them. Her concern over the increasing difficulty of that struggle in her contemporary South grew to dominate her last novels.

After *Barren Ground* she turned to the first of three comedies or tragicomedies placed in Queenborough, the "distilled essence" of all Virginia cities. A "perverse imp of humour" within her demanded laughter—"delicate laughter with ironic echoes." Ironic echoes because the little world of its own that became her Queenborough reflected also the mood and mental climate of the larger world in the postwar decade of the twenties: "Everywhere in the world outside old cultures were breaking up, codes were loosening, morals were declining and manners, another aspect of morality, were slipping away" (221). Yet always through the ironic laughter pervading these novels Ellen Glasgow's devotion to the continuity of the South's moral heritage shines forth. The disasters, comic and tragic, that beset those attempting to perpetuate that heritage in an antagonistic modern society were to preoccupy her for the rest of her literary career. But her emphasis lay always on the possibility, indeed, the promise, of realizing the Southern dream in an alien atmosphere.

The Romantic Comedians (1926), the first novel of the Queenborough trilogy, deals with the restlessness of a group of "happiness hunters," traveling relentlessly "on roads that are circular and lead back again to the beginning" (216). In Judge Honeywell, the principal figure and a composite portrait of the old school Virginia gentleman, Ellen Glasgow tried to isolate and observe not only the illusion of perpetual youth but "the universal hunger for a reality that is timeless" (223). At sixty-six, Judge Honeywell finds his only timeless reality in a fleeting instant of selflessness when he promises to divorce and provide for his twenty-three-year-old second wife who has run away with her lover after a few months of marriage to the Judge. The happiness he hoped to find with a lovely young wife, he discovers instead only in continued devotion to unattainable perfection, in continued practice for the millennium of the Southern Eden. As for Annabel, the lovely young wife who has fled with her lover, the judgment of the novel pronounced by the impartial observer, Mrs. Upchurch, is that her daughter must pay in future suffering for her flight. For Ellen Glasgow still insists that the young and strong of will and heart, however pragmatic their pursuit of happiness, are yet bound by the code of their fathers.

This conviction dominates *They Stooped to Folly* (1929), the second book in the trilogy of tragicomedies. But in this novel Miss Glasgow finally, grudgingly, concedes that the manners of the great tradition cannot be salvaged—a major concession since she had always held that manners and morality ought to be inseparable. More striking yet is her treatment of the inherited morality of the tradition here. She shows it surviving as a habit of mind in old and young alike rather than providing a patterned path to glory. This failure of purpose will never do for any American, especially a Southerner, for the point of the code, its very rigor and complexity, has always been meant to ensure the fruition of the dreamer's dreams. The iron-veined innocents of this novel test the code under the new freedom of the twenties, test it and find it wanting.

In *The Sheltered Life* (1932) Miss Glasgow acknowledges the final inadequacy of the inherited tradition for those preserved from experience and self-awareness by their patterned existence. Tragedy here is precipitated by innocence—the innocence of cultivated blindness to evil. And, most important, the great dream of the great tradition, the promise of a communal Eden on earth gained by careful attention to the inherited pattern has faded beyond recognition for the young. The world of *The Sheltered Life* is the prewar Queenborough of 1914, an autumnal world, dust-blown and fading, where two old families struggle alone to cover the gap between the old order and the new, struggle until the evil odor of their own inner decay rises to mingle with the chemical stench of the new Queenborough industries.

Still, however strong Ellen Glasgow's rejection of the old paths to glory in this work, her insistence on and hope for the discovery of new paths is equally determined. Her civilized old man, General Archbald, peacefully delivers his sense of responsibility for his world's perfection into the hands of the young, civilized John Welch. For if young John's outspoken certainty furnishes the General both amusement and apprehension, he is yet secure in the knowledge that John possesses both the moral indignation and the iron determination to continue the fight for the dream of perfection. The important consideration is that although the dream may have altered, it should not, it must not die. While the old myth has proved too strenuous for most, there must be somewhere, somehow, a fairer design for civilization—a design that can be realized.

But it is to those who believe parts of the traditional design for living still durable and, most particularly, to those in whom the pattern of the old dream still endures that Ellen Glasgow dedicates her final novels. In *Vein of Iron* (1935) and *In This Our Life* (1941), Miss Glasgow searches for and finds victories for the iron-veined individualists devoted to perfecting their ancestral dreams amid the modern chaos. Ada Fincastle, the heroine of *Vein of Iron*, is a Dorinda Oakley who leaves her narrow Shut-In Valley to carry on her family's heritage in the hostile city. Her reward for success in her endeavor is the return of her family to their manse in the valley to restore its ruins and weed its garden for the future of their heritage and the perpetuation of their dreams. But the iron-veined characters of *In This Our Life*, Roy Timberlake and her father, Asa, forge their uncertain victories and persistent dreams without reward from the heart of the city's hostility.

Asa Timberlake, a man overwhelmed and rendered powerless in a world without moorings, is a man still upright, holding to hope with no visible supports. He certainly lacks the daring heart, the brave impulses, the youthful determination to search on for perfection and happiness that spur young Ada Fincastle of *Vein of Iron* and his own daughter, Roy, to pit their heritage of strength to the end against soul-shattering obstacles. He has neither the protective naiveté of a Virginius Littlepage or a General Archbald nor even the protective metaphysics of a John Fincastle to shelter him from an environment in which both his convictions and his efforts no longer seem applicable.

Nevertheless, Asa's refusal to surrender his search to recover the lost certainty of his tradition symbolized for Ellen Glasgow "one of those rare defeats that are victories" (257). His vision of fulfillment might remain out of reach in the present, but there could be no future without the vision. *In This Our Life* came to a pause, not an end, and she planned to fill out the "unfinished destinies" of that work, to write of Timberlake's "hard-won freedom, and of its effect upon other lives, in a novel . . . already named *Beyond Defeat*" (264). This last work, completed in manuscript form, she did not publish, and, indeed, it may be argued that the most striking contribution of "Beyond Defeat" to Miss Glasgow's central thesis lies in its commitment to the necessity of rejecting both tradition and certainty in order to realize any vision of fulfillment, any portion of one's dreams. But she left behind her a lifetime of novels in which her main preoccupation had always been the creation of characters who were beyond defeat in their aspirations to recover the communal Eden of their heritage, the Eden that guided their visions. And she knew whereof she spoke when she said that her central theme lay in "the conflict of human beings with human nature, of civilization with biology"—a constant warfare, but a battle tragic "not in defeat, but in surrender" (250). For the promise of the Southern dream demanded unceasing effort; the practice for the new Eden a never-ending struggle against man's vagaries. But the fight to preserve any dream seems endless, and Ellen Glasgow's Southern Eden, like all American dreams, promised a glorious victory in a future meant to be very much present.

SO I DETERMINED THAT I WOULD WRITE, NOT MERELY ABOUT
SOUTHERN THEMES, BUT A WELL-ROUNDED SOCIAL RECORD OF
VIRGINIA FROM THE DECADE BEFORE THE CONFEDERACY DOWN TO
THE PERIOD IN WHICH I WAS THEN LIVING. —ELLEN GLASGOW

Above all dedicated to unveiling through her fiction those aspects of
individual character and consciousness invulnerable to time and
circumstance, Ellen Glasgow never swerved from this initial commitment. Yet she chose as the medium in which to accomplish her
purpose not merely the novel of manners but a literary chronicle of
manners. From 1899 until after World War I most of the novels she
published contributed directly to her developing pattern of a
complete social history of Virginia since the Civil War. Even those
works written during this time that did not purport to erect a
fictional framework on the historical background of a specific
period embraced one or more of the varied facets of Virginian
society. After the war epoch ended she felt she "had finished with
history," was able to "break fresh ground, and at least to lay the
foundations of a more permanent structure,"[1] but, in fact, her later
novels from *Barren Ground* to *In This Our Life* were also arranged
to fall within the broadened scope of her original historical design.

Perhaps if Miss Glasgow had been a British novelist her selection
of a social chronicle would not be especially noteworthy. The social
fabric of the English novel is traditionally as thick and rich as the
American material is thin, poor stuff. And whether the British
craftsman chooses to concentrate on the so-called novel of manners,
the novel of morals, or the artful mixture of a Jane Austen, a

[1] *Certain Measure*, p. 5.

Meredith, or a George Eliot, the world in which his characters live
and act has a concrete reality, a solidity of outline, in short, a clear
place and sphere for each of his figures to move about in. A
comparable achievement is usually held to be impossible for American novelists, who must, it appears, write in what amounts to a
relative social vacuum owing to the "fluidity" of our social structure. So it is that in view of America's fluid society, a history of
Virginian manners may well appear at first consideration a self-
defeating subject matter for a novelist like Ellen Glasgow, who
proposed to reveal "universal human chords."

True enough, two of Miss Glasgow's feminine contemporaries,
Edith Wharton and Willa Cather, projected their novels against
specific American cultural backgrounds, but both of them held the
societies, and hence the values they celebrated to be dying of the
traditional American malady of social mobility. Moreover, their
ranges tended to be narrow and limited; each concentrated her
major efforts on a more or less uniform "class" in a relatively small
area at a particular time in American history. And even William
Dean Howells, sometimes cited as Miss Glasgow's Northern counterpart, who purposefully selected representatives of many of the
fluid classes in our post-Civil War society to set in contact and
conflict with one another, was markedly unsteady when dealing
with the very rich or very poor under conditions he did not know
thoroughly. Most important, these novelists, however they might
differ in their sentiments about the past, were agreed that no past
could be recovered.

In the light of the difficulties attending Ellen Glasgow's hope to
illuminate the Southern dream for the future by rekindling the
Virginian past, a "well-rounded social record of Virginia" appears
at once a dangerously inaccessible and an absurd ambition. Dangerously inaccessible, obviously, because such a record would require
both a social structure sufficiently concrete and immobile to bear a
long-term examination, in itself an American rarity, and a broad yet
exact knowledge of the whole of that structure during the extensive
time span to be covered—a knowledge difficult to come by at best

but heretofore impossible for American novelists. An absurd ambition because, however irritated one might be with the persisting inanities of the Southern legend, one could scarcely hope to undermine an inherited mythology or a decayed code of manners by rewriting or re-creating the myth after one's own inclinations. Even the determination to attempt such a project casts a dubious shadow over the author's avowed interests. If she sincerely deplored the provincial and romantic nostalgia of the South, if she really wished to write of the universal and permanent, surely the better course was a departure from rather than a variation on the traditional historical romances which almost exclusively provided the South's scanty literary contribution.

Certainly Ellen Glasgow's chosen framework left her open to the charge that she was, after all, a victim of rather than a victor over the past of the South. And despite her many and repeated protests against the character of Southern fiction at the time she began to write, she often appeared, in the very midst of her objections, a lady who did protest too much:

It was not that I disliked legend. On the contrary, I still believe that a heroic legend is the noblest creation of man. But I believe also that legend to be a blessing must be re-created not in funeral wreathes, but in dynamic tradition, and in the living character of the race. I had grown up in the yet lingering fragrance of the old South; and I loved its imperishable charm, even while I revolted from its stranglehold on the intellect. Like the new South, I had inherited the tragic conflict of types.[2]

Captivation by the "imperishable charm" of the old South, however reluctant, clearly does not strengthen the likelihood that a fictional treatment of it will proceed on either an impartial or a penetrating basis. Both the absurdity and the danger of Miss Glasgow's goal seem only heightened by her fondness for phrases such as "heroic legend," "dynamic tradition," and "character of the race." For these phrases sound suspiciously like the cant of the myth-bound "aristocrats" she accused of denying reality in their persistent,

[2] *Ibid.*, p. 12.

though fading, tyranny over Southern life and attitudes. What could be more natural, after all, than that she should succumb to the "sanctified fallacies" of her surroundings—a young woman who grew up in the very midst of this feudal autocracy at Number 1, West Main Street, Richmond, Virginia, "in a charming society, where ideas were accepted as naturally as the universe or the weather."[3]

Yet Ellen Glasgow somehow achieved her social record with a scope and penetration rarely equalled in American letters. More significant still, she made the problem of Virginia in these novels serve as an enduring problem founded on individual integrity and force of character. Peculiarly enough, part of her ability to achieve a quality of permanence and an overarching importance through an historical approach may have stemmed from the very hidebound rigidity of the society she treated. The Virginia she knew best, the Virginia of her most authentic novels, comprised only a small but unique area of the "great South." Even W. J. Cash, who devotes much effort and emphasis in *The Mind of the South* to exposing the baselessness of the cavalier-colonial aristocracy thesis, says of Revolutionary Virginia:

Here, indeed, there was a genuine, if small, aristocracy. Here was all that in aftertime was to give color to the legend of the Old South. Here were silver and carriages and courtliness and manner. Here were great houses—not as great as we are sometimes told, but still great houses. . . . Here were names that were sometime to flash with swords and grow tall in thunder.[4]

And of those historians in our century who have devoted so much space and scholarship to assessing the exact origin and development of the concept of the Southern aristocrat, most have attempted to establish precisely what Cash concedes—the genuine nucleus from which the aristocratic legend arose. Indeed, orthodox historians differ from Cash and Ellen Glasgow on this point chiefly in their

[3] Kazin, *On Native Grounds*, p. 191.
[4] (Garden City: Alfred A. Knopf, Inc., 1941), p. 5.

more sanguine view of the genuine qualities of this aristocracy simply because their major emphasis is on what the aristocracy was and not, as with Cash and Miss Glasgow, on the ways in which aristocratic ideals became distorted.

Thomas Jefferson Wertenbaker in *Patrician and Plebeian in Virginia* argues ingeniously that the Virginian aristocracy established by the time of the American Revolution was a genuine, completely homegrown product of the plantation system, an aristocracy that developed its character, its code, and its ideals from the economic and political conditions confronting the Virginia planter. In *Virginia: A New Look at the Old Dominion* Marshall W. Fishwick speaks of Virginia's "unique rural aristocracy" developed in colonial days by settlers who had been for the most part "city-bred Englishmen, often in poor straits," planters who, if unable to claim aristocratic lineage, to make aristocracy an actuality in early Virginia, nonetheless took it as the ideal to be sought after, and in their search found "rare and fine things."[5]

Moreover, the pioneering work on the plantation legend in fact and fiction, Francis Pendleton Gaines' *The Southern Plantation: A Study in the Development and Accuracy of a Tradition* supports Cash by pointing out that the traditional social order beloved of the romances actually existed "in tide-water Virginia, in the rice districts of South Carolina, in the lower Mississippi Valley, and, to a smaller extent, in certain Piedmont sections."[6] And while he emphasized the frequently mentioned point that belief in the growing legend of the plantation aristocacy was of more compelling importance than the actual number of bona fide aristocrats who originally existed, Francis Butler Simkins in *A History of the South* asserts that Virginia was ever the model of the Southern elite, "the focal point on which they patterned their houses and their manner of life. It was not the Virginia of Richmond and other towns, but the Virginia of plantations, of manor houses, of a simple home life, of

[5] New York, 1959, pp. 32, 22.
[6] New York, 1925, p. 144.

courteous squires, and of Washingtons, Jeffersons, Randolphs, and Lees."[7]

Ellen Glasgow was not battling merely the facile illusions of Southern romanticism, then, when she chose to strike out against the stubbornly clinging fictions of Virginia's withered gentility. The distorted legends by which her contemporary Virginia elite blindly continued to abide had once had a basis in reality; the pale, ineffectual shadows who insisted that they descended, possessed of divine rights of leadership, from a courtly aristocracy might claim kinship with ghosts of the past who had once embodied a genuine nobility. Virginia could claim a real legend, a tradition, and a "race" stemming from Revolutionary times more sharply defined, more enduring, and more binding, perhaps, than those of any other section of our nation. Viewed in this light, Miss Glasgow's desire to resurrect the true values of this society begins to make sense. For here in Virginia's past lay the source of the vein of iron—the qualities of behavior and the code which might restore the dynamic force to a tradition well worth preserving, might bring back the "living character" to the race.

But what of her treatment of the race itself? Surely her achievement here depended on the breadth of scope and the sensitivity she could command when dealing with Virginia's classed society. Again the fact that Virginia actually had a more or less stable class structure was an advantage. Above all, however, she succeeded through her own ability to see beyond the artificial atmosphere created by the minority who composed the privileged society surrounding her. She perceived, it would seem intuitively, that the vein of iron existed in more Virginians than the handful of gentlemen adventurers who contributed color and, too often, false glamour to the legend of the South. She saw that it was, in fact, the natural birthright of the more enterprising yeomen farmers and backwoodsmen. In these individuals, often misleadingly classified under the collective label, "poor whites," she found the determina-

[7] New York, 1953, p. 151.

tion and ambition to conquer life on its own terms most characteristic of the heirs to the vein of iron.

Of course it may seem only natural that this should have been the case. Miss Glasgow's concept is one derived from the qualities associated with the pioneer and frontiersman—qualities commonly attributed to our more presentable specimens of wilderness conquerers from New England to the far West. And, as Cash points out, Virginia emerged much as New England began: "from a primitive backwoods community, made up primarily of farmers and laborers." The few existent gentlemen languished at the expense of the enterprising former redemptioners and servants unless they possessed a comparable stamina, for this land, like most sections of our country, "had to be wrested from the forest and the intractable red man."[8] Actually, Ellen Glasgow's insight into this matter, an insight developed in her novels as early as the turn of the century, approaches the extraordinary for one of her milieu. C. Vann Woodward, who sees her as "the forerunner of a new age in the South," expresses most strongly the enigma surrounding the origin of her convictions:

The standard of revolt was lifted in a Richmond rose garden of the nineties, and the bearer was neither beachcomber nor jail bird, but the sheltered daughter of an aristocratic Victorian home. The rebellion of Ellen Glasgow can, as yet, only be recorded, not explained, for of all the strange mutations in this age of the South's transition hers was the most unaccountable.[9]

Not that there was no fictional precedent at least for her intuition. William R. Taylor in his very valuable *Cavalier and Yankee: The*

[8] Cash, p. 6. The overwhelming proportion of former servants and small freeholders among those doing the wresting is made clear by T. J. Wertenbaker: "In conclusion it may be said that in the first fifty years of the colony's existence conditions were very favorable for the graduation of the servant into the class of small freeholders, that the records amply prove that many succeeded in doing so, but that at this period a fair proportion of free immigrants also came to the colony. Before the expiration of the Commonwealth period was formed from these two sources, perhaps in not unequal proportions, a vigorous, intelligent, independent yeomanry, comprising fully 90 percent of all the landowners" (*The Planters of Colonial Virginia* [Princeton, 1922], p. 83).

[9] *Origins of the New South, 1877-1913* (Baton Rouge, 1951), p. 434.

Origins of the Old South as a Cultural Ideal shows that, contrary to the popular conception of the typical plantation novel as a sustained celebration of the aristocratic qualities of the gentleman planter, a conception, incidentally, shared by Miss Glasgow, the "commoner and the genteel half-breed" received much attention in novels written by Virginia and seaboard authors in the generation preceding the outbreak of the Civil War. Taylor concludes that "the gentleman planter . . . became less a cultural ideal than a touchstone against which the emerging stock could measure its historical credentials, its vitality, and its promise. The result of this fictive introspection was a virtual revolution within the social world of the novel, a near overturning of the social order on the legendary plantation and the emergence of the Scotch-Irish yeoman as a chivalric hero second to none."[10] He is referring specifically, however, to such novels and characters as William Caruthers' *The Cavaliers of Virginia or A Recluse of Jamestown: An Historical Romance of the Old Dominion* (New York, 1834), with its portrait of Nathaniel Bacon; John Pendleton Kennedy's *Horse-Shoe Robinson* (New York, 1835) which has as its hero a Scotch-Irish yeoman of the South's new immigrant population; Beverley Tucker's Virginia mountaineer, the Black Dutchman, John Keizer in *George Balcombe* (New York, 1836) or his Christian Witt of *The Partisan Leader* (Washington, 1836).

The writers of the Southern literary revival of the eighties, with whose work Ellen Glasgow was doubtless most familiar, Taylor does not number in this group. Listing these writers as George Washington Cable, Joel Chandler Harris, Thomas Nelson Page, and James Lane Allen, C. Vann Woodward dismisses them with the blanket assertion: "Among them, however, one will search in vain for a realistic portrayal of their own times."[11]

What is more, as late as 1941 Cash could still point out that by popular doctrine supported by "practically all the standard histories of the United States" the great, confused mass of so-called poor

[10] New York, 1961, p. 178.
[11] *Origins of the New South*, p. 168.

white Southerners were yet held to have descended from the congenitally inferior stock of the Southern farmers and backwoodsmen. This breed was considered so uniformly shiftless and criminal "that these characters, being inherent in the germ plasm, were handed on to their progeny, with the result that the whole body of them continually sank lower and lower in the social scale."[12] A naive and even preposterous notion, perhaps, in view of the fact that most regions of our nation were first settled by men of comparable background. But it is a curiously compelling and persistent idea, nonetheless, and one still important because it is deeply entrenched in Southern legend.

Its significance for the South and more particularly for the social pattern of Ellen Glasgow's novels lies in the fact that the "aristocracy" and the masses alike have accepted its widespread truth. The form in which this concept of class superiority and inferiority imposed itself was, however, a positive expression of the degrees of honor and responsibility due from representatives of various social positions. In the minds and hearts of the new cotton planters, this positive attitude toward the consequences of their class superiority assumed forms as naive, preposterous, and influential as their notions of class inferiority. In short, the power of positive wishful thinking became at least as pervasive and compelling as its negative counterpart.

But the picture of the new planters in *The Mind of the South* which has them zealously wielding the ideals of aristocratic probity and *noblesse* almost in the same manner and at the same time that they wielded their axes to clear the frontier lands they had seized is only the first in a series of acid dipped sketches. The next scene illuminates the quick propagation of the new faith among both the planters and the masses about them. As for the planters: "No group of people anywhere, indeed, ever more constantly represented to themselves and to the world that they were absolutely under the domination of these ideas and the Christian virtues, to which they

[12] Cash, p. 6.

wedded them."[13] The masses not only accepted these planters as paradigms of honor and social responsibility, they began to accept honor and responsibility as their own highest aspirations. And just as this scene begins to look dangerously crowded or at least top-heavy with professing aristocrats, Cash presents the picture of a postwar South in which military discipline has preserved the hier-archy on which aristocratic paternalism depends:

Moreover, and for all the genial looseness which indubitably had characterized it, military discipline had done its work here as every-where. Upon the common fellow the habits of following and of obedience were far more deeply engraved than they had been before. . . . In these four years there had begun to grow up in him some palpable feeling . . . of the *right* of his captains, of the master class, to ordain and command.

The captains themselves, of course, having intimately observed the commoner, were now convinced that he was essentially an irrespon-sible child who must be directed. "And, as the issue of it," these captains "were decidedly more imbued with the imperious convic-tion of their own right, and not only their right, but their duty, to tell the masses what to think and do."[14]

So it is that we have unveiled for us the picture of the South "like nothing so much as a veteran army" for a generation following the war. Of course this strange overlay on the surface of the Southern

---

[13] *Ibid.*, p. 74.

[14] *Ibid.*, p. 111–12. Stark Young, commenting on the persistence of this attitude and point of view "induced by the Southern way of life," not only defines the aristocratic view as implying "a certain long responsibility for others; a habit of domination; a certain arbitrariness," but indicates wryly that half of the virtue attributed to and deference accorded aristocratic leadership arose from the high-handed manner in which the aristocracy assumed and carried out their roles: "Undoubtedly [the aristocratic manner] had to do with a certain fineness of feeling, an indefinable code for yourself and others, and a certain continuity of outlook; but what it inherently implied was something like that which Lord Melbourne, the celebrated minister to Queen Victoria, meant, when he observed that, of all the coveted orders in England, the one he admired most was that of the Garter—'there was no damn merit about it'" ("Not in Memoriam but in Defense," in John Crowe Ransom *et al., I'll Take My Stand: The South and the Agrarian Tradition* [New York, 1951], pp. 349–50).

frontier tradition, composed as it was of the back-country independence common to most sections of the country, had to be
squared with that individualism. Cash resolves the contradiction in
this way:

The common Southerner's growth in the sense of the right of his
captains to prescribe the public course was possible, in the last analysis, only because their prescriptions, never, until the nineties at least,
crossed his ego; because it never entered his head that they might
conceivably run counter to his aims and desires. More accurately
still, it was possible only because, like every other good Southerner,
he so absolutely identified his ego with the thing called the South
as to become, so to say, a perambulating South in little, and hence
found in the prescriptions of his captains great expansion for his
ego—associated the authority yielded the master class not with any
diminution of his individuality, but with its fullest development
and expression.[15]

Miss Glasgow undertook her literary career in the nineties at the
very time when paternalism did begin to cross the ego of the
yeoman and backwoodsman, when decay began to manifest itself
among "these long-realized aristocrats," the Virginians, a decay
arriving "not so much through any even partial surrender to the
demands made upon them as through the inevitable consequences of
their failure and their refusal thus to surrender."[16] Perhaps the clue to
Ellen Glasgow's perceptive genius can be found in her focusing
at this point on "a newly discovered social revolution in the moment
of triumph." For she saw emerging from this period of moral, social,
and economic disintegration in Virginia and, indeed, the entire
South, a few Virginians of all classes who dedicated themselves to
the extension of their long-standing notions of *noblesse* and integrity despite the chaos of the moment.

These individuals she re-created in her novels as the iron-veined
heroes and heroines of the post-Civil War South, emphasizing
always the unique factor in their Virginian heritage which simultaneously set them apart from their fellow pioneer-individualists in
other parts of America and accorded them universal stature: a

[15] *Ibid.*, p. 113.   [16] *Ibid.*, p. 154.

consciousness that worth might be measured in terms of obligation. The obligation was to images of the past—not so much to the amorphous mass known as "society," but rather obligation to "stand for" certain principles and to prove oneself in terms of those principles. The obligation was to oneself first and last and to the world only incidentally.

That a social revolution of sorts began in the South during this period no historian would deny. But from the beginning of her career Miss Glasgow was as selective in characterizing this revolution as she was in choosing the revolutionaries that interested her. C. Vann Woodward concedes an element of "moral regeneration" in the Southern atmosphere during this period and describes the philanthropic crusades of the period as animated by a mixture of paternalism and *noblesse oblige*—"the most authentic heritage the dominant middle class got from the old ruling class."[17] He also emphasizes, however, the importance of the essentially "immoral" ingredients that also figured in this revolution: the influence of Northern capital which began to flow into the South at this time, capital that led to Southern industrialization and the rise of business and political leaders whose perversions of the very legend of the old South they popularized Miss Glasgow was to find an increasing danger to the triumph of the revolution she had in mind.

Understandably enough her disgust with the evasions of Southern life and literature led her initially to attempt portraits of sturdy-fibered rebels cut loose from their enervating environmental ties with the South, but never from their Southern heritage. The two pairs of heroes and heroines who dominate her first and second novels merely move to New York in order to assert themselves. In fact the strongest and perhaps best of the lot, Anthony Algarcife of *Phases of an Inferior Planet* (1898), left his birthplace in childhood when as an orphan he was given into the protection of an Anglican clergyman. And if it is difficult to see how he might be counted a Southerner at all in this case, whatever his origins, he nonetheless envisions retreat to a Southern farm with his wife as his "second

[17] *Origins of the New South*, p. 401.

chance" to find heaven on earth—much as Nick Carraway of *The Great Gatsby* regards the Midwest as his land of last resort. For Ellen Glasgow, whether consciously or not, looked on the Southern heritage as bred in blood and bone, as a pattern of values inherited along with physical traits, values never surrendered, however betrayed. Miss Glasgow, moreover, was actually quite in line with an established, if not then recognized, Southern literary tradition in giving all her early heroes obscure or dubious backgrounds. As William R. Taylor reveals, the "effective characters," even though they are not the designated heroes of pre-Civil War romances, "are apt to be 'orphans' . . . or men of mixed, unknown or unspecified ancestry, or even yeomen of Scotch-Irish or German ancestry from the South's 'new' immigration."[18]

Admittedly, Algarcife does not make the most of either his instincts or his rebellion against the false and distorted concepts by which men, and especially Southerners, cheat reality. Almost a ridiculous caricature of the fair-minded individual, he dedicates himself repeatedly to high purposes and higher sacrifices only to find himself always assailed by circumstances or by doubts about the worth of his pursuits. He insists during his college years upon writing on both sides of every question, and we leave him in his maturity an Anglican priest refuting his own sermons anonymously in a journal called *Scientific Weekly*. Yet if he serves unwittingly as a symbol of Miss Glasgow's own early bewilderment over the nature and purpose of her revolt from the South, he may also stand as the prototype of many of his fellow sufferers in her novels.

Algarcife differs, however, from Michael Akershem, the young revolutionary of her first anonymously published novel, *The Descendant* (1897), in one important respect—his origin. While Akershem forces his way to prominence from a background of feeding hogs as a bastard orphan in Plaguesville, Virginia, Algarcife's childhood memories hold shadowed glimpses of an aristocratic mother who read Victor Hugo from an invalid's couch and caressed his

[18] *Cavalier and Yankee*, p. 154.

brow with the approved slender, blue-veined hands of the Southern lady. And origins, pretty versus ugly images, we feel uncomfortably, make all the difference in these first two novels. Only in Henry James' work do we find characters who suffer as acutely as Miss Glasgow's from sordid surroundings.

If it is appropriate that Algarcife should devote his youth to a treatise on "Transmission of Acquired Characteristics," it is equally significant that Akershem should expend his energies as volcanic editor of the revolutionary *Iconoclast* in lashing out against the social customs and institutions that his bastard birth violated. It is clear that the contemptuous scorn and neglect meted out to him from the upholders of custom and ceremony motivate Akershem's outbursts rather than any abiding feeling of kinship with the downtrodden and outcast. His actions, ambitions, deepest longings mirror in retrospect only the fevered hungering after and savage pursuit of respectability found in Faulkner's Snopeses.

John Driscoll, his "civilized" mentor, sees in Akershem "not the man revolting against the system, but the abnormal development revolting against the normal," beholds in him "an expression of the old savage type beaten out by civilization, and yet recurring here and there in the history of the race to wage the old savage war against society."[19] Poor Michael is both too much and too little a revolutionary, and the world can afford neither to ignore nor to accept him. Characteristically he meets his nemesis when in a fit of rage he kills a fellow journalist who questions the integrity of his desperate attempt to establish himself as a respectable citizen. Broken and remorseful, the young savage is left to decay in prison until he emerges a wasted and whining specter who sees himself "a cur that the stones of mankind have beaten to death."[20] But while his savagery and dramatic downfall may serve to establish only the strength of young Ellen Glasgow's romantic imagination, his ambitions and his career are nonetheless significant.

Michael Akershem as a primitive rages loudest to be permitted

[19] Ellen Glasgow, *The Descendant* (New York, 1897), p. 246.   [20] *Ibid.*, p. 275.

recognition and admiration as a human being of worth; if he is abnormal, his abnormality is chiefly a matter of the sustained vigor he exercises in his efforts to find a place for himself and his kind in civilized society. He is a bogus savage most eager to be tamed. To the degree that we suspect his creator of showing that, given legitimate birth and a thoroughbred ancestry, Akershem would have had little cause to revolt, his revolutionary role remains dull. Instead, his initial effort to remold social institutions, his final would-be capitulation to conventions, and his abiding shame over the irregularities of his own origin represent a singularly overpowering need to cast himself in a secure and well-thought-of social role. More shallow than his "fine upstanding" counterpart, Algarcife, and therefore less pitiable in his failure, he questions less often and demands much less.

Young Akershem wants essentially the identical splendor that Carrie Meeber sees behind the wall of wealth, the prestige of aristocratic largess Gatsby seeks. But despite his expensive tastes and instinctive recoil from squalor, he never imagines that money can achieve his desire. And herein lies the basic difference between the Northern naif and the Southern innocent of Miss Glasgow's novels. If Michael's career stands for anything, it signifies not the need to overthrow the standards and patterns of existence which compose the ideals of Southern tradition both for him and his creator, but rather the necessity to lower the barriers separating class from class. In short, Ellen Glasgow is pleading only that the poor white trash be given a chance to measure up to their superiors. For Akershem as she draws him is undermined both by his conviction of his own inferiority and by the reality of inferiority that accompanies substituting a "sense of gratitude" for a "sense of duty." Yet, she implies, if his vigor and vitality had been given scope, who knows what nobility might have emerged. "Yes, he wanted the opportunities that men open only to men who are like themselves. He wanted his reputation repaired. What an excellent thing it was that one had the power to repair one's reputation!"[21] It was Michael's pathetic

[21] *Ibid.*, pp. 234–35.

misjudgment of his own power, or that of any man to repair "reputation," that finally destroyed him.

Ellen Glasgow's purpose was to repair the inevitability of such misjudgment. It is clear that even in *The Descendant*, published anonymously when she was twenty-four, her "revolt" took the form of a "conserving revolution," a pattern she was to retain to the last. As Shields McIlwaine observes: "Miss Glasgow has never been interested in the Virginia poor-white for himself; . . . she is concerned incidentally with the lower or primitive levels of folk only as they represent a relation to or progress toward the goal of all society: a culture of social justice and gentle living."[22]

To the potentialities of nobility and justice existing in Southerners of the "lower class," Miss Glasgow next turned her attention. Furthering the breakdown of class barriers in the post-Civil War South apparently seemed sufficiently revolutionary to satisfy her rebellious tendencies and at the same time allowed her to define what the Southerner ought to be attempting in order to carry on his heritage. Greeting the twentieth century with her third novel, significantly titled *The Voice of the People* (1900), she chose as her hero a second poor white farm boy. Nicholas Burr, however, differs from Michael Akershem in several important respects. The legitimate son of toil-ridden parents bound soul and spirit to the meager soil that enslaves them, he nonetheless descends from sturdy stock. His forbears number at least one would-be scholar whom Nick envisions as "a man with a great brow and a twisted back, with brawny, knotted hands—an unlearned student driving the plough, an ignorant philosopher dragging the mire."[23]

This romantically conceived ancestor failed to break away from his plough even as Akershem failed ultimately to rise above his deficiencies, but Nicholas, through a better-directed and less egocentric determination, goes far. As fiercely proud, independent, and

---

[22] *The Southern Poor-White from Lubberland to Tobacco Road* (Norman, Okla., 1939), p. 185.

[23] Ellen Glasgow, *The Voice of the People* (New York, 1900). Page references to future quotations from this novel in Chap. 1 are given in parentheses or brackets after the quotations.

overconscious of his "low origins" as the young editor, Nicholas Burr shares the "primitive" impulses that caused Akershem to strike out against all opposition and finally to destroy himself. Burr, too, meets his end in "a blind fight for he cared not what," as "the old savage instinct blazed within him—the instinct to do battle to death—to throttle with his single hand the odds that opposed" (441). But Burr dies a hero, for his "red rage" consumes him at the sight of a lynch mob defying the law he defends in an attempt to murder a helpless, if guilty, Negro. Kingsborough, Virginia,[24] and its best elements have cultivated his instincts far beyond the distorted ideals that Plaguesville and New York developed in Michael Akershem. Nicholas has learned to be a primitive only when it is proper.

In Nick's childhood, Judge Bassett, "secure in the affability of one who is not only a judge of men but a Basset of Virginia"(4), overcomes the opposition of Mrs. Jane Webb, paradigm of Southern prejudice and virtue, to allow young Burr to be educated "above his station" with his own son and hers. Judge Bassett represents the best qualities of the aristocracy whom the war left unchanged as Mrs. Webb represents the worst. But the Judge's gesture of generosity in admitting Nicholas to his school is presented as one grounded in kindly, determinedly fair-minded paternalism rather than as a concession to the realities of the new order or the New South. Indeed, he is uncomfortable at gaining a victory over Mrs. Webb because it violates his sense of the proper respect and deference that ought to be accorded a Southern woman, and he feels that he has somehow taken advantage of her and betrayed his

[24] Old Williamsburg served as the model for Miss Glasgow's Kingsborough, a model that she took care to transcribe with great fidelity to minute details according to her observation in *A Certain Measure*, pp. 61–63. She relates as well her precision in copying the externals of the Richmond of her youth that serve as the background of the latter part of the book and her attempt to describe "without exaggeration" the Democratic State Convention in Roanoke into which she had been smuggled in 1897. But as proud as she was in her youth of her efforts to reproduce external verisimilitude" which seemed to her evidence of her alienation from romanticism, she came to realize in her maturity that "sound psychology" was more important than "accurate geography" (*Certain Measure*, p. 213).

loyalty to what she stands for. He and his confrere, General Battle are, like Mrs. Webb, influential only as private leaders representing the standards of their "class." Their sons may "adjust" to the new order by involving themselves in politics; they do not. General Battle shows his refusal to reconstruct his society in the smallest particular when he insists on restricting all conversation with Nicholas to discussion of crops, which are for him their only conceivable common interest. Judge Bassett reveals awareness of political concerns only when, from the standpoint of a Virginia Funder convinced that Virginians are bound by "honor" to repay their war debts in full, he condemns the Readjusters in the revised version of the novel. His attack was upon "Mahonism" in the original version (316). As McDowell points out, the revision is more appropriate in illuminating the Judge's principles, but the original seems rather more faithful to the Judge's autocratic abhorrence of individuals capable of the political tactics that characterized the flamboyant leader of the Readjusters, William H. Mahone.

Although the representatives of the antebellum plantation aristocracy personified in Mrs. Webb, General Battle, and the Judge do their best to make Nicholas realize in his childhood the difficulties that will confront a young man "in his position," that position is clarified for him only in his young manhood. For a while he endures the usual hardships associated with poverty in securing his education, it is not until he confronts squarely "the shade that had arisen from the gigantic gulf between separate classes" (252) that he realizes how long, how difficult, how lonely his battle must be.

His enlightenment emerges from an incident involving a ruined Kingsborough maiden. Rumor charges Nick with the guilt, and his childhood classmate and love, Eugenia Battle, daughter of the General, implores his denial on the grounds that even Bernard, her brother and his friend, believes him responsible. Infuriated by Eugenia's failure of trust and aware of Bernard's own guilt and cowardly evasion, Nicholas Burr storms off in true melodramatic grandeur, cursing Bernard roundly and bitterly casting off Eugenia for her suspicions. Curiously enough, given that our sympathy for

Nicholas is supposed to remain steadfast, it is Eugenia who first realizes and then justifies the finality of their differences:

The pride of Nicholas was not individual, but typical—the pride of caste, and it was against this that she had sinned—not in distrusting his honour, but in offending it. It was in the clash of class, after all, that their theories had crumbled. He might come back to her again—she might go forth to meet him—but the bloom had gone from their dreams—in the reunion she saw neither permanence nor abiding. The strongest of her instincts—the one that made for the blood she bore—had quivered beneath the onslaught of his accusation, but had not bent. Wherever and whenever the struggle came she stood, as the Battles had always stood, for the clan. Be it right or wrong, true or false, it was hers and she was on its side [252].

Ellen Glasgow never suggests that Eugenia's determination to cling "to that unswerving instinct which had united individual to individual and generation to generation" (254) lacks nobility. She does insist, however, that Eugenia Battle's loyalty, if not misplaced, is misapplied, for the South has too long used its gracious ladies to protect the sins of its worthless scamps. Years later when Eugenia admonishes Bernard's long-deserted wife for failing to greet with delight his anticipated state's pardon for manipulating funds and his consequent impending return, Bernard's wife is made to reply: "Oh, but I'm not a Battle. . . . Battle sins are just like other people's sins to me" (372). And while Eugenia responds with irritable wonder "that a Battle should have married a woman who did not know how to behave in a crisis," Miss Glasgow comments wryly, "The loyalty of the Battle wives had been as a lasting memorial to the Battle breeding—which, after all, was more invincible than the Battle virtue" (373).

The limiting strengths by which Eugenia is irrevocably bound have cut off the possibility of a life of shared understanding with a Nick Burr. Clearly, if Ellen Glasgow can conceive of love and even of admiration between the best specimens of two Southern classes this early in her career, she cannot yet imagine that they might live together successfully. Separately, she allows them each a fairly fruitful and contented existence. As the wife of Dudley Webb, a persuasive and charming politician, Southern style, Eugenia fits well her role as a decorative and useful accessory to Dudley's ambitions.

Her affection for Dudley had grown so into her nature that it was like the claim of kinship—quiet, unimpassioned, full of service —the love that is the end of many happy marriages, the beginning of few. . . .
She made the best of her life today, as she would have made the best of blows and bruises. It was the old buoyant instinct of the Battle blood—the fighting of Fate on its ground with its own weapons. She had insisted strenuously upon her own happiness—and she had found it not in the great things of life, but in the little ones. She was happy because happiness is ours in the cradle or not at all —because it is of the blood and not of the environment [382].

Nick Burr's achievement is for Ellen Glasgow also a matter of blood rather than environment—even though his blood is of a type incompatible with the Battle group, even though it needed the fortification of Battle training to triumph. Yet Nick, with a misguided idealism no Battle would ever entertain, never stops trying to perfect the Virginian masses by decree. He achieves distinction in the political arena, but he does so in the manner of a Southern Abe Lincoln rather than with the easy geniality and empty, if impressive, oratory of a Dudley Webb. Winning the Democratic nomination for Governor of Virginia over Webb and other candidates by his sheer honesty which is illuminated during a forthright defense of his opponent, Webb, against a charge of lobbying, he succeeds as a matter of course to the governorship. But while he insists on abiding by his convictions, however unpopular, and on appointing the most qualified men to official posts, whether or not he has their political support, his chief adviser among the Southern gentry points out the folly of Burr's actions: "My dear governor, you are the one great man in State politics, but that unimportant fact would not have landed you into your present seat had not the little revivalistic episode befuddled the brains of the convention" (330). And to

Burr's wistful assertion that he has, after all, "the confidence of the people," his adviser retorts:

The people! How long does it take a clever politician to befuddle them? You aren't new to the business, and you know these things as well as I do—or better. I tell you, when Dudley Webb begins to stump the State the people will begin to howl for him. He'll win over the women and the old Confederates when he gets on the Civil War, and the rest will come easy. There won't be need of bogus ballots and disappearing election books when the members of the Democratic caucus are sent up next session [330–31].

All things considered, it is this mood of cynical distrust of the "people" which dominates Ellen Glasgow's conclusions in *The Voice of the People* The people, she shows, may select the leader with the proper vision to voice their needs, but their selection is all too likely to be based upon caprice, their allegiance merely momentary enthusiasm. Once their representative begins to speak out for the changes that will realize their dream, they refuse to heed his pleas, and if he persists, the people are always capable of choking him into silence, as they do Nick Burr.

Miss Glasgow's continuing rebellion against the South's entrenched illusions is only emphasized by the final chapter in the novel. Here she gives us a brief, ironic glimpse of Nicholas Burr's aristocratic associates settling back into the comfortable complacency of their established way of life while the "people" give him an elaborate funeral. The final impact of Nick's career is revealed by Sally Bassett, Eugenia's friend, who says soothingly of Burr's dramatic death three days before the Senatorial election in which he was to have opposed Eugenia's husband, "And, after all, it is perhaps better that he died just now. He would have tried to lift us too high, and we should have fallen back. He was a hero, and the public can't always keep to the heroic level" (443).

In life, Nicholas Burr was a voice crying in the Southern wilderness. In death, his voice cries no more, and the wilderness remains. McDowell suggests that even though Nicholas' triumph comes within the Democratic party, his career and death are meant to

reflect the rise and fall of the Populist reform elements in Southern
politics during the eighties and nineties, a challenge to tradition
defeated, as Nicholas is defeated through death, by the Southerner's
compulsive dedication to white supremacy.[25]

This is certainly a possible reconstruction of Burr's amorphous
political background, although given Miss Glasgow's own reminis-
cences of her presence at the 1897 Roanoke convention, it is more
probable that she simply modeled her hero after her impressions of
the silver Democrats who figured prominently there, such as J.
Hoge Tyler, a man who knew and sympathized with the needs of
the farmers and the man who was actually elected governor. The
fact that her father, Francis T. Glasgow, was a "Gold Democrat" in
1896 and chairman of the Richmond Committee Opposing Free
Silver may serve to support Ellen Glasgow's familiarity with the
current political issues as well as her sense of radical rebellion in
creating her hero. But despite this and her youthful enthusiasm for
Henry George, John Stuart Mill, and Fabian Socialism, *The Voice
of the People* contains neither economic nor political theory, and its
social ideals are Miss Glasgow's own. That she was faced with
unusual difficulty in her attempts to translate the political confusions of this time into any clear-cut design becomes apparent from
even a brief examination of Virginia politics during this period.[26]

Not that she does badly with the "psychology" of her characters
in *The Voice of the People;* indeed, her rendering of the separating
claims made upon Nicholas Burr and Eugenia Battle by their
disparate heritages is, perhaps, her most remarkable achievement in
this novel despite the fact that at this stage she was not able to
accomplish it without appearing to shift the focus of sympathy
away from Nicholas while attempting to illuminate Eugenia's stand.
The difficulty with her handling of detail in this novel is rather that
in her treatment of Nicholas Burr's political career, she neglects

[25] Frederick P. W. McDowell, *Ellen Glasgow and the Ironic Art of Fiction,*
p. 60.
[26] See, for example, Allen Wesley Moger, "The Rift in Virginia Democracy in
1896," in *The Rebuilding of the Old Dominion: A Study in Economic, Social,
and Political Transition from 1880–1902* (Ann Arbor, 1940).

what she might have called the psychological detail she needs in favor of literal detail far less important to her purpose. She does not, perhaps could not, translate Burr's political ideals and aspirations into convincing political actions; the pictures in his library may be faithful fictional copies of actual pictures on the walls of the Governor's mansion in Richmond; her hero sitting in the Governor's chair seems to have been imposed on the scene. We understand his desire to sit there and the ideal role he hopes to play, but we are not shown clearly or convincingly how he managed to get there (despite the convention scene) or how he fulfills his role once he does arrive. He fails to emerge as an ideal political leader not because he lacks ideals but because he lacks politics.

Nick Burr's role as Ellen Glasgow's hero remains important, for in that role he dramatizes the shaping vision of her dream for the new South. Undeniably, in his heroism Nicholas Burr is as Southern as the setting of Miss Glasgow's dream. Perhaps the heroic heights of his personal and public demeanor appear to be only that elevation to which any reasonably conscientious leader of men might aspire. If that demeanor, however, is as Miss Glasgow indicates—a product of Nick's "adjustment of individual needs to the Eternal Laws" (361), surely the Eternal Lawmaker in *The Voice of the People* had a Southern upbringing—a background which it is necessary to examine closely.

The girl, the money, and a happy life ever after: this is the classic American success pattern retold countless times during Miss Glasgow's long career by Northern novelists. But Nicholas Burr is deprived of the girl, of any girl, through circumstances alien to the Northern novel if not to its British counterpart. Even more significant, perhaps, is the fact that money never figures at all in his story except as an incidental advantage. Above all, a happy life ever after is permissible only within a very strictly bounded circle of conventions—which Nick denies successfully only by a series of lucky accidents. And from the encroaching consequences of that denial, he is rescued only by death.

Nicholas Burr has not gone far when he dies. Indeed, beyond his refusing a bill to restrict suffrage in Virginia, we are given little evidence that he does anything at all unusual as governor. But to Americans the really disturbing feature of this novel is probably its preoccupation with "class." Disturbing primarily, of course, since the assumption our society has usually operated on appears to be that class is a matter of adaptability, which is clearly not meant to be the case in *The Voice of the People*. True enough, Howells suggested that the Silas Laphams must do something beyond learning to hold their liquor and select their forks in order to acclimate themselves thoroughly in "higher circles." And Dreiser's *Sister Carrie* and *An American Tragedy* often seem unwitting confessions of his own as well as his protagonists' bewilderment over the means and manners necessary to achieve the "happiness" of the elect. Furthermore, a Nicholas of the next generation proclaimed in *The Great Gatsby* the truth, terrible in its very simplicity, that there were deficiencies in the Horatio Alger myth as well as in the delusions of the wealthy. But never had a Northern novelist produced a character so conscious of his "place" in society as Nick Burr so evidently was.

Indeed, it seems only proper that the major efforts of our more perceptive novelists should be devoted to showing us that the real divisions in our society are not a matter of more or less money, for surely this is the error that lies enshrouded in the misty vapor of the American dream. Yet if Ellen Glasgow judged correctly in this and later novels, we must look behind another cloud altogether to pierce the mist enveloping the Southern scene, to penetrate the vision that motivates her Southerners. And if we are successful in illuminating this vision, it may prove to be founded, peculiarly enough, on ideals of honor, responsibility, and achievement identical with rather than divided from those that shape the dream of Northerners. Only we must understand that the Southern path to glory is a different celestial byway altogether, marked with detours and pitfalls never occurring on Northern paths to paradise, blocked by barriers essentially alien, even unreal, to Northern eyes. The classed society, so much to most of us a prerogative of the British novel, is foremost among these barriers—a roadblock strange enough in our culture to seem absurd, an obstacle only for the simpleminded. But the assumption that erected such a barrier on the Southern byway may not be too different from the assumptions marking the works of the Northern novelists who also deal with "closed" societies—namely, the idea that certain values cannot be acquired, nor even comprehended, until an individual has been exposed to the full strength of those values for generations.

For such values, although of necessity carried on by individual endeavor, belong to no individual, nor even irrevocably to any group or clan, nor yet to a specific age. They remain intangible ideals to be borne onward or buried by members of each generation, to be distorted almost beyond recognition or adapted to new conditions but never to be surrendered wholly. Obscured by the haze of time through which anything belonging to history must be viewed, their origin and emergence into a definitive code of manners, a "well-organized" way of life is mysterious only in that it belongs to the irrecoverable and, therefore, slightly unreal past. However, these values are further obscured in fiction by being examined critically only at their most elusive stage—when the society in which specific ideals are cherished has begun to make a caricature of them, when form has turned to formula, and only the heroes may hint that it was not always so and need not always be. In the North, Edith Wharton dramatized a society in which hereditary ideals were on the decline. Willa Cather wistfully mourned a West where nobility and courage declined as the virgin prairie vanished. John Marquand, of course, revealed a code of manners mangled by the plentiful blockheads to the manner born, at best held in hesitant allegiance by his bumbling heroes, who are sufficiently perceptive to see beyond the clichés governing their class to the ideals governing the clichés, but not sufficiently articulate to express the ideals without repeating the clichés.

Ellen Glasgow's novels, then, present a twofold problem. Initially they must be viewed apart from the so-called main stream of American fiction lest the problems they suggest seem altogether trivial or unreal. But finally they must be examined by the same criteria with which we judge the values of any novel. And once the Southern viewpoint she delineates is clear, her chosen dilemmas become significant and valuable. Judging the importance of the values she ultimately leans on is, however, a more difficult matter.

In most novels the revolt from the village or society or status quo is a relatively simple and justifiable process. The revolt *to* a new way of life, a more enduring and less perverted code of conduct, a value system based on a sensitive analysis of individual needs and, unfortunately for utopians, individual potentialities, is the real challenge. This challenge, if met at all, is met most often, perhaps, with alternatives as inadequate or as superficial as the deficiencies they propose to remedy. Or the ideal is left submerged in misty mid-regions of nowhere. And no sooner had Ellen Glasgow emancipated her poor whites by admitting them into the society of the elect than she was confronted with the need to make them do something and, while they were about the doing, justify their actions by reference to some permanent standard. This standard she sought in the misty mid-regions of the past—the days of the glory and the despair of the Old South—the Civil War epoch, when values were clear and unquestioned, but, alas, only for a moment in eternity.

IN *THE BATTLE-GROUND*, I HAVE TRIED TO PORTRAY THE
LAST STAND IN VIRGINIA OF THE ARISTOCRATIC TRADITION. . . . ANY
FAITH THAT MOULDS AND INFLUENCES THE PLASTIC CHARACTER OF A
PEOPLE HAS VALIDITY FOR THOSE WHO LIVE UNDER IT AND BELIEVE
IN IT. THE CULTURE IT CREATES AND ESTABLISHES IS A REALITY SO
LONG AS IT SURVIVES. — ELLEN GLASGOW

A new aristocracy born out of the war-ravaged ruin of the old way
of life: this is the hope and the promise of *The Battle-Ground*
(1902), Ellen Glasgow's fourth novel. Looking back upon this
work at the end of her career, she found it the product of a "long
departed spirit"; although not a romance, "nevertheless, the work of
romantic youth." Her sense of alienation, one suspects, arose not
from the final unreality of the old way of life she conceived but
from a shattered vision of the new, from a mocking hope and
promise too long deferred by the perpetuated last stand of an old
aristocracy that should have been and was, in truth, dead. Dead, yet
surviving still, an immense, distorted parasitical growth, withering
the life on which it fed. Once a graceful, living faith; now only a
grotesque living past. What more bitter to one for whom the there
and then of *The Battle-Ground* had been dedicated to the here and
now?

The there and then of pre-Civil War days in Virginia receives
gentle, loving treatment in this novel. An idyllic, sunlit world where
even the children behave as gallant gentlemen and ladies, and where
the gallant gentlemen, who often behave as children, may be smiled
at and soothed, for their outbursts scarcely ruffle the surface of the
pervading serenity. A world of plenitude, leisure, and quaint cour-
tesy in which the deepest shadows are the small daily anxieties over
the children, large, small, black or white, shadows that serve best to

enhance the saintly luster glowing from the eyes of the plantation mistress.

A legendary, highly exclusive world this, which Ellen Glasgow knew well enough never quite existed, and, even at its most splendid hour, she shows us, was fading before the exigencies of time and circumstance. For alongside old, well-nurtured memories of ministrations to black children, care which extended even to free Levi in his lonely hut on the turnpike, lay equally old, troublesome memories shrouding figures like Sarindy, Levi's wife, sold up the river as a consequence of the same master's death that freed Levi—because she was a field hand and he a body servant. Nor did the practice of purchasing unneeded slaves in order to keep families together, a practice indulged in by supercivilized gentlemen like Miss Glasgow's tenderly conceived Governor Ambler, afford any real comfort to these sensitive souls. Such men knew well enough that they were merely quieting their consciences in the face of an indefensible and uncontrollable institution, indefensible perhaps chiefly because it could not be controlled.

The society sufficiently rigid in its class distinctions to mete out different fates to field hand and body servant was, nonetheless, incapable of maintaining that rigidity where it was most important. And just as the Governor Amblers could not share the faith of the more numerous Major Lightfoots in the "divine right of slavery," so the Governor was denied any real share of Major Lightfoot's triumphant conviction that slavery could be preserved as a gentleman's institution. The Major might rejoice in quelling the newly rich Rainy-Day Jones whose abused slave he rescued; he did in fact feel that he was tempering the rightful wrath of his private justice by allowing Rainy-Day to survive at all, having decided that "he didn't want such dirty blood upon his hands" (88). And, conveniently enough, Rainy-Day sidled away in appropriate skulking fashion under the Major's tirade:

Don't open your mouth to me, you hell hound . . . or I'll have you whipped clean out of this county, sir, and there's not a gentleman in Virginia that wouldn't lend a hand. Don't open your mouth to me, I tell you; here's the price of your property, and you can stoop in the dirt to pick it up. There's no man alive that shall question the divine right of slavery in my presence; but—but it is an institution for gentlemen, and you, sir, are a damned scoundrel [88–89].

But Peyton Ambler was all too well aware that the Rainy-Day Joneses outnumbered the "gentlemen," and, even more sadly, that the gentlemen themselves were most often dangerously myopic.

Dedicated to at least maintaining the infallibility of their own superiority in Virginia, the Major Lightfoots are seen as humorously, almost lovably pretentious when unchallenged. But, as conflict threatened their position, their unshakable outlook loomed steadily more ludicrous until it became vicious in its self-satisfaction. A well-bred discussion among gentlemen in support of Virginia's claim to the titles "school for gentlemen" and "mother of presidents," a modest observation that General Lafayette no doubt acquired his dignity and ease by early association with Virginian gentlemen, seemed harmless enough, even endearing. Considerably less endearing was the gentlemen's impatience to vindicate Virginian honor by a war of gentlemanly fisticuffs calculated to bloody the collective nose of the upstart North. Still, if hardly endearing, perversely how convincing. Their attitudes so caricatured the behavior of a legendary aristocracy that the gentlemen would scarcely have dared attempt such poses had they not been sincere.

In this delightful children's world created by their elders, the young grew up cheerfully dedicated to preserving this world's delights. What better assurance that nothing would change than to imitate all and question nothing. Young Dan Mountjoy, Miss Glasgow's hero, rides off to college doubly secure in the innocence of one who accepts both his world's rewards and the way to keep them. Indignant at finding the son of Rainy-Day Jones admitted to an institution for gentlemen, he promptly refuses to shake hands or fight with a man who is not of his class, while, at the same time, he donates his allowance to a straitened young man of his own circle

whose family has lost its money. As might be expected, he and his
cousin Champe remain robustly unaffected by their college years,
their summer tour of Europe, and Virginia's increasingly precarious
status in the growing turmoil between North and South. Indeed,
when they think of war at all, they share their Grandfather Lightfoot's eager satisfaction at the possibility of administering a good,
sound beating to those who try to tread on Virginia's toes—and of
gaining glory in the process. After all, the Major's attitude toward
battle has weathered two encounters with his personal enemies in
1812 and the years of the Mexican War, encounters that he still
contemplates with the same fondness he holds for memories of
conflicts between contemporary hotbloods who picked fights at
every twinge of gout or hangover. Why, then, should the young
dispute a veteran view that the young are predisposed to envy?

Clearly dissidents like Peyton Ambler can scarcely hope to be
heard in such an atmosphere, let alone heeded. And when Virginia's
secession follows hot upon Lincoln's request for Virginian troops
to invade the South, even Ambler hesitates no longer; he must fight
for his own. With sorrow equalled only by determination, he joins
the eager young men dashing off to battle while the enthusiastic
cries of the old Major Lightfoots urge them on. If Peyton Ambler's
presence in the front lines is ironic, the comparable positions of Dan
Mountjoy and Champe Lightfoot, the novel suggests, are doubly
so. Ambler's case is after all the more or less classic one of a man
who feels he must fight against a cause he believes in to defend a
way of life that plagues his conscience for reasons that fail to
vindicate him to himself.[1] He lacks even the dubious comfort of a
clear-cut necessity to kill Northerners to avoid killing closer neigh-

---

[1] Thomas Nelson Page testifies to the historical basis of responses such as
Governor Ambler's when he comments: "Men who had been the most earnest
advocates of the Union went into the Southern army to resist Invasion. Even
men like Governor Perry of South Carolina and General Wickham of Virginia,
who had fought Secession to the last moment at length went with the people
of their States 'ready,' as the former said, 'to go to the devil with his own
people'" (*The Old Dominion: Her Making and Her Manners* [New York,
1908], pp. 240–41).

bors. His decision taken, he can at best attempt to bury himself in the mindless immediacy of battlefields conveniently crowded with fleeting glories and horrors. Between times he has only the doubtful solace of fighting to perpetuate the imperfect manner of life that is, as a matter of fact, his own, and as such may justify his actions in the mystical realms of self-defense. On the other hand Dan and Champe, for whom personal honor and Virginian ideals are identical, see the scrapping as a splendid chance for assuring the triumph of their individual aspirations and their immortal society. The possibility that a man might prove his worth in terms other than those dictated by the code of his society never occurs to them—indeed, cannot, so long as to be a man, for them, is to be a Virginian.

It is this faith that distinguishes their innocence from the innocence of Henry Fleming of *The Red Badge of Courage* whose battleground experiences they share. And finally it is this faith that renders their coming of age on that battleground so much more precarious than young Henry's awakening. Fleming enters battle from a background of robust misgivings, distrusting the war as "some sort of play affair"[2] that he already suspected lacked "distinctly Homeric" qualities. In place of Major Lightfoot he had only his mother, contemptuous of his patriotic ardor, effortlessly supplying endless reasons why he was much more important on the farm than in the battlefield, reasons so convincing that she commanded his belief "that her ethical motive in the argument was impregnable" (4). The ideals dominating Henry's world appear most distinctly in the always shadowed and essentially specter-like figure of the "tattered soldier." To be sure, the tattered soldier clutters the scenes of many of Henry's most vivid experiences and haunts his memories in the aftermath of battle. But he is always cast in his rags as a kind of "public conscience" with whom Henry's private conscience undeniably must deal, yet never as one who might rightly absorb or judge Henry's whole self. At most, Henry fears the tattered soldier as one who might expose his "vivid errors," his "sins,"—his mo-

---

[2] Stephen Crane, *The Red Badge of Courage* (New York, 1951), p. 4.

mentary weaknesses. And at last, with surprising and convincing ease, he puts this public conscience "at a distance," chiefly by his assurance that the tattered soldier is, after all, inadequate to judge the qualities of his newfound manhood, but at least partly by associating that bedraggled repository of his sins with the originator of the "brass and bombast of his earlier gospels" (156).

This last association is Ellen Glasgow's fondest dream for the youth of Virginia in *The Battle-Ground*. Like Henry they must learn that the hovering image of war-ravaged Virginia, who carries with her the knowledge of their too human efforts in her behalf, is the same Virginia who taught them a brass and bombast that their battlefield experiences deny. This Virginia she would have them put also "at a distance," but rather in favor of a new image than a new individuality. Ideally her heroes must emerge from battle as they entered, holding hard to the identity between being a man and being a Virginian. After the battle is over, however, they must remold the Virginian image according to the knowledge of their new maturity. The old Virginia, they must see, is dead, in many ways ought to be dead—long live Virginia!

Nonetheless, through Dan Mountjoy's experiences during the war years Ellen Glasgow presents a compelling picture of the second chance for Southerners she feels the Civil War ought to have created. Dan, in fact, appears to discover rather more than young Henry Fleming about his world and his place in it, if only because his initial innocence is so much more complete. The outbreak of conflict finds Dan in disgrace, playing at temporary stagecoach driver since he knows nothing so well as horses. Expelled from college and banished from the Lightfoot acres because of a duel fought over a barmaid[3] (the college authorities objected to the

---

[3] The practice of duelling was apparently an authentic part of the Tidewater tradition, extended by the time of the Civil War into the Valley of Virginia, where "Chericoke," the Lightfoot estate, is located. T. J. Wertenbaker, in the process of his effort to establish the native origins of the Virginia aristocracy in *Patrician and Plebeian in Virginia* (Charlottesville, Va., 1910), presents some interesting statistics designed to show that while duelling all but disappeared in colonial Virginia, it grew increasingly popular again as a device for defending honor with the progressive conversion into aristocrats of the descendants of the original mercantile-minded settlers.

duel; his grandfather, of course, to the barmaid), he knows literally
no place to turn until the splendid chance for sanctioned fighting
intervenes.

His plight and his rescue by enlistment serve as a comic commen-
tary on the Southern "tendency to violence," a trait Miss Glasgow
usually treats with rather more than tolerable respect. Since she
assumes the habit of violence, the touch of primitive savagery, a
kind of elemental blood urge, as a more or less distinctive and
universal Southern characteristic, she is at pains throughout her
novels to stress both the dangers and the possibilities of this tendency. Uncontrolled violence, that is, violence in a spotted cause, she
finds only self-destroying, as in Dan's duel (one cannot help feeling
that Ellen Glasgow's objection, like the Major's, is to that brazen
barmaid) and Michael Akershem's enraged pistol firing. Yet a too
watery blood urge, a failure to sustain even the savagery that is
essential to preserve the self, destroys equally—a phenomenon she
describes at greatest length in the lives of Virginia Pendleton and
Eva Birdsong.

The tendency to violence is, of course, a standard ingredient of
the Southern legend. Francis Pendleton Gaines appears to assume
that a violent temper, at least, is a characteristic Southern trait
attributable to the effect of the slave system, one which served as a
minor expression of the South's feudal outlook. He notes, however,
that as far as the tradition is concerned, the quality of violence is
almost always indulgently viewed "as a fine imperiousness, or at
worst, unreasoning hot-headedness."[4] W. J. Cash extends this
explanation to include the frontier heritage of private justice alongside the plantation system encouragement of such justice.[5] William
R. Taylor labels the Southern "Hot-Head" an archetypal figure in
the South's pre-Civil War literature; he finds the hot-head awarded
the role of hero in the light of the same hope that Ellen Glasgow
embodied in Dan Mountjoy—the writer's faith in the strength of a

[4] *The Southern Plantation: A Study in the Development and Accuracy of a
Tradition* (New York, 1926), p. 144.
[5] See *The Mind of the South*, pp. 42–44, and elsewhere.

character of violent passions made tractable through the "civilizing agent" of the gentleman planter's code.[6]

What is really needed, then, is a worthy cause in which to channel violence, and Ellen Glasgow finds this worthy cause to be the lessons of the Civil War and its after-confusion for the legions of young men like Dan Mountjoy. Where battles are lacking, her heroes and heroines have only to seek salvation by a kind of physical equivalent of warfare, a concept flexible enough to include Nick Burr's fistfight to the death and Dorinda Oakley's determined ploughing. The theory is most appealing, smacks least of feminine tidiness, when Miss Glasgow admits its weakest point: the scarcity of physical equivalents of warfare—the dilemma of those who, having turned their swords obediently into the recommended ploughshares, still lack gardens to cultivate.

But Dan Mountjoy has both battlefields and a ruined Virginia to cultivate. Even his temporary disgrace proves providential because it deprives him of his horse and his commission, "forcing" him to enlist in the infantry. To be sure he is attended throughout the fighting by his body servant, Big Abel, who behaves consistently in the manner of a faithful retainer. Moreover, he finds himself surrounded chiefly by other languorous, merry gentlemen, each accompanied by his own Big Abel: volunteers who discover themselves in the ranks on foot through deference to the patriotic ardor of feminine admirers. Yet even in the prebattle atmosphere dominated by the spirit of undergraduates preparing for a wild party,[7] small awakenings stir. As scornfully indignant at the annoyance of

[6] *Cavalier and Yankee*, p. 321.

[7] George William Bagby in his chapter "An Unrenowned Warrier," in *The Old Virginia Gentleman and Other Sketches* (New York, 1910), gives an account of the prebattle spirit of some Virginia recruits as he observed it in the early days of the war. His chapter contains many of the elements Ellen Glasgow incorporates into this portion of *The Battle-Ground*—the festival mood of the young Virginians, their hatred of discipline, their resentment of officers whose origins they consider inferior to their own. Ellen Glasgow must have known this essay, as she once commented: "His sketches have always been a part of my Virginia heritage. The vital warmth and humanity of the writing give him a permanent place in the literature of Virginia" (Marshall W. Fishwick, *Virginia: A New Look at the Old Dominion* [New York, 1959], pp. 156–57).

discipline and drill as the rest of the "men," Dan is doubly chagrined to find as his lieutenant his old adversary, the son of Rainy-Day Jones. But this time Dan condescends to smash the Lieutenant's nose for "impudent" insults to his drilling prowess only to be surprised into admiration for the Lieutenant's cheerful courage under the impact. And then there is Pinetop, the tall, blue-jeaned mountaineer, about whom "the boys raised a row" (293) when he entered the mess. Pinetop was first accepted under duress as "company fool" and finally adopted amidst joyful astonishment at his imperturbable self-possession.

Training camp conditions affect the merry gentlemen very little; they insist upon behaving as though they were off on a grand fox hunt and must spare themselves for the ball to follow. Only now they have discovered fellow huntsmen who follow the rules of their game where before they saw only fellow men unfit to follow the dogs. Yet it is difficult to say whether their battle experiences teach them anything more unsettling or more important than the worth of the Lieutenant Joneses and the Pinetops.

The battleground does test the ideals of Dan and his fellows. Above all, it makes of honor, duty, and responsibility a code to be lived, a standard to struggle for instead of a schoolboy's game one is born to play.

Francis Butler Simkins illuminates the importance of Ellen Glasgow's focusing on the distinction between the inherited game and the necessary revaluation the war should have brought when he remarks that the virtues of the Confederate leaders became weaknesses when they were unable to see that the war in itself made necessary a new interpretation of the rules of the game. "They were gentlemen who regarded war as a game of the governing classes, its cruelties regulated by the code of chivalry."[8] For Miss Glasgow's young gentlemen in the ranks as well as the leaders, the game had been the real training ground. Little wonder, then, that in their first engagement they confuse the battlefield with the playing field.

[8] *A History of the South* (New York, 1953), p. 226.

Dan Mountjoy is as unnerved as Henry Fleming in his first battle, and both express almost identical feelings of weariness, bewilderment, suffocation, and horror as they prepare to fight. Henry can discover no proper "battle scene" and Dan looks in vain for the "prancing horses and uplifted swords" (311) of old engravings. But the consciousness of "being welded into a common personality which was dominated by a single desire" (38), the surrender of self to regiment or cause in crisis that sweeps over both in the fury of the fighting comes to Henry as a surprise and temporary gratification. For Dan it is only a quickening of long-prepared instincts, a heightened source of strength he expects and waits to feel. Robert Penn Warren attempts to explain this communal strength enjoyed by any individual who identifies himself with his society:

Today, we can scarcely imagine a commander saying what Pickett said to his men as they dressed lines for the fatal charge: 'Don't forget today that you are from Old Virginia!' It is absurd— and romantic. But it carries the nostalgic appeal; for the notion of place has a natural relation to the notion of identity in community, in the shared place.

Ultimately, it is the same appeal, even more romantic, which we feel when the old words duty and honor are spoken by tnose men. No doubt then many a rogue laid tongue to the words, and no doubt now many a man acts in duty and honor without using the words; but the words speak to us across time of a world of joyfully recognized obligations to the self and to society, and for some even to God.[9]

Appropriately, at the instant of the charge, Dan loses himself effortlessly in emotion: "He knew that he loved every man in the regiment beside him" (310). And,

he was not afraid, for he had been here long before . . . As he bent to fire, the fury of the game swept over him. . . . All the primeval instincts, throttled by the restraint of centuries—the instincts of bloodguiltiness, of hot pursuit, of the fierce exhilaration

---

[9] *The Legacy of the Civil War* (New York: Random House, Inc., copyright, 1961, by Robert Penn Warren).

of the chase, of the death grapple with a resisting foe—these awoke suddenly to live and turned the battle scarlet to his eyes [312].

Artificial primitivism, hothouse tribalism, but glorious! Poor Henry found unexpected assurance, comfort for his "pestered animal" exasperation in the noise of the men around him; Dan had only to immerse himself in long-accepted melodrama.

Moreover, after the battle initiation, while Henry examines himself and his feeling in "an ecstasy of self-satisfaction," Dan hardly pauses to admit nausea and near hysteria from overexercised emotions before beginning to worry about the afterbattle disorder of his fellows. "He asked himself almost impatiently if this were the pure and patriotic army that held in its ranks the best born of the South? To him, standing there, it seemed but a loosened mass, without strength and without cohesion, a mob of schoolboys come back from a sham battle on the college green" (317). In truth, they were all still schoolboys, Dan among them. One quick triumph had merely reinforced their schoolboy code. The only significant revelation the day held for Dan lay in a chance bit of campfire conversation with Pinetop, whose code came from no school. But both Dan and the mountaineer himself were yet too unprepared to appreciate its significance.

Ellen Glasgow remarks of the fervor sustaining young Mountjoy and his college mates in their first encounter that it sprang from a patriotism appealing as romance rather than religion. Theirs was the "fine Southern ardour" that responded instantly, and no doubt uniformly, "to the sound of the bugle, the fluttering of the flags, the flash of hot steel in the sunlight, the high old words that stirred men's pulses" (299)—things theirs "by blood and right of heritage." Not Pinetop's. Speaking to Dan of his feelings about the fight, the mountaineer says:

I ain't never owned a nigger in my life, and what's more, I ain't never seen one that's worth owning. 'Let 'em take 'em and welcome,' that's what I said. Bless your life, as I stood out thar I didn't see how I was goin' to fire my musket, till all of a jiffy a thought jest jumped into my head and sent me bangin' down that hill.

'Them folks have set thar feet on ole Virginny,' was what I thought. 'They've set thar feet on ole Virginny, and they've got to take 'em off damn quick' [323]!

And, after a reflective moment:

What I can't make out for the life of me . . . is how those boys from the other states gave thar licks so sharp. If I'd been born across the line in Tennessee, I wouldn't have fired my musket off today. They wan't a-settin' thar feet on Tennessee. But ole Virginny—wall, I've got a powerful fancy for ole Virginny, and they ain't goin' to project with her dust, if I can stand between [324].

Presumably, then, Pinetop's patriotism arises from a "religious" conviction about Virginia, for surely the bleak and narrow acres of the mountain farm which must be his "Virginny" are more promising as grounds for faith than for romance. In any event, the mountaineer's initial fervor springs from a soil very unlike that in which Dan's Virginian romance was cultivated. Yet disparate as their images of and faiths in their cause may be, that cause is for both from the outset more single, more vivid than it is ever to be for Henry Fleming. Henry must test everything continually, must weigh and judge his world, his society, his surroundings by the feelings of the moment in the pit of his stomach, and at every interlude against the current sum of those feelings. But for both Dan and Pinetop Virginia is always the given ideal; their discoveries they consider new perceptions of that given Virginia, their changed conceptions new insights into their roles as Virginians. And what Miss Glasgow might term the fortuitous fellowship of the battle-ground does allow them to become aware of the validity of one another's Virginia. Moreover, for Dan at least, this new awareness entails the necessity of taking both Virginias into account in his visions of the future.[10]

[10] Howard W. Odum refers to the possibilities for the future in the "understanding" cultivated between the sons of aristocrats and mountaineers who fought and marched side by side during the war. However, he speaks of the realization of these possibilities as a "might have been" that never materialized to mitigate the "bitter and pathetic" class struggle which he saw still characterizing many parts

Indeed, in one sense Dan adopts Pinetop's brand of patriotism after his first battle. For the terrible days that follow mark the death of his romantic ardor, and his unshakable loyalty to his South is upheld through the terrible years to come by a dogged faith in the necessity to struggle onward or be damned. The jesting defiance of his manner in the face of danger and suffering is still as far from Pinetop's silent, plodding determination as the distance of their origins might lead one to predict, but they worship one goddess, the many-faced Virginia. Years of fighting beside Pinetop gradually disabuse Dan of the notion held "in the lofty isolation of his class" that the "plebeian" is, after all, but "an alien to the soil" (442), yet the war is almost at an end before a chance discovery allows him to see Pinetop's true position. Coming upon the mountaineer struggling to master a child's first primer by firelight, Dan grasps in an instant both the degradation to which his own "genial plantation life" had doomed the "white workman" and his identity with that man.

In his sympathy for the slave, whose bondage he and his race had striven to make easy, he had overlooked the white sharer of the negro's wrong. To men like Pinetop, slavery, stern or mild, could be but an equal menace, and yet these were the men who, when Virginia called, came from their little cabins in the mountains, who tied the flint-locks upon their muskets and fought uncomplainingly until the end. Not the need to protect a decaying institution, but the instinct in every free man to defend the soil, had brought Pinetop, as it had brought Dan, into the army of the South [443].

So it is that, as defeat hovers, one would-be plantation master and one mountaineer find themselves closer than sudden victory or even

of the South of the 1920s (*An American Epoch* [New York, 1930], p. 44). In a more sanguine spirit, Marshall W. Fishwick suggests that battle solidarity prefigured Southern solidarity, gave rise to the "veteran army" mood that dominated the post-Civil War South in the view of W. J. Cash: "What no documents can tell is how battles and defeats cemented an army and a people together. Eventually, these soldiers knew how to speak to one another, to arrive at a tacit understanding. Their attitudes toward life were alike" (*Virginia: A New Look at the Old Dominion*, p. 129).

peace might ever again allow. And Dan's feeling for Pinetop is at the last much like his feeling for Virginia in her hour of defeat–a curious compound of pity and respect. Newly awakened pity for irremediable inadequacies, unfair deprivations; newly reinforced respect for the human qualities of courage and perseverance her soil nurtures in its humbler as well as its loftiest inhabitants. While Henry Fleming finds the flag he carries in a victorious charge a "creation of beauty and invulnerability . . . a radiant, imperious goddess" to be endowed with power "because no harm could come to it" (125), Dan grips his "helpless flag" in final retreat out of the mingled pity and respect beside which "he held his life as nothing." "The cause for which he had fought, the great captain he had followed, the devotion to a single end which had kept him struggling in the ranks, the daily sacrifice, the very poverty and cold and hunger, all these were bound up and made one with the tattered flag upon his arm" (473). And that may have made for all the difference that was to develop between Henry and Dan.

When Dan returns again to the charred remains of his grandfather's plantation, his sanguine spirit returns with him. He is made to reflect somewhat sententiously "with the smiling patience that suffering brings to the brave" that "now in his approaching poverty he might put away from him forever" (494) the single memory that had really troubled the "jovial ease" of his old life–the haunting figure of the poor black wretch saved by the Major from the power of Rainy-Day Jones. "He had never been a coward and he was not one now. The years had taught him nothing if they had not taught him the wisdom most needed by his impulsive youth–that so long as there comes good to the meanest creature from fate's hardest blow, it is the part of a man to stand up and take it between the eyes" (493–94). Hardened alike by the necessary courage of privation, he and his childhood sweetheart, Betty Ambler, the Governor's daughter, vow to begin again. A new life with a new wisdom.

Commentators on this "new wisdom" vary as much in their beliefs about its substance as Dan's moods of hope and despair in regarding his future. The outlook of the optimists, before radical reconstruction at least, is best represented by Thomas Nelson Page when he insists: "There was no feeling of indignity, no repining. A man who had hitched the horses to a gun under fire and brought it off under a storm of shot and shell could drive a streetcar without chagrin. He expected to be a brigadier-general then; now he expected to be some day president of the line."[11] This description of the defeated Southerner effortlessly transferring his allegiance from the Southern to the Northern version of the American dream is credible surely only if we see it as a dream about dreamers by a gentleman undeniable only for the grandeur of his dreams. Francis Butler Simkins generalizes about postwar optimism somewhat less exuberantly and certainly more convincingly: "The whites faced their difficulties with superb courage. . . . Women cheerfully retreated to the kitchen and men turned to manual labor. A philosophy of hard work and close economy was preached, and every expedient which might lead out of the impasse of poverty and social stagnation was advanced."[12] But Simkins, whose analysis is much closer than Page's to Ellen Glasgow's fictional representation of the postwar spirit, also comments on the Southern despair Miss Glasgow suggests in this book and makes the subject of her next novel: "A few dreamed of the day when the landed aristocracy would be restored to social dominance; a larger number resigned themselves to supine admiration of a past that they knew could not be revived."[13]

That the new wisdom and hope were denied many Miss Glasgow was certainly aware, but that faith in future glory departed or ought to have departed, she rejected strenuously. C. Vann Woodward, whose comments on the South's necessary loss of American innocence and the myth of Utopia in its Civil War experiences may at first suggest a denial of Miss Glasgow's major theme, actually comes closest to outlining the framework within which she hoped the new wisdom and the new South might emerge from the postwar period. Woodward feels that the South's defeat gave them what amounts to a unique heritage of failure in American history:

[11] *The Old Dominion: Her Making and Her Manners*, p. 322.
[12] *A History of the South*, p. 256.   [13] *Ibid.*

For Southern history, unlike American, includes large components of frustration, failure, and defeat. It includes not only an overwhelming military defeat but long decades of defeat in the provinces of economic, social, and political life. Such a heritage affords the Southern people no basis for the delusion that there is nothing whatever that is beyond their power to accomplish.[14]

Although Woodward emphasizes that the South's postwar preoccupation "was with guilt, not with innocence, with the reality of evil, not with the dream of perfection," his emphasis seems born of fears which, like Ellen Glasgow's, are for those who continue to dream of a dead South, "darling of divine providence." If he and Miss Glasgow differ at all in their respective assessments of the advantages inherent in the Southern burden of history, their difference lies in the conception of what a dream of perfection must consist of. Both deny the possibility of realizing such a dream by Northern standards. Ellen Glasgow merely insists on the enduring strength of a dream of perfection that provides for Woodward's "reality of evil." Indeed, she appears to qualify remarkably well for the role of Woodward's "hard to come by" ironic historian so much needed by the South—one not "so hostile as to deny the element of virtue on the one side, nor so sympathetic as to ignore the vanity and weakness to which the virtue and strength have contributed."[15]

Beginning anew in the South's postwar wilderness—the second chance Betty and Dan Mountjoy of *The Battle-Ground* promise themselves—is, of course, sacred to American tradition, all but an unquestionable right which we are not allowed even to doubt. And we need not doubt the bright promise of the future for Dan and Betty because from the outset of the strife both their inclinations and their experiences have helped prepare them for further battling. But what of those for whom the new Southern wilderness promises only despair: those like Champe whom the war left unchanged; the Major Lightfoots and the Mrs. Amblers who lost all they knew and believed in? Obviously Ellen Glasgow in her youthful enthusiasm hoped that the vanguard of the Dans and Bettys might lead these out

[14] *The Burden of Southern History* (Baton Rouge, 1960), p. 19.
[15] *Ibid.*, pp. 173–74.

of the wilderness. Yet even in this novel she makes Dan reflect on
the heritage of hopelessness he shares with his fellows:

For a country that was not he had given himself as surely as the
men who were buried where they fought, and his future would be
but one long struggle to adjust himself to conditions in which he
had no part. His proper nature was compacted of the old life which
was gone forever—of its ease, of its gaiety, of its lavish pleasures.
. . . The army was not the worst, he knew this now—the grapple
with a courageous foe had served to quicken his pulses and nerve
his hand—the worst was what came afterward, the sense of utter
failure and the attempt to shape one's self to brutal necessity. In
the future that opened before him he saw only a terrible patience
which would perhaps grow into a second nature as the years went
on. In place of the old generous existence, he must from this day
forth wring the daily bread of those he loved, with maimed hands
from a wasted soil [492–93].

For Dan Mountjoy this melodramatic pose of the defeated aristocrat passes quickly. Even as the grim demands of the forced march
to Romney killed his romantic visions of battle only to awaken a
sustained determination to resist the defeat of submission, so the
insistent demands of his grandfather's wasted acres promise to bury
the dark vision of his role as maimed toiler beneath his newly
plighted role of restorer and preserver. But for many the dark vision
did not die. And it is to this legion of the disinherited that Ellen
Glasgow turned in her next novel, *The Deliverance* (1904), attempting, as she later realized well enough, to deliver them out of
darkness by force of will:

Had I been older and possessed of a wider experience, I should
have left out, or at least subordinated, the part that romantic love
plays in the triumph over revenge. The book would have been
stronger, I think, if I had narrowed down the range of the theme,
and held it firmly to the bare anatomy of inherited hatred. Certainly the novel would have gained firmness of structure by this
logical simplification.[16]

Projected upon an epic canvas, *The Deliverance* was meant to be
a Southern *Wuthering Heights*, complete with raging elemental

[16] Ellen Glasgow, *Certain Measure*, p. 34.

passions of desire and revenge and a blonde, comely, fallen aristocrat as Virginia's Heathcliff communing mystically "with the earth
which had moulded both him and his race." But Ellen Glasgow, as
she herself points out,[17] was never to be the South's Emily Brontë,
although she did finally achieve in *Barren Ground* much of the epic
celebration of the land she attempted in *The Deliverance*.

Nonetheless, for all its inadequacies, *The Deliverance* does capture much of the Southern dream world Ellen Glasgow found so
destructive of the true Southern vision—"A native country of the
mind, where protected by inaccessible barriers, the sensitive dream
life may exist safely," and where, too frequently, "the fields within
are no more than an extension of some lost and remembered earlier
surroundings."[18] The pivotal figure of the novel is the fantastic Mrs.
Blake, blind for twenty years, and ever since the downfall of the
Confederacy serenely secure in the dream world where the lost
Blake Hall, Blake plantation, and three hundred Blake slaves continue to flourish and to celebrate the triumphal inaugurations of
successive Confederate Presidents. An improbable figure, of course,
and yet surely authentic as a cherished personification of the
sanctified past of the South. Nor, as Miss Glasgow realizes, is Mrs.
Blake's actual blindness really necessary to the preservation of her
fantasies:

So profound had been her former sense of security and permanence,
so unreasoning her belief in a personal Providence, and her
veneration for religious and social taboos, so invulnerable her
pride of name and estate, that even had her eyes been suddenly
opened, in all likelihood she would have looked on her fallen
fortunes merely as a sort of inopportune masquerade.[19]

In fact, when William Fletcher, the former overseer who has
dispossessed the Blakes, becomes furious at what he sees as un-
bearable Blake treachery and tries to inform her of the real situa-

---

[17] "In looking back on *The Deliverance* after thirty-four years, I can but
realize that the theme was not completely developed. . . . For the pure romancer, intuition may be all that is necessary, especially when, as with Emily
Bronte, it is the intuition of genius. But I was never a pure romancer any more than
I was a pure realist" (*ibid.*, p. 27).

[18] *Ibid.*, p. 31.   [19] *Ibid.*, p. 36.

tion, she merely erases the postwar years from her mind, living out her last days as the plantation belle of her youth.

Yet it is the reverence with which the Blake family regards Mrs. Blake's delusion rather than the impenetrable dream existence itself that forms the really significant criticism of the novel. The elder daughter, Cynthia, finds her only security in devotion to her mother's deception, and at Mrs. Blake's death discovers herself lost.

Released from her daily sacrifice and her patient drudgery, she looked about her with dazed eyes, like one whose future had been suddenly swept away. There was nothing for her to do any longer —no risings in the gray dawn to prepare the day's stealthy work, no running on aching feet to answer unreasonable complaints, no numberless small lies to plan in secret, no stinting of herself that her mother might have her little luxuries. Her work was over, and she pined away in the first freedom of her life. The very fact that deception was no longer necessary seemed to sweep her accustomed moorings from beneath her feet . . . to her surprise she found almost an indecency in the aspect of the naked truth.[20]

In Cynthia's despair at awakening to an existence empty save for an indecent reality, Ellen Glasgow foreshadows the plight of future daughters of the new South like Virginia Pendleton, reared in dedication to a dead fantasy. Foreshadows their plight, but as yet hardly equals its depths of delusion; for Cynthia at least is still aware of the distinction between illusion and reality. Her toneless lament, "It's all so dull when you have to stop pretending and begin to face things just as they are. I've lied for almost thirty years, and I reckon I've lost my taste for the truth" (486), suggests a rejection of reality which, however hopeless, is yet based on a realization of alternatives Virginia never possesses.

Cynthia's worship of her mother's fantasy is, of course, understandable as devotion to a world she consciously prefers. But Lila, the younger Blake daughter, reared in disinheritance, is wholly a

[20] Ellen Glasgow, *The Deliverance* (New York, 1904), p. 485. Page references to future quotations from this novel in Chap. 2 are given in parentheses or brackets after the quotations.

child of the new South. She and her twin, Christopher, born on the eve of the war, fifteen years younger than Cynthia, have only fleeting memories of Blake Hall life. Not at all unhappy in her present life, Lila nonetheless accepts, although she cannot understand, being "spared" the household drudgeries of her present condition. Her dream of complete fulfillment consists simply of marriage to Jim Weatherby, a prosperous farmer of "good people." Yet knowing that her mother, albeit inexplicably to Lila, could never bear the thought of a union with one who was not of their class, Lila waits submissively for her own life until Mrs. Blake can no longer be made unhappy by her marriage. And, curiously enough, Lila's position after her years of waiting have ended is an enviable one. Under the Weatherby roof, which is to her a household differing from her own only in its prosperity, she is cherished as the Blake her mother believed her to be; for the Weatherbys are at one with her mother in their persisting regard for class distinctions. So it is that Lila in the Reconstruction twilight enjoys the best of two worlds, although for her kind, Miss Glasgow hints, the enjoyment may be but bitterness deferred as generations pass and her "superior descent" is conferred as a mocking heritage upon her children.

Perhaps the most curious veneration of Mrs. Blake's delusion, however, is that accorded by her brother, Uncle Tucker, now a crippled veteran soldier (once the daredevil Colonel Corbin) who has lost an arm and a leg in battle. In his declining years Tucker has become *ad nauseum* an immovable celebrant of the way things are. Consequently, he rejoices at his sister's imprisonment in youthful memories as her only possible happiness even as he prefers for himself aimless musing amid the sunlit fields and singing birds that compose his last horizon. He assures the embittered Christopher that the best is yet to be, that his despair is but youth's rage for action, for extravagant follies to look back upon with laughter and chagrin in the contentment of maturity. And he refuses equally to accept any prediction save earthly bliss for Lila and any permanent loss of Cynthia's taste for truth. After all, Lila is blessed with the temperament for happiness, and Cynthia needs only the "change" of visiting the Weatherbys to tend her sister's cold.

Of course, Tucker is most irritating when his idealistic pronouncements seem most probable, as they almost always do. But he irritates only partly because of his bland smiling at sunshine in the midst of what are intended as perfectly good personal tragedies; his really disturbing quality is his "civilized soul." Admittedly, he was one of Ellen Glasgow's first attempts at "this rare pattern of mankind," and she herself saw that his portrait suffered "from the quixotic idealism which clashed with decadent sensationalism at the end of the century."[21] Yet she insists that "his crutch also was firmly planted on the common ground," and this is surely only literally true. It is not only that Tucker refuses to make claims on life. After all, only rarely do such figures achieve "worldly fulfillment," even in novels, and then, as with the Knightlys and Vernon Mitfords, their measure of the world's desserts comes to them as they stand and wait. The real trouble with Tucker is that he is more than apart from the life of his time; he is past that life.

In *A Certain Measure*, Ellen Glasgow says of her fondness for such figures:

Even when I was very young, I liked to write of old people, because the old alone have finality. What is true of the young today may be false tomorrow. They are enveloped in emotion; and emotion as a state of being is fluent and evanescent. It is impossible for anyone, even for an interpreter of human psychology, to place the centre of experience in a perpetual flux. But the old not only *know*, they have *been*. They are settled in the kind of peace that dwells always in the heart of a storm [45–46].

But, having *been*, Tucker can serve only as a dubious and confusing model for Miss Glasgow's youth, whom she prods constantly to be up and doing—the right things, of course. For he represents not the final contentment of one who has fought the good fight of the iron-veined for his convictions, but the permanent inertia of one old and

---

[21] *Certain Measure*, p. 39.

grey and full of sleep who has realized at last the futility of struggle and has given up all pretense of resisting his fate. He is a strange dream figure of the future without foundation in the carefully realized past or present chaos of Ellen Glasgow's Virginia. He is also a dream figure with a past in Southern literature, a man who would have to be called a Southern Hothead turned Southern Hamlet in William Taylor's classification of Southern archetypes. The Southern Hamlet, labeled by Taylor "The most interesting kind of Southern gentleman to make his appearance in this fiction," is characterized as "introspective, given to brooding—one in whom the springs of action have become somehow impaired."[22] Tucker is behaving according to type in serving, however indirectly, as a model to check and balance the excesses of the Hothead Christopher in whom all future hope is placed.

Certainly Tucker's world never touches that of Christopher Blake, the most violent devotee of Mrs. Blake's dream existence. As a Virginia Heathcliff, Christopher possesses origins almost ludicrously clear, and his passions roar only on behalf of his heritage. In fact, Christopher is meant to have descended to his role through "a long line of generous livers" whose idle excesses have imparted "a certain coarseness of finish" (13) to his features, not neglecting his perceptions. The circumstances of his disinheritance have served only to deepen what Miss Glasgow was first pleased to call the "suggestion of sheer brutality upon the general impression of a fine racial type."[23] Turned out of his Blake Hall life at the age of ten, put to work in the few remaining acres owned by the Blakes, Christopher cultivates his tobacco fields with sullen success fired by vindictive loathing. His loathing is fairly equally divided between disgust at his lot and hatred for the man he holds responsible for his disinheritance. The green testimonial of the tobacco juice staining his thumbs repells him, and though this repulsion may merely be

[22] *Cavalier and Yankee*, p. 160.
[23] *Ibid*. She did modify this phrase in the Old Dominion Edition, substituting effect" for suggestion" and "family pattern" for "racial type" (see *The Deliverance* [Garden City, 1929], p. 11).

deference to his creator's estimate of the plant, Christopher cannot possibly be held responsible for any communion with the soil save that of bitter necessity. He does have an almost mystic regard for the lost Blake acres, but even this regard is rather for the hereditary role of those who ruled the Blake estate than for the land itself. And his mystic feelings are kept well clouded by his overshadowing desire, not to be restored to his status as hereditary ruler of the Blake plantation, but rather to destroy the present usurper of his role, his father's former overseer, Will Fletcher.

The only peace that Christopher knows arises from a childhood memory of the "rare exhilaration" he felt as he crouched by the roadside with a squirrel gun awaiting Will Fletcher's footsteps and Blake vengeance. A Blake servant who stumbled upon him had struck the gun from his hand even as he raised it, and so deferred "justice." Yet Christopher soothes himself in later years by remembering how near he had come to righteous murder, soothes himself and awaits a second chance. A savage and childlike giant dedicated to realizing his mother's dreams by adolescent vendetta, his kinship with his forebears stirs most vigorously in his veins through wild soarings of imagination. "At such times he liked to fit heroic tortures to heroic crimes—to imagine the lighted stake and his enemy amid the flames" (92). Surely he is a grotesque figure, and yet, Ellen Glasgow would have it, the prototype of the decayed aristocrat in "the power of malignant circumstances." There were enough "real" Christophers in the postwar period, of course, to vindicate the origins and manner of life of Miss Glasgow's fictional creation. Frank Lawrence Owsley in "The Irrepressible Conflict" points out that the younger sons and daughters of Civil War leaders "between 1865 and 1876 or later grew up wild and uncouth, either unable to attend school or too proud to attend school in company with their former slaves."[24]

There seems no chance of redemption for Christopher, no possible reconciliation with the Fletchers, save in pools of mingled

[24] *I'll Take My Stand*, p. 64.

blood. But Miss Glasgow cannot tolerate such total annihilation of the aristocracy, and so she allows the very "hereditary fibre" that damns Christopher to his smouldering perpetual infancy of discontent, "the tendency of native impulse nurtured by tradition and legend,"[25] to save him. And while his salvation appears to be rather confusingly encouraged by his love for Will Fletcher's niece, this melting of classes is meant to provide additional hope for the New South.

Christopher's revenge, which conveniently entails his penance, is curious in its implications. He manages it by slowly tempting to destruction Will Fletcher's weak young grandson, heir to the Blake plantation. Young Will, lost in adolescent admiration of Christopher's skills with rifle and hounds, is willingly set at odds with his grandfather, taught to drink and defy old Fletcher's hopes with curses, taunted into marriage with a golden-haired young tramp and finally into the bitter fury at his disinheritance that culminates in his murdering his grandfather. But even before Will's frenzied last blow descends upon old Fletcher, Christopher, awakened by his love for Maria Fletcher, has realized his full guilt: "he knew himself for what he was—a man debased by ignorance and passion to the level of the beasts. He had sold his birthright for a requital, which had sickened him even in the moment of fulfillment."[26] And, his creator insists, he is fully aware of the weight of his responsibility:

To do him justice, now that the time had come for an acknowledgment he felt no temptation to evade the judgment of his own mind, nor to cheat himself with the belief that the boy was marked for ruin before he saw him—that Will had worked out, in vicious

[25] *Certain Measure*, p. 34.
[26] *The Deliverance*, p. 427. In the Old Dominion edition of 1929, Christopher is made to characterize his actions as deeds motivated by "vengeance" rather than merely "requital" (p. 363). The more damning "vengeance" does help to convince us that Christopher is as fully aware of how and why he has "sold his birthright" as his creator insists he is, but, as she also knew, the force of Christopher's acknowledgment of his own responsibility for the loss of his hereditary status is considerably weakened by the alacrity with which he is allowed to regain that "birthright."

weakness, his own end. . . . It was a human life that he had taken in his hand . . . a life that he had destroyed as deliberately as if he had struck it dead before him. Day by day, step by step, silent, unswerving, devilish, he had kept about his purpose, and now at last he had only to sit still and watch his triumph [427–28].

But now, of course, he is unable to sit still. Seeking escape from the guilt of his successful revenge, Christopher contemplates leaving his family, Maria, and Virginia and striking out anew on his own. Instead he rejects this possibility for escape into an hereditary responsibility that prepares him for his final expiation. For the weeks he spends in the backwoods tending the family of a former Blake servant dying of smallpox are scarcely past when Will Fletcher approaches him in the moonlight, full of the nightmare horror of murdering his grandfather. With the dawn, Christopher calmly and contemptuously sends Will on his way North, assuming Will's guilt proudly in the memory of the dying phrase spoken by one among his gaily sinning ancestors: "I may not sit with the saints, but I shall stand among the gentlemen" (533).

The novel's prevailing attitude toward Christopher's sentence of five years' imprisonment for the murder is stated flatly by one of the local farmers when he comments that "it was a good deal, when you come to think of it, for a Blake to pay jest for gettin' even with a Fletcher" (535). But that jail term is made to pay for a good deal. Christopher's mental and physical suffering while in prison is meant to atone for all Blake crimes against all Fletchers, past and present. If, as Ellen Glasgow would like to think, William Fletcher and his grandson belonged to a breed that "used to be called, with unsentimental accuracy, 'a bad lot,' "[27] this might be possible. But old Will

[27] *Certain Measure*, p. 37. If overseers considered as a "class" are not quite dismissed as a bad lot by historians, they do emerge as a breed who, by and large, had few desirable qualities to recommend them. Ulrich Bonnell Phillips, after conceding that records do attest to the existence of a handful of enterprising overseers, most often sons of planters learning the trade, remarks: "Most overseers were not eligible as mates for heiresses, nor were they notable for zeal, intelligence or ambition. As a rule, on the contrary, they were crude in manner, barely literate, commonplace in capacity, capable only of ruling slaves by severity in a rule-of-thumb routine, and needing fairly constant oversight by their employers" (*Life and Labor in the Old South* [Boston, 1929], p. 310).

Fletcher's only known offense was possessing seven thousand dollars to purchase Blake Hall at a time when Christopher's family was bankrupt. And although this outrage is shrouded in blackest suspicions, although Fletcher is seen as displaying the ignorant cruelty and greed of a thoroughly "vulgar soul," even his creator is troubled about how his soul came to be vulgarized. ("Was he the victim of prolonged social injustice and the functional derangement of civilization?"[28])

Whatever the case with the Fletchers, Christopher, the Blake representative, must be set free to begin anew. And freed he is after three years when Will's overseas confession to a priest filters back to Virginia. Freed, and once more presumably in possession through Maria of Blake Hall. We find him at the last "starting clean" after his release; beginning to "breathe anew the spirit of life": "With a single bound of the heart the sense of freedom came to him, and with it the happiness that he had missed the evening before pulsed through his veins. Much yet remained to him—the earth with its untold miracles, the sky with its infinity of space, his own soul—and Maria" (543)! Maria is, of course, a new acquisition, firmly characterized by Miss Glasgow even in 1938 as "the higher offspring of a lower form" who fails as a "test" because "she had inherited a better strain from her mother."[29]

So it is that in *The Deliverance* Ellen Glasgow sturdily recovers the disinherited aristocrats lost in dreams rather than awakened by the Civil War. And yet, almost despite what she later saw as her too rash inclinations toward enforced salvation, she allows her hero to reveal clearly the true confusion of his kind. When upon Chris-

[28] *Certain Measure,* p. 37.

[29] *Ibid.,* p. 39. The extent to which Ellen Glasgow was departing from tradition by allowing this marriage to occur at all, however, may perhaps be appreciated by comparing her views on such marriages to those of William Byrd II. As Louis B. Wright points out: "Throughout his life Byrd held to a strict belief in the superiority of his class. When, in *A Progress to the Mines,* he reports the unfortunate marriage of a planter's daughter to her uncle's overseer, he takes occasion to observe: 'Had she run away with a gentleman or a pretty fellow, there might have been some excuse for her, though he were of inferior fortune; but to stoop to a dirty plebeian, without any kind of merit, is the lowest prostitution'" (*The First Gentlemen of Virginia: Intellectual Qualities of the Early Colonial Ruling Class.* [San Marino, Calif., 1940], p. 340).

topher's release, Cynthia reproaches him with her failure to understand his original confession, he is made to reflect:

They would not understand, he knew, none of them—neither the world, nor Cynthia, nor his mother who was dead, nor Maria who was living. They would not understand, and even to himself the mystery was still unsolved. He had acted according to the law of his own nature; this was all that was clear to him; and the destiny of character had controlled him from the beginning. The wheel had turned and he with it, and being as blind as fate itself he could see nothing further [542].

But Ellen Glasgow had determined to see much further. In her next novel, *The Wheel of Life* (1906), the turning is complete; her dispossessed aristocrats are now expatriates in New York,[30] and only their controlling "destiny of character" and their inability to foresee their future course connect them with the Blakes. The city-pent sufferers here dedicated to a life of gay, aimless pleasure-seeking or reduced to nurturing in neglected eccentricity long outmoded disappointments foreshadow the communities of lost souls in Ellen Glasgow's last novels—the trilogy of tragicomedies beginning with *The Romantic Comedians*, and her final book, *In This Our Life*. Where the atmosphere is illumined by the artificial glitter of carefully sustained hypocrisy and deceit, where life revolves around affairs, divorces, the latest scandal, the Southern code avails only to snub the most shameless cads and behave chivalrously to the variously fallen ladies. And the eccentrics who attempt to preserve the past like Aunt Angela, who has spent a lifetime of cloistered seclusion for a youthful sin, and Uncle Percival, whose "excess of goodness invariably resulted in producing petty annoyances if not serious inconveniences,"[31] are ignored in their ridiculous isolation by a world that has no place for them.

[30] Jay B. Hubbell in *Virginia Life in Fiction* (Dallas, 1922), observes that the period of decay following the Civil War led to "wholesale emigration" from the South, often to Northern cities. "The ruined gentry migrated in larger numbers than any other class, and they carried their traditions with them, often their only asset" (p. 18).

[31] Ellen Glasgow, *The Wheel of Life* (New York, 1906), p. 21. Page references to future quotations from this novel in Chap. 2 are given in parentheses after the quotations.

In fact, the comfortable, often lavish, always mindless world of urban sophistication that dominates *The Wheel of Life* has no real "place" for any of its inhabitants; the majority find nothing to do short of drifting further into final disenchantment, and drift they do. This is the world of the 1900s, the world of the Fowlers from which Miss Glasgow's enterprising future heroine, Gabriella Carr, was to make her escape. But few escape here, and no one in *The Wheel of Life* enjoys Gabriella's upward flight into a new and vigorous, if rather overpowering, world. If the majority of the characters in this novel were potential George Fowlers or Florrie Spencers, they might be dismissed safely as incorrigibles. Ellen Glasgow never wasted either her sympathy or her reforming impulses on weaklings of this stamp. She preferred to ignore them as beyond the pale or, if they encumbered her protagonists, to push them toward ruin and the grave as she did Roger Adams' drug addict wife in this work and George Fowler in *Life and Gabriella*. But most of the inhabitants of this restless, sense-ridden world are far from hopeless degenerates. Rather, they are of a breed that was always to perturb Miss Glasgow—those who in succumbing to their momentary inclinations or sensual impulses still retained some concern for right and wrong, or for at least the proprieties of right and wrong, which their observer felt ought properly to be the same thing.

So it is that Ellen Glasgow approaches the pleasure-seekers of *The Wheel of Life* with an attitude of irritated wonder. Perry Bridewell is presented as a handsome, unthinking savage whose "life had corresponded so evenly with his bodily impulses that the perfection of the adjustment had produced in him the amiable exterior of an animal that is never crossed. It was a case in which supreme selfishness exerted the effect of personality" (7). Yet Perry repents lavishly after each of his unending casual entanglements and quivers with fury at the cad who lures Connie Adams to her final ruin. As for Perry's lovely wife Gerty, the young Southern innocent of the novel, one of many fascinated by her radiance is immediately convinced of her "deep disgust, a heavy disenchantment, which her ostentatious gaiety could not conceal. Even her beauty gave back to him a suggestion of insincerity, and he wondered if the brightness of her hair and her mouth was as artificial as her brilliant manner. It was magnificent, but, after all, it was not nature" (72). Maxwell Geismar points to the close similarity of this appraisal and Nick Carraway's observation of Daisy Buchanan's "basic insincerity" in *The Great Gatsby*. Even more interesting is the parallel between Fitzgerald's conclusions about his characters and Ellen Glasgow's judgment of the figures in *The Wheel of Life*.

The Bridewells, with rather better instincts and intentions than the Buchanans, are equally lost. Both couples are purposeless, dangerously afflicted with boredom, and above all addicted to a self-centered view of life which makes them capable of destroying their fellows with a "vast carelessness." But the consequences of the Bridewell egotism are peripheral here. A more commanding, more ruthless egotist plays the central villain while his intended victim is a bluestocking Nick Carraway. Even at the height of Arnold Kemper's infatuation for Laura Wilde, rising young poetess and the last "perfect flower of artistic impulses" (21) blooming on an eccentric family tree, Kemper feels himself caught. His one firm principle in pursuit of pleasure has been to avoid permanent entangling alliances. He tries to lull his uneasy thoughts at his approaching marriage by conjuring up images of a peaceful old age and a dutiful young heir but manages to quiet his unrest most efficiently by reviving a tempting old passion for Madame Alta, opera singer. Ellen Glasgow treats Kemper's comedy of self-deception effectively as she does that of the Bridewells. Her attitude toward the consequences of this deception is, given her abiding assumptions, at best complex, at worst irritatingly confused.

Laura Wilde escapes to the South to nurse her broken hopes, but finds nothing there—"soft air or the cold made little difference . . . when, as she said, she could feel neither" (464). The prevailing implication remains that neither she nor the sensation seekers can go back again. They are in truth too far past that, even as Nick Carraway has come a long way from the Midwest to which he proposes only as a matter of fact to return. All this is convincing.

Nor is the suggestion disturbing that the sins and omissions of the lost egotists might have been somewhat redeemed or at least curtailed had they been enclosed by the familial fences of Southern society. (A suggestion echoed by Nick's conjecture that he and his fellows "possessed some deficiency in common which made us subtly unadaptable to Eastern life."[32]) What does disturb is Laura's complete turning away from those with whom she had at least a distant past in common, a turning away much more final than Nick Carraway's. Of course Laura had no Gatsby whose great dream would not die, and that may have made all the difference. But Ellen Glasgow had her own Southern vision, and if she did not desert it in *The Wheel of Life,* she cloistered it thoroughly. For Laura's salvation here is a very private awakening. To be sure, when she begins to "live anew," she is meant to prove "one of those nobler spirits who in passing through the tragedy of disillusionment drain from it the strength without the bitterness that is its portion" (469). But although her love, "which had recoiled from its individual object," Kemper, is meant in its renewal to touch "the boundries of the earth," surely it does not do to march off as Laura marches to tend the slum children of New York, leaving all those poor Southerners to burn on in their Eastern hell.

In this deliberate isolation from her fellows Laura is much more alone than Christopher Blake, who, if conscious that his family could never understand his attempt at retribution, is yet secure in his shared mystification, knowing that, just as they, he moves with the turning wheel of life according to "destiny of character." But although the destiny of Laura's compatriots can only be lasting damnation, she is cut off from them in her "resurrection" by the "widening distance that divided her dream from her awakening" (473). Nick Carraway's reflections on the believers in "the green light, the orgiastic future that year by year recedes before us" spring from a wisdom as lonely as Laura's, but it is wisdom tempered in its inevitability by the determined communal sympathy

[32] F. Scott Fitzgerald, *The Great Gatsby* (New York, 1951), p. 186.

of "it eluded us then . . ." and "so we beat on." Laura can only say
with finality of her elaborate plans for slum service: "It isn't that the
poor need help any more than the rich . . . but the poor are the
only ones that I can reach" (470). A dubious conclusion at best, for
Laura has joined the thin ranks of Ellen Glasgow's "civilized
souls"—thoroughly admirable beings all, but characterized always,
like Uncle Tucker of *The Deliverance* and Roger Adams of this
novel, by a total inability to reach anyone not of their own kind.

The reason for the unsatisfactory quality of Laura's awakening
may lie in the fact that it was indeed a uniquely private awakening,
as Ellen Glasgow confesses in a letter to Bessie Zaban Jones, dated
Richmond, April 18, 1938:

You can't imagine how amused I was to find that he [Howard
Mumford Jones, the recipient's husband] had discovered the auto-
biographical basis of my New York novel, *The Wheel of Life*.
Most people have thought I was writing of strange ground, but
this was, in fact, the only one of my books that was taken directly
from experience. That may be why it was so much less convincing
than the Virginia books. I was too close; for the mystic phase, and
even the incident of the little blue flower, really occurred. But that
book was not a good novel, and I have long since disinherited it.[33]

Ellen Glasgow's own "mystic phase," fortunately for her art of
short duration, was occasioned by the death of her one great love, a
married Wall Street financier identified in *The Woman Within*
only as Gerald B., a man she knew and loved for seven years. It
appears fairly certain that when Miss Glasgow transferred her
emotional responses to incidents or individuals in her private life
directly to characters in her novels, the result was a weakening of
her art and her controlling purpose.

There is evidence of such confusion of purpose not only in Laura
Wilde's mystic transfiguration and equally mystic turning to social
service in the 1906 *The Wheel of Life* but, as Miss Glasgow also
acknowledges, in the sympathy she cannot prevent from intruding

[33] *Letters of Ellen Glasgow,* ed. Blair Rouse (New York: Harcourt, Brace &
World, Inc., 1958), p. 238.

on the ironic detachment with which she intended to render the plight of Virginia Pendleton (*Virginia*, 1913), a character modelled all too closely on her memories of her mother.

Ellen Glasgow does not comment on the extent to which the short idyllic phase of her twenty-year relationship with the man she calls Harold S. (identified by McDowell as Henry Watkins Anderson, 1870–1954, Richmond lawyer, railroad executive, and active Republican) may have influenced her novels written during or immediately after World War I. Whatever the case, an alien spirit of impetuous and too groundless optimism allows her to conclude *Life and Gabriella* (1916) with the prophecy of a life of wedded bliss for the ill-matched hero and heroine; a comparable spirit permeates the idyllic and untenable rendering of David Blackburn's political dreams for the future of the South in *The Builders* (1919). And there is much in the character and actions of the self-made Harold S. as she presents him that is echoed in both Ben O'Hara (a man she confesses having drawn from life) and David Blackburn; there is more than a little of Ellen Glagow's hopes and aspirations for her own happiness in both Caroline Meade and Gabriella.

The larger question of the abiding effects for good or ill on Miss Glasgow's art of her emotional entanglements and personal trage- dies must, I think, be left largely to conjecture. One may assert, as does McDowell, that Ellen Glasgow wrote "one of her strongest books, *The Deliverance* (1904), when she was in love with Ger- ald," but the "strength" of this book is at the least open to question whatever may be said for her prevailing euphoric mood during the period of its composition. Moreover, while one might allow that only the first of her three novels written during the seven-year period of her love affair with Gerald has an "unhappy" ending, this novel, *The Voice of the People* (1900) shows neither less nor more of anything that might be called the "influence" of her emotion than *The Battle-Ground* (1902) or *The Deliverance*.

It is undeniable that her next three novels written during her period of despair following Gerald's death "show her talent at its thinnest," as McDowell points out. But the slender qualities of these

three works could be attributed as easily to Ellen Glasgow's inse-
cure grasp of her material gleaned from a society in rapid transition,
or to her own evolving conceptions of that society, as to her
emotional turmoil. In addition, one might note that all three of these
novels written during the period of agony have what are meant to
be triumphant conclusions.

A similar objection may be brought against McDowell's conjecture that the "grim force" of *The Miller of Old Church* (1911) and
Virginia (1913) may well derive from her suffering as a result of a
brother's suicide and a sister's death during this period. If these
novels do have "grim force" (and it seems to me that they have
very little that may justly be termed "grim" however forceful they
are in their castigation of aristocratic illusions), this quality may
have arisen from a number of sources totally unrelated to Ellen
Glasgow's emotional state. Indeed, one might more easily attribute
the force of *Virginia*, for example, to Ellen Glasgow's developing
maturity in craftsmanship—or to a fortuitous choice of material that
allowed her ironic perspective, insofar as she maintained it, to
emerge more fully than it had in earlier works.

McDowell is on surer ground when he observes that Ellen
Glasgow most accurately accesses the influence of her own private
emotional state on her work in *The Woman Within* when she says
that her best novels were written when her most intense emotional
reactions "had diminished to the throb of remembrance." And, as
she expresses it, "Analysis, if it comes at all, must come later." Her
delightfully dispassionate treatment of the romantic entanglements
of two lawyers in her tragicomedies, Judge Honeywell of *The
Romantic Comedians* and Virginius Littlepage of *They Stooped to
Folly*, suggests the effective literary use she was able to make of her
relationship with Harold S. long after that relationship was over.

Yet whatever its origins and despite its deficiencies, Laura
Wilde's rebellious awakening marks a new vision in Miss Glasgow's
prolonged Southern dream. Laura has been made to see the final
futility of attempting to preserve unchanged the code of a vanished
past in a clamorous and chaotic present. And even her pathetically

ludicrous turning to "reach" the poor is meant as a very hopeful sign. For, to Ellen Glasgow, it was never enough that a hero or heroine should merely recognize the need for change, for reconciliation of old and new. Once recognition descended, her protagonists had only two choices: action or defeat, and until her final tragicomedies she concentrated her enthusiasm on crusading spirits, pausing only in *Virginia* for a last, almost unintentional, lament over those powerless to change.

AS AN EMBLEM, SHE FOLLOWED CLOSELY THE MID-VICTORIAN IDEAL, AND THOUGH HER SORT WAS FOUND EVERYWHERE IN THE WESTERN WORLD, IT WAS IN VIRGINIA THAT SHE SEEMED TO ATTAIN HER FINEST AND LATEST FLOWERING. — ELLEN GLASGOW

With this rather vague and hesitant explanation Ellen Glasgow, thirty-five years after creating her, attempted to justify Mrs. Blake of *The Deliverance*, a lady fantastically, willfully preserved in her blindness from change. Mrs. Blake, "legendary" even to her creator is, truly enough, an emblem—the first of several ideal and less than ideal feminine emblems in Miss Glasgow's fiction. And like all of her kind, she is at once too much and too little to accept joyfully. Still, Mrs. Blake and her more exact counterparts in later novels (Victoria Littlepage, Eva Birdsong), however incredible as ideals, however incurable as neurotics, have an easier task than the emblematic characters who must acknowledge change to some degree, who are asked to look at and perceive the actual, no matter how little they may "deal" with it.

In three successive novels written during the second decade of the century, three ideal young ladies are called upon to look at the monster "change" who threatens their serene oblivion. The monster devours the first lady, but she learns at least and at last that she has been overwhelmed, if not how or why she has come to be swallowed. The second lady first defies, then tames the monster, and the third, after penetrating his disguise, welcomes him as a reforming hero—although not even she may live happily ever after with him.

Virginia Pendleton, heroine of *Virginia*, is conceived as more than an emblem of the Victorian lady, Southern style. She is, indeed, claimed to be "the feminine ideal of the ages," the patterned image of womanly perfection that "had embodied for centuries the thwarted human longing for the beautiful and the good."[1] And, apparently, the dumb. For this "candid portrait" of a Richmond gentlewoman who reaches womanhood if not maturity during the mid-eighties hardly invites questions, as Miss Glasgow imagines, because "the lady has become almost as extinct as the dodo." Rather, Virginia Pendleton is at once an anachronism and a worthy subject because she is a dodo—even in the eighties and even in Virginia.

Undeniably Ellen Glasgow is aware of certain of Virginia's dodo qualities. She emphasizes the responsibility of the community for creating Virginia as a waxen image molded in the worship of the cult of "evasive idealism." The senior Pendletons, cherishing the conviction that to acknowledge evil is to "countenance its existence," do their best to hand down their illusions as sacred heirlooms to their only offspring. And Virginia learns readily enough that "taking a true view of life" means believing the pleasant instead of the painful, whatever the evidence. In an atmosphere of proud poverty Mrs. Pendleton enforces the principles if not the practice of ancestral ideals by rising with the dawn to scrub floors and clean furniture before the neighbors, or for that matter, her husband or daughter awaken.[2] It is she who repeats the phrase "spare Virginia" in her daughter's hearing until it takes on "almost a religious significance"—or meaning enough to hold Virginia immobile in the traditional pose of a lady. Above all Virginia's mother strives to perfect in her child the vacant, dreamlike stare in the face of unpleasantness and cruelty, the unseeing gaze that in the "old days" allowed Mrs. Pendleton to "know where the slave market stood, without realizing in the least that men and women were sold there" (67).[3]

---

[1] *Certain Measure*, p. 96.

[2] The importance of the tradition of the sacred secrecy of the house-cleaning ritual is attested to by George William Bagby (*The Old Virginia Gentleman and Other Sketches*, pp. 23–24).

[3] Howard Odum in *An American Epoch* speaks of this cultivated blindness as a part of the heritage of the plantation mistress. "Many things she was not supposed to see, and if seeing, was not to record and, if recording, was not to let see the light either in her own consciousness or in the records of posterity. Thus this remarkable character became a symbol for a certain type of hypocrisy, super-

To Miss Priscilla Batte of the Dinwiddie Academy for Young Ladies, whose courageous innocence "feared nothing except opinions," the Pendletons entrust Virginia's more "formal" education. And Virginia is marked by Miss Priscilla as a docile and consequently excellent pupil. For,

The chief object of her upbringing, which differed in no essential particular from that of every other well-born and well-bred Southern woman of her day, was to paralyze her reasoning faculties so completely that all danger of mental 'unsettling' or even movement was eliminated from her future. To solidify the forces of mind into the inherited mould of fixed beliefs was, in the opinion of the age, to achieve the definite end of all education. When the child ceased to wonder before the veil of appearances, the battle of orthodoxy with speculation was over, and Miss Priscilla felt that she could rest on her victory.[4]

Apparently Miss Glasgow's description of Virginia's education not only caricatures but characterizes the quality of instruction in Virginia in the eighties. The historian Marshall W. Fishwick cites the novel as a work demonstrating that Ellen Glasgow was "keenly aware" of the prevailing power of Virginia's entrenched social structure over education.[5] Even enterprising young ladies who refused to succumb to the imposed orthodoxy of the Miss Dinwiddies' Academies like Virginia's friend, Susan Treadwell, found nowhere to turn for another sort of education. Had they not been prohibited by their parents' sanctified objections from attending college, as Susan was by her mother's tradition-bred opposition to such impropriety, they would still have been unable to discover an educational institution worthy of the name in Virginia that was willing to admit them.

Virginia Pendleton's elders achieve stature by the very strength

ficiality, and rationalization wherever reality was concerned, and this symbolism carried over into the reconstruction period and far into the twentieth century" (pp. 46–47).
[4] The quotation is from Ellen Glasgow, *Virginia* (Garden City, 1913), p. 22. Page references to this novel in Chap. 3 are given in brackets or parentheses after the quotations.
[5] *The Virginia Tradition* (Washington, D.C., 1956), pp. 20–21.

of their stern evasiveness, their steady refusal in the name of their cherished ideals to face facts. A part of this dignity, even nobility, derived, no doubt, from the origin of their convictions. Unlike Virginia, who was tutored after the fall to believe in an enduring Southern Eden, they learned to cherish their past when that past yet existed. And vividly painted over the often unsightly reality of the things that were living was "this impassioned memory of the thing that was dead. . . . The young were ignorant of it, but the old *knew*" (39). Knew, perhaps, not only that the manners they clung to as the last precious fragments of a lost glory had once belonged to a real glory, but that even in the days when that glory abided, its sustaining grandeur depended upon perfected "looking away."

For surely there is a sense in which the Pendletons must be upheld in their conviction that to acknowledge evil or even imperfection is to countenance it. If an evil is looked upon and realized, it must be taken into account. And until that evil has been explained away, or even more dangerous because more arduous, has been "dealt" to death, the vision of glory, to say nothing of the life of glory, must remain submissively in the background out of reach. No one can have the beautiful, the good, and the slave market if he persists in looking at the slave market. On the other hand, if the slave market is there as a part of what is believed beautiful and good, it must be absorbed by that beauty and goodness. Where there can be no looking away, there can be failure to see. Once the beautiful and good are found, it is safer to avoid examining them; they cannot be improved, and if their possessors prod them, they may shatter to reveal heaven knows what unholy shapes.

But Virginia is of the young who remain ignorant. Her strength is but the strength of submissive loyalty to a code she accepts without understanding; her dignity is only the dignity of dumb immobility. Molded with good instincts, lightly powdered with dust, a waxen lady makes an appealing figurine in a museum of antiquities, out of time behind a glass case. A lovely emblem perhaps, a living lady never. Virginia melts when the heat is on. Melts, droops, diminishes, behaves in short as the elder Pendletons and Miss Priscilla Batte would never allow themselves to behave under stress. Ellen Glasgow denies that Virginia's progressive droop and slow death-in-life originate in weakness. "On the contrary, she was a woman whose vital energy had been deflected, by precept and example, into a single emotional center. She was, indeed . . . the logical result of an inordinate sense of duty, the crowning achievement of the code of beautiful behavior and of the Episcopal Church."[6]

She was, indeed. But Virginia's sense of duty, beautiful behavior, and Episcopal Church ideals were, of course, not hers but those of her parents, of Miss Priscilla Batte and Miss Willie Whitlow, the spinster seamstress. They belonged to those who knew, and Virginia had only been taught them too well, too superficially. Possible discrepancies between appearance and reality never occurred to her until too late. And since neither change nor adaptation was part of her training, when at last she vaguely perceived a distinction between precepts and practices, she remained lost. Virginia could not grow; she merely shrank into herself, of which there was very little anyway—a self growing always more dim and vague as the years and the world whirled by. Miss Glasgow sees her as a pathetic victim, not so much because she believed, indeed, became a part of the myths her elders taught her, but rather because the myths grew progressively mythical. Virginia, to her creator, is a victim of "time" because time means change and change always, somehow, is finally loss.

But time, her antagonist, had conquered. Minute by minute, with the slow wash of the tides on a beach, time had worn away her loveliness, her innocence, her flushed expectancy, her radiant belief in life, which was dimmed but never extinguished. One after another, like sands drifting, all the little graces, all the small things that made up the sweetness of life, slipped by and were gone. More slowly still, under those soundless waves of the years, the larger things also began to pass from her, the dependence of her children, the imperative desires of her husband, the multitude of daily services that had once filled the present emptiness of her

[6] *Certain Measure*, p. 83.

heart. Nothing but constancy was left to her and constancy, when it was outlived its usefulness, is as barren as fortitude. Time had not crushed her, but, little by little, the years had nibbled away the very roots of her life [90].

Still, Virginia remains uncrushed only in the sense that any myth remains uncrushed. There is nothing individual enough in her to be broken. The years may be, as Ellen Glasgow claims, "powerless to destroy that inviolable essence which is the self within the self" (91). Alas, Virginia herself never violates that inner self by recognizing its existence. She is allowed occasional flashes of insight, all of which seem "the result of some outside vision rather than her own uncritical judgment" (444). But these moments of vision do make her recognizable as an admirable and interesting representative figure, if hardly as an aspiring human being.

Newly in love with the "strong-minded" Oliver Treadwell, Virginia at twenty pauses while dressing for a ball, steps out of her world of enchantment for a moment, and reflects "how hard life had been to her mother . . . how pretty she must have been in her youth." But Ellen Glasgow knows perfectly well that this youthful Virginia is incapable of conceiving "that her mother, like herself, was but one of the endless procession of women who pass perpetually from the sphere of pleasure into the sphere of service" (55). And Virginia, married, surrounded by children, and duly transported to her own sphere of service, is almost as incapable of conceiving the desires and expectations that she looked upon as her right during the brief enchantment of her sphere of pleasure. Moreover, the tender, often syrupy sympathy with which Ellen Glasgow persists in rendering Virginia's plight, despite her ostensible criticism of that plight, creates an aura of pathos around Virginia's activities that all but challenges the touchy "modern" reader to emphasize the heroine's worst qualities. Half apologizing much later for this "intense pathos," Miss Glasgow commented that she had "loved and pitied" the original Virginia in her mother. Only occasionally does Virginia even contemplate a lapse from perfect behavior, but intermittent and fleeting as her temptations are, they give her substance. It is to these momentary crises, then, and to the rare interludes of selfish honesty Virginia permits herself that we must turn to find the significant irony of her position that Ellen Glasgow originally intended to dominate her story.[7]

The conflict that enthralls Virginia is first dramatically revealed in her reaction to Dinwiddie gossip linking Oliver's name with that of the town belle, Abby Goode. Instantly determined to meet this crisis as a "gentlewoman," she immediately resolves that Oliver is blameless and that all possible slanderous rumors will be stifled if she merely accompanies Oliver and Abby on a foxhunt. Occupied with the details of preparation, she secures her mother's promise to look after the children during the hunting expedition and leaves her house to borrow a horse. On the street she glimpses Oliver and Abby returning from one of their frequent afternoon rides glancing happily at one another as they canter in the direction of Abby's home. Suddenly, sharply jealous, yet clinging to the wistful hope that Abby's virtue is after all to be trusted, Virginia proceeds to borrow the horse and is returning home when she sees in a shop window a length of hyacinth-blue silk "which she had remotely coveted for weeks."

For the first time in her life that immemorial spirit of adventure which lies buried under the dead leaves of civilization at the bottom of every human heart . . . this imperishable spirit stirred restlessly in its grave and prompted her for once to risk the future. In the flickering motive which guided her as she entered the shop, one would hardly have recognized the lusty impulse which had sent her ancestors on splendid rambles of knight-errantry; yet its hidden source was the same [319].

One recognizes, perhaps, quite readily in Virginia's giving way to her impulse to enforce "her desire upon destiny" a mood kindred to,

---

[7] "Although, in the beginning, I had intended to deal ironically with both the Southern lady and Victorian tradition, I discovered, as I went on, that my irony grew fainter, while it yielded at last to sympathetic compassion" (*ibid.*, p. 79). She also says: "Although the irony has grown fainter, it is still there at the end, interwoven with the pathos and the tragedy" (*ibid.*, p. 91).

or at least the feminine counterpart of, the "primitive savagery" with which Miss Glasgow's earliest hero, Michael Akershem, lashed out at the society that refused to contain him, and the "red rage" that drove Nick Burr, her more cultivated poor white, to enforce justice with his fists. Virginia, product of generations of gentle breeding, is more conscious of the genuinely revolutionary quality of her mood than either of her predecessors were despite the comparatively thin and comic silken symbol of her rebellion.

She knew that [the impulse] was a rebel against the disciplined and moderate rule of her conscience, but this knowledge which would have horrified her had she been in a normal mood, aroused in her now merely a breathless satisfaction at the spectacle of her own audacity. The natural Virginia had triumphed for an instant over the Virginia whom the ages had bred [320].

Ruthlessly the natural Virginia goes on to triumph in the fox hunt and seals her victory over "the Virginia who had learned from the ages to stifle her desire" by agreeing to join Abby and Oliver in a jaunt to Atlantic City. But the hunt had no sooner ended than "the excitement of the chase had ebbed away. . . . She had neglected her children, she had risked her life – and all for the sake of wresting a bit of dead fur out of Abby's grasp." And her consent to accompany her husband and Abby had no sooner been given than she felt the exultation of victory and the "fugitive excitement of pleasure" depart. "Like other mortals in other triumphant instants, she was learning that the fruit of desire may be sweet to the eyes and bitter on the lips. She had sacrificed duty to pleasure, and suddenly she had discovered that to one with her heritage of good and evil the two are inseparable" (329).

The rest of Virginia's life is dedicated to reinforcing the inseparability of her duties and her pleasures. Her Atlantic City trip cut off when her son contracts diphtheria, she hovers over him in a frenzy of devotion long after she learns that he will recover. And when her doctor informs her of Oliver's return and his refusal to let Oliver see the boy for fear of spreading contagion, she murmurs, "Poor Oliver . . . it is terrible on him. He must be so anxious." Yet even as she speaks she is aware of a sense of unreality, "as if she were speaking of a person she had known in another life" (360).

Of course, Oliver Treadwell had never shared anything with Virginia beyond youthful mutual illusions and a common heritage. The slow and painful souring of a relationship based on adolescent ideals, cruel as silly misconceptions of needs and desires, is predictable enough in or out of fiction. But the force of a shared heritage that can hold two such alien souls to the end is a rare thing. Although Oliver grows completely away from Virginia before many years pass and finally, in fact, resolves on a divorce which no true Southerner would permit even in fancy, he remains a very conscious and very Southern cad. As a "true Treadwell" Oliver comes of an upstart strain; he is possessed of the "universal Treadwell spirit" that demands power, authority, and finally, "success" from its exertions. And if he never achieves the status of his Uncle Cyrus, the controlling industrialist of Dinwiddie who is rapidly converting his own little portion of the South to most unchivalrous Northern practices and values, Oliver does manage to change his play writing tactics sufficiently to produce hits based on very popular "rot." Nonetheless, he insists bitterly on the inferior quality of each progressively more resounding success and suffers as Virginia is temperamentally incapable of suffering over the dissolution of their marriage and his tortured growing love for the heroine of his plays, Margaret Oldcastle.

In his middle years he is deprived of even his youthful illusion that, whatever came, he at least belonged to the select circle of fighters for truth. Made acutely conscious by his growing awareness of the way things are that he stood "with the safe majority" who are "neither for God nor for His enemies" (403), Oliver Treadwell is truly a pitiable figure. And it is to his creator's credit that she encourages our sympathy for Oliver throughout the most intense of Virginia's pathetic reactions. Perhaps the more so because in his rigid indecisions he curiously but constantly calls to mind the contemporary dilemma of the grey-flannel suited. Like theirs, his "imperative," as Miss Glasgow points out, had even been the

opposite of Virginia's—not "I must," but "I want" (404). This observation is deleted from the Old Dominion (1929) and Virginia
(1938) editions. As Oliver's imperative represents, from Miss Glasgow's point of view, the most damning defect in individual perspective, the deletion is important. It is also puzzling, for she omitted
along with it the original accompanying passage which indicates
Virginia's share of responsibility for encouraging Oliver's self-
indulgences: "If only in the beginning she had upheld not his
inclinations, but his convictions; if only she had sought not to soothe
his weakness, but to stimulate his strength; if only she had seen for
once the thing as it was, not as it ought to have been—". Given Ellen
Glasgow's sympathy for what Virginia represented, one can see
readily enough why she did not want Virginia to appear culpable in
practicing a conception of duty for which Dinwiddie was responsible. On the other hand, the deletion in its entirety cannot be taken
as one that indicates a harsher later judgment of Oliver, as
McDowell imagines. There is, however, considerable evidence in
Miss Glasgow's later novels that she grew increasingly aware of the
impossibility of defining a strong character as one like Virginia in
whom duties and desires did not conflict. She reserved motivation
by self-interest ("I want") alone for her genuinely evil or entirely
self-seeking characters such as Angelica Blackburn of *The Builders*
(1919) or Stanley Timberlake of *In This Our Life* (1941). Oliver
obviously does not belong with these. So her early explanation of his
imperative most probably seemed to her an inadequate oversimplification of the motives of a man she insisted to the end upon
viewing as "an idealist," who is "burdened by imagination and the
temperament of an artist." And to the end Oliver Treadwell, like his
disconsolate brothers in grey flannel suits, sustains a natural "lofti-
ness of purpose" alongside a fading capacity to resist "opportunity."
Alas, poor Oliver; he wants so much to be a good man, yet his world
refuses to supply a convincing guidebook to the attainment of his
fond aspirations. Grown beyond the Dinwiddie-inspired "Duty"
that controls Virginia, Oliver is not only "like his age . . . adrift
among disestablished beliefs"; he is aware, as Virginia can never be,

of forces for good that go far beyond her limited and limiting creed. He has learned from living in and with his time of concepts of morality and responsibility wider, deeper, and doubtless more charitable than those Dinwiddie could hope to cull from its fading past for imperfect distribution to its more rapidly fading present. Oliver has learned of them; he merely cannot bring himself to apply them to his own actions. For "these things had been weakened in his character by the indomitable egoism which had ordered his life. There was nothing for him to fall back upon, nothing that he could place above the restless surge of his will" (460–61). And so he did not. But always it is the Dinwiddie creed that Oliver feels he has failed to live up to, and never his new wisdom—the past and not the future of the grey flannels preserves his guilt. Miss Glasgow says of his moments of most intense misery: "Though [Virginia] was not penetrating enough to discern it, there were times when his pity for her amounted almost to a passion, and at such moments he was conscious of a blind anger against Life, as against some implacable personal force, because it had robbed him of the hard and narrow morality on which his ancestors leaned" (457).

But there were other, increasingly frequent interludes in which Oliver held Virginia responsible for his backsliding. Truly enough, she spent a quarter-century upholding his inclinations, soothing his weaknesses, and viewing their marriage, as everything else, so constantly as it ought to be by her traditional canons that she failed to see that he had withdrawn from her completely. At forty-five, confused and hurt by his flippant ridicule of his work and deprived of the "supreme topic" of the children's school reports, she realizes occasionally that she bores him and after her custom silences her honeyed, rippling chatter about inanities. When her older daughter marries, Virginia knows a vague restlessness and wistfully mourns the years ahead with "nothing to do" unless her younger daughter comes home to be wed. But through the years she has felt "no cause for unhappiness" in her own marriage or her lot. For after her fleeting jealousy of Abby Goode, Virginia secures her fears on the ground that Oliver really "does not have that side to his nature," and she can conceive of no comparable delinquency that might permanently mar their union.

So it is that she is initially disturbed rather than alarmed over her apprehension about Oliver's relationship with Margaret Oldcastle. Bolstered by her son's glowing report of the actress and her conviction that the framed photograph Oliver keeps reflects an "honest woman," she cannot consciously resolve her uneasiness. Only in an intuitive instant, alone in her house after gazing at the photograph, does Virginia perceive "that life had treated her as it treats those who give, but never demand. She had made the way too easy for others; she had never exacted of them; she had never held them to the austerity of their ideals" (444). The illuminating instant fades quickly, and Virginia, returned to normal, reproaches herself for her thoughts—until the next day when she discovers that Oliver, for the first time, has neglected to take her picture with him and that the photograph of Miss Oldcastle is missing from its frame.

Firmly banishing the fear and the wound of her discovery, Virginia still refuses to acknowledge anything amiss. With sincere innocence she wonders aloud at Oliver's informing her upon his return that he has established a separate income for her, murmurs confidingly to her friend Susan that it "makes her smile" to consider the contrast between the Don Quixote Oliver of her youth and the money-minded Oliver of the present, and is gently amazed at Oliver's embarrassed attempts to dissuade her from attending his new opening in New York. Only the alien city is brutal enough to thrust the truth upon her. Oliver's infatuation and her own death sentence are hurled at her in overheard scraps of gossip in an hotel lobby. And Virginia is perceptive enough to realize that with this forced knowledge her life is ended. Her remaining strength is only the strength of passive endurance; there is no longer any real question of refusing to surrender. Momentarily reaching out toward "that lost spirit of youth that had once carried her in a wild race over the Virginian meadows," Virginia goes to see Margaret Oldcastle only to find that, confronting her, she can say nothing. Nothing at all, for Virginia sees dimly, almost unconsciously, that

Margaret Oldcastle, like Oliver, is of the present while she herself belongs to a way of life that is past. A way of life fading permanently, but strong enough still to demand of Virginia the best possible vindication of its precepts. Her inherited obligation to keep life's surface sweet, her instincts of breeding, all the "principle" she has learned, principle "filtering down through generations . . . so inseparable from the sources of character, that it had passed at last through the intellect into the blood" (488), conquer in this crisis, as they must, the outcry and struggle of the self in revolt. Virginia stands silent before Margaret Oldcastle, wrapped in "unassailable gentleness" and the dignity of "defeat that surrenders everything except the inviolable sanctities of the spirit," shielded by that gentleness and dignity from pity and resentment. "Then, because it was impossible to say the things she had come to say, because even in the supreme crises of life she could not lay down the manner of a lady, she smiled the grave smile with which her mother had walked through a ruined country, and taking up her muff, which she had laid on the table, passed out into the hall" (487). This Virginia is, then, what blood and Dinwiddie have made her, and just as surely, this Virginia is damned.[8]

Had the lady been allowed to fade into the distance complete with grave smile and muff, both her blood and Dinwiddie might have come off better. Instead she returns to her empty home to play the role of martyr quietly, to shut out even Dinwiddie, to make a last stand for Pendleton idealism against the nasty evil of the actual; but even she knows that her purpose, like Oliver's letter begging for culpable liberation that she throws on the fire half read, is crumbling to ashes. Declining to acknowledge openly the fact of Oliver's departure, refusing to realize the "processes" leading to his freedom, sparing the children knowledge of her tragedy, all these are gestures without meaning or power for her now despite lifelong perfection in comparable subterfuge. Meant to be only pitiable in her inability to understand where she has failed, Virginia becomes, despite Ellen

[8] Ellen Glasgow remarks somewhat testily that Virginia's instinct was "a mere anachronism" only to the "vulgar or undisciplined" (*ibid.*, p. 93).

Glasgow's intentions, almost contemptible in her helpless hysteria of despair. But the measure of our contempt can only equal the strength of Dinwiddie's hold over Virginia, a hold that does not diminish even with her realization that the world has passed beyond Dinwiddie's standards. In her final delirium of despair, when even her Pendleton idealism can find nothing left to evade, Virginia tries once more to act, only to find that the code which permits her to undertake Oliver's "salvation" prohibits accomplishing that salvation. She may convince herself that Oliver must be saved from himself, from sin and utter damnation; she may even travel to New York for a final appeal; she cannot commit the "vulgarity of thrusting her presence into his life."

Returning by train to Dinwiddie, she overhears an angry cleric decrying politics as civilization's foremost menace. Lastingly enveloped in that total innocence which is so irritatingly allied with total depravity in hope for recovery, she can only wonder at the absurdity of imagining that "civilization could make any difference to anybody on earth" (523). And even Ellen Glasgow is not much comforted by the bond between Harry and his mother that precipitates the concluding note of the novel to let us know that Harry is homeward bound.[9]

But Virginia's final disillusioned quandary is one worth pondering. There can be no doubt that "civilization" is to her one half an equation balanced by Dinwiddie precepts and practices. More significant, Ellen Glasgow is, consciously or not, to remain in accord with Virginia by subscribing throughout her novels to the idea that civilization must be equated with Dinwiddie concepts of responsibility, discipline, and goodness. She has been balking only, as she continues to balk, at Dinwiddie practices—the refined evasions the Southern community has perfected to maintain the myth of a flourishing Utopia. For, and this is never really disputed, Southern "civilization" is the only way to maintain a perpetual Garden of

[9] She can only comment feebly, "in emphasizing the strength of this bond, whether as an ideal or an actuality, I am rendering the truth of an individual experience" (*ibid.*, p. 92).

Eden with so many snakes in it. Dinwiddie is totally responsible for
Virginia, but Dinwiddie deserves blame not for "civilizing" Virginia but for neglecting to educate her to overcome the ways of
ungrateful serpents. The snakes are always the real difficulty in
Ellen Glasgow's works. They are perpetually hidden, not only
from her characters and her readers, but from Ellen Glasgow
herself. None of her would-be villains are really villains, harboring
vipers in their bosoms. Like Oliver, they are merely permanently
bitten or hissed out of mind. N. Elizabeth Monroe, annoyed by this
vagueness, insists that Ellen Glasgow has no sense of evil.[10] But this
seems unfair. The snakes are there in plenty; they are only unat-
tached.

Indeed Miss Glasgow opens her autobiography, *The Woman
Within*, with a description of disembodied evil—her "earliest remembered sensation." As an infant staring out the window "as
contented and as mindless as an amoeba," she sees staring in at her "a
face without a body . . . a vacant face, round, pallid, grotesque,
malevolent." Terrorized at the "bloated mask of evil," the unchang-
ing face that she alone can see, she is wracked by convulsions. And
although one feels in reading her melodramatic rendering of this
experience that a part of her knows perfectly well that she is
recounting a common childhood response to the mysteries of sun-
sets, shadows, or imagination, nothing is more clear than her demand that we recognize her childish fear of the staring malevolent
mask that dominated her first moment of consciousness as symbolic
of a haunting consciousness of evil that dominated her life—"terror
of the formless, the unknown, the mystery, terror of life, of the
world, of nothing or everything?"[11]

Perceptive enough to realize that the Dinwiddie Edens of the
South are decaying, snake-infested gardens, Ellen Glasgow maintains only that they have been attempts to perpetuate orderly and
flourishing beauty. In her view these Southern Shangri-las are
withering partly because time and change are proving many of their

[10] N. Elizabeth Monroe, *The Novel and Society* (Chapel Hill, N.C., 1941), p. 176.
[11] *Woman Within*, pp. 3–4.

remedies for snake bite ineffective, but most of all because they have too often tried to outwit the snakes by pretending that they were not there. Still, the gardens were created by a society that felt the necessity for an Eden. The new order seems to produce only a violent irreconcilable disorder: a helpless tangle of rare new flowers of truth, the same plentiful weeds, and worst of all, the same multitude of snakes, too often disguised as flowers. If we cannot go back to the Edens of Southern yesterday, and Ellen Glasgow emphasizes this impossibility, we dare not reject standards of conduct that perpetuate the possibility of cultivated gardens. Why? Merely because tangled weed-patch societies lead to confused anarchies which are intolerable, as surely every upstanding inhabitant of the universe will agree. Moreover, Miss Glasgow doubtless would continue snappishly, prune and pluck those standards though we may and should, only the vulgar will dissent about the meaning of responsibility, discipline, and good, about the greenery to be nurtured. And that's that. Move on to plant new flowers alongside the old, but be orderly about it; there is no other way. Otherwise all will be barren, eroded, lost.

Many of the Glasgow novels following *Virginia* dwell heavily on the "otherwise" of the new order and the mess it has created. But even in *Virginia* Ellen Glasgow suggests an answer to the how of orderly moving on—though most particularly addressed to the Dinwiddie born and bred. Increasingly relishing the modern dilemma in which squirming facts exceed squamous minds so that returning to old faiths becomes an absurdity, she nevertheless manages to reinforce that answer in her next two novels: *Life and Gabriella* (1916) and *The Builders* (1919). In many ways the ideal standards of conduct she conceives for her heroines are hopelessly Southern and even silly in their assumptions and limitations. Miss Glasgow herself did not long remain sanguine in her attitude toward them. Nonetheless, she manages to make such standards conceivable, if not altogether believable; necessary, if not sufficient, in a cause few contemporaries even recognized until the twenties.

Susan Treadwell, confidante and counterpart of Virginia Pendleton, embodies the hope of the South in the saga of Dinwiddie. Subjected to an upbringing and education identical in most respects to that which doomed Virginia to her paralysis of innocence, Susan still brings off a neat little personal revolution. Yet her triumph, if modest, is as thoroughly convincing as it is thoroughly Southern. All Susan gets is the man she wants rather than a spinster's lot as superior servant to aging parents. At that, she manages marriage only by moving her husband into her father's house. But her management is skillful enough to combine adherence to Dinwiddie standards of duty and responsibility with a meaningful and even happy personal life; it is also good enough to defy old Cyrus Treadwell and make him like it. Surely not only chance and circumstance separate the fates of Virginia and Susan. Nor is the difference a matter of their comparative intelligence, no matter how often or how sorely tempted we may be to believe that it is.

Although Susan never measured up to Miss Priscilla Batte's standards for the ideal, docile pupil as Virginia did, although her perceptions are undeniably keener, her convictions about right and wrong are much the same. Miss Glasgow allows Susan an aristo-cratic, if decaying, mother and a father of stern and sturdy Calvinist stock. Much is apparently to be made of this combination. Ellen Glasgow herself descends from comparable parents; so do later heroines like Dorinda Oakley and Ada Fincastle, who in conse-quence are significantly labeled as ladies who have inherited a "conflict of types." The difficulty is that while we know that the heritage of a conflict of types is important for Miss Glasgow, we never really know why. Perhaps she was merely adhering to the time-tested notion that too much inbreeding produces idiots, even in Virginia—a notion that she herself exploited in the best of her short stories, "Jordan's End," *The Shadowy Third and Other Stories* (Garden City, 1923). (If so, as we have secretly hoped all along, the lovely last bloom of the Pendleton line may be merely a case in point.) Just as probably she may have felt that at a time when all traditions seemed to be wearing thin, two traditions were better than one. Actually I think we must be content to allow Miss

Glasgow her favorite heritage as a private conviction or symbol. If we do, we can readily see that a heroine who inherits both romantic if idle visions and real if ruthless power to realize her ambitions is likely to be more personable as well as more successful than one who has only visions or only power.[12] Thus, Susan Treadwell's success.

A more significant, even startling triumph is won by Gabriella Carr of *Life and Gabriella* (1916). As the title suggests, her victory is over the life of her Southern upbringing. Refusing, as Susan Treadwell refused, to conform to the South's ideal of femininity, Gabriella seeks and finally wins a fulfillment at once more revolutionary and more complete than Susan would have dared to imagine. Nonetheless Gabriella's is not a conquest through rejection; she preserves as steadfastly as Susan, as completely as Virginia Pendleton, the commitments of her heritage to honor, duty, and responsibility. The chronicle of her achievement Miss Glasgow intended as both the concluding volume in her history of manners and as "a companion piece" to *Virginia*. Of course, *Life and Gabriella* is far from Ellen Glasgow's last word on the history of manners, however much she may have thought she shifted her perspective in later novels; it is an interesting companion piece to Virginia.

Gabriella's world was the world of the nineties and Virginia's that of the eighties, but as their creator points out, worlds quite different. "Although Gabriella lived only a decade later than Virginia, a whole era of change and action, one of the memorable epochs in history, separated the two women."[13] In the eighties the past as "a state of mind" lingered on, and the value of the Southern woman still lay "in sentiment," or at any rate, in her ability to

[12] While Miss Glasgow's conception and labeling of the heritage of a "conflict of types" may have been private, it fits nicely within what William R. Taylor establishes as the pervasive legend of the dual origin of American national character, a legend in which the ideal American emerges as a mixture of the best stereotyped traits of the Cavalier and the Yankee. Of course, throughout her novels Ellen Glasgow rather neatly (and quite justifiably if we accept Cash's emphasis on the strength of the South's frontier heritage) ascribes a Southern origin to both the Cavalier and Yankee traits.

[13] *Certain Measure*, p. 97.

ornament "civilization" combined with her legendary powers to subdue if not to obliterate the male nature. But by the nineties the hungry and defiant younger generation, over-weary with the denials of a stubbornly reconstructed Virginia, had achieved a spiritual and in some instances a real exodus. Ellen Glasgow's own career is a case in point, and it may well be that while she saw her mother's fate in that of Virginia Pendleton, she conceived Gabriella's achievements from the stuff of her own dreams and aspirations.

The Southerners' migration from their home ground had begun in the Reconstruction period among those of the former gentry who would not or could not be reconstructed, as Miss Glasgow points out in *The Wheel of Life* (1906). As she makes clear in this novel in her portraits of the Fowlers, many of these former aristocrats now faced the necessity of adapting themselves to the standards of their new way of life, a necessity they met with various degrees of enthusiasm and success. Gabriella, however, is meant to represent the youthful emigrés of the next generation, emigrés whose rebellious, enthusiastic departure from their place of birth is often cited as the controlling reason for the South's persisting backwardness. Marshall Fishwick states this position most forcefully when he says: Virginia's chief export for a generation was brains."[14] Whatever the case, the dominant impression the novel creates is that of recording the success story of a Southern Miss Alger. Its real interest lies in the disparity between Gabriella's assumptions and those of her Northern fictional counterparts. For the obstacles she hurdles, albeit with ladylike grace, are as standard as her accomplishments—including her final marriage to a genuine Northern Horatio. Her inhibitions and attitudes are not standard at all.

Although born an "incarnation of energy"[15] battling from birth the powers of decay and inertia that surround her, Gabriella has

---

[14] *Virginia: A New Look at the Old Dominion*, p. 151.

[15] *Ellen Glasgow, Life and Gabriella* (Garden City, 1916), p. 16. Page references to future quotations from this novel in Chap. 3 are given in parentheses or brackets after the quotations.

modest ambitions. Given her choice, Miss Glasgow tells us, "she would have instinctively selected, guided by generations of gregarious ancestors, the festive girlhood which Cousin Pussy so ardently described" (31). Actually, Gabriella consciously refuses her instinctive choice and the murmured advice of her relatives because her widowed mother's "reduced circumstances" necessitate dependence on those willing, although comparably reduced relatives, and Gabriella finds intolerable a dependence Virginia Pendleton assumed necessary. Of course she has the advantage of a constant horrible example before her in the person of her sister Jane. A decade married to an irresponsible scapegrace, the saintly Jane thrives on a martyrdom commanding incessant attention, advice, and aid from her hovering family. Rejecting Jane's sanctified helplessness at the same time that she rejects a totally decorative youth for herself, Gabriella assumes that money is, after all, the commodity most needed to remedy both Jane's and her own dependence.

An innocent, reasonable, and obvious assumption surely; an assumption, moreover, defended in terms of honor, duty, responsibility, and an assumption that no Alger hero would ever be without. But Gabriella's decision to earn money by working in a local millinery shop entails the decade's revolution that separates her world from Virginia Pendleton's and Jane's. It is, after all, a decision defying the whole social structure in which she lives, shaking dangerously the moldy but firm foundations of life in a Southern community. No lady, as Gabriella knows very well, ever works in a store; it is permissible, if one is pressed, to teach, to sew or crochet in one's home, to make lampshades, to send some of one's prize angel food to the Woman's Exchange, but never to accept a situation in a shop. That, her relatives chorus, destroys one's social position. But Gabriella dismisses "social position" as firmly as she dismisses her family's numerous "acceptable" suggestions. She is convinced that selling hats is the most attractive way to make the most money; therefore, she will sell hats.

The necessity of making Gabriella a thoroughgoing revolutionary by her stand on selling hats may have been brought home to

Ellen Glasgow by the abortive millinery career of one of her own
"relatives." Stark Young in *The Pavilion* mentions that his Aunt
Julia, orphaned as a child and sent to live with her mother's sister
and her husband, Dr. Gholson, the brother of Ellen Glasgow's
mother, decided on a postwar career in the millinery business as her
planter husband's fortunes sank lower and lower. "She would open
a millinery shop; now there, she said, you could make a fortune.
Various cousins suggested the loose atmosphere that clung to the
name of milliners and mantuamakers, the only women in Victorian
days who, we were to assume because of their Parisian origins, had
frankly scattered their charms."[16] Aunt Julia's fortune never materialized as all the possible customers in her small town of Como,
Mississippi, were either relatives or friends to whom custom made it
improper to sell anything. The result was that she spent her life
renovating her friends' hats in her own home for gracious thanks.

In her more determined revolt, Gabriella does not cast off her
large, good family, nor they her, but much is lost in her denial of
their preferences that she maintain her "own station in life," and
even more is forsaken by her rejection of their "proper feeling" that
none of theirs must come to want, let alone work, as long as the
family can help. Gabriella does cast off Arthur Peyton, her childhood sweetheart, before entering Brandywine's millinery department. Again she feels compelled to deny the old for the new.
Arthur, a young man "always in perfect order" from his immacu-
late linen to his inherited conceptions, is distressed at the prospect of
his vision of Gabriella as "a star shining serenely above the sordid
struggle" (36) being blotted out by old Brandywine and his environment. His "sentiment is against it," and although he offers no
opposition other than that of sentiment, Gabriella is aware that
accepting Arthur involves ignoring poverty and submitting to his
sentiment—"who ever heard of a woman of good family starving in
Virginia" (39)? Already committed to the notion that poverty
cannot afford sentiment and remain honest, she not only refuses

---

[16] Stark Young, *The Pavilion* (New York, 1951), pp. 86–87.

Arthur but enlarges on her honesty by informing him that she doesn't really love him.

Still, she is sufficiently a product of her Richmond upbringing to be genuinely surprised that her revelation scene impresses her as matter-of-fact, even rather foolish. At the least, she had imagined herself collapsed in tears on the same sofa "sacred to the tragedy of poor Jane"; instead she not only finds herself without inclination to weep, but nerved to confess her attraction to George Fowler, expatriate Southerner from New York with whom she was scandalously smitten during his brief visit to Richmond a few months earlier. All this is a bit hard on poor Arthur, who, bound by traditional responses, can only mutter, "I'll never give you up," and "I thought women were more constant than men!" And Gabriella scarcely comforts him by agreeing that she, too, considers her behavior shocking and strange, even contrary to possibility, since she ought to have virtuously held to her engagement and she ought not to have fallen in love with George first. But she did love George, whether George returned her love or not, and she found herself merely "being false" by fighting to remain true to Arthur.

Despite her clinical detachment in the rejection scene, Gabriella was not as free of Arthur and the life he represented as she thought. Arthur was to haunt her, much as Jason Greylock later haunted Dorinda Oakley, well into her middle years, as the dream she ought to have espoused. Meanwhile, Gabriella feels only that her refusal of Arthur, like her decision to work, is reasonable, if improper. For she knows full well that being reasonable violates the cultivation of "exquisite sensibility." "The most disagreeable thing about Gabriella, Jane had once said, was her inveterate habit of being reasonable" (36). Determined that exquisite sensibility, however desirable, is a present luxury yet more disagreeable than reason, Gabriella goes on after banishing Arthur to practical success at Brandywine's. Her short career as a Richmond business woman is soon cut off by her marriage to George Fowler, but she strenuously renews her struggle to weigh sense and sensibility.

Indeed, Gabriella's marriage almost founders before it begins owing to her insistence that her mother must live with her to be cared for properly. To Gabriella this demand is only sensible; to George it is only irritating obstinacy, and his furious reaction is darkened by a dreary vision of a lifetime in Mrs. Carr's company. Although George threatens that she must choose him or her mother, although life without George seems a tragic prospect, although she exonerates him by judging his declaration that he wants her to himself a natural instinct, even "reasonable" sensibility, Gabriella remains firm. She wants above all to give in to George; she feels she cannot because she ought not. So she doesn't. Her "vein of iron," a militant faith in "the moral law, stripped bare of clustering delusions" (188), compounded of the "Berkeley conscience" inherited from her mother's people and the "fighting spirit" of her father, long dead in the Confederate cause, guides her in her youth as it is to guard her later. Undeniably the Berkeley conscience, even in Gabriella, appears composed of at least one part exquisite sensibility (a generous stipend for one's mother if she is living or sentiment if she is dead is all that is required of any Alger hero), and the rest seems hardly more than Southern smugness about the moral law. Still, it is her father's fighting spirit that makes Gabriella's revolt effectual, for the Berkeleys specialize in graceful surrender; and just as that fighting spirit triumphed initially in the millinery sortie, so it controls the strength of Gabriella's Berkeley belief in her quarrel about her mother. Even more important, it is to combine increasingly with Gabriella's "sensible" revisions of "the moral law" during her later experiences.

Winning her point openly with George, Gabriella marches happily into marriage. Then, pleading poverty, George fails to make provisions for her mother to live with them. That failure of trust marks him as a cad and a boor, for he has violated a part of the code Miss Glasgow cherishes and, above all, violated it in a servile and wholly unchivalrous manner. In fact, George is soon revealed as a totally spoiled and worthless ingrate, dependent on his parents' generosity for his livelihood. Moreover, transplantation to New York has not only corrupted George thoroughly but has reduced the senior Fowlers to Northern marketplace standards. George's father, though gentlemanly enough, relies for alternate affluence and near bankruptcy on the fluctuations of the stock market, and the Fowlers feel constrained to "keep up appearances" in any event. Gabriella early discovers a discrepancy in the New York and Richmond manner of maintaining these appearances when, during a period of economy, she notices Mrs. Fowler's willingness to purchase cheap underwear. Mrs. Carr's standards had always demanded that she keep up appearances even to herself, and although Gabriella reflects that on the whole she prefers "the safe middle distance between two exacting standards of living" (168), Miss Glasgow permits no doubt that if the choice is between preserving one illusion or another, Mrs. Carr's thoroughly mended underwear of good quality must be preferred. Indeed, while her heroine is dedicated to denying all illusions in the name of honorable honesty, and while much of the gaiety and humor of this novel turn on Gabriella's Southern-bred naiveté in this regard, the line between illusory and real values is meant always to be sharply drawn. The real values are assumed, of course; they are never meant to give trouble, and they don't.[17] Narrow, even foolish as we may find them, they are constantly, comfortingly clear.

So it is that Gabriella's growing disillusionment with George can justifiably turn to disgust when, after four months of marriage, he comes home drunk. His behavior, not his drinking, is the issue, for George is "revoltingly" sick all night, and Gabriella reasons that he must be lost not only to respect but to common decency to appear

[17] It was not only within novels that would-be Southern revolutionaries like Gabriella enjoyed the advantage of being able to assume the real values. Miss Glasgow in undertaking her individual revolution could do so as well; so could the group of her latter-day contemporaries who came to be called the "Southern Agrarians." Donald Davidson makes this point in retrospect when he says: "But as to attachments and assumptions, it is only the backward look that now allows me to distinguish them as a kind of discovery. Our great good fortune was that we shared pretty much the same assumptions about society, about man, nature, and God. And we were most fortunate in not even having to ask ourselves whether or not we were on common ground in such matters" (*Southern Writers in the Modern World* [Atlanta, 1958], p. 6).

before her in that state. But as she has determined that reason, not emotion, must govern her actions, so she decides to continue her marriage and ignore George.

All her life she had suffered from an unrestrained indulgence of the virtues—from love running to waste through excess, from the self-sacrifice that is capable of everything but self-discipline, from the intemperate devotion to duty that is as morbid as sin. Balance, moderation, restraint—these seemed to her . . . to be the things most worth striving for [183].

Either moderation and restraint or her almost amiable acceptance of her husband's weaknesses permits Gabriella to continue with George for six fairly comfortable years. Permanently relegating him to the ranks of the weak and unregenerate, she can assume responsibility for her mother and her two children without despairing unduly over his defections. In fact, when she learns at last that George has "taken up" with another woman, her habit of self-reliance is so strong that it allows her only brief moments of humiliation. Within the hour of her enlightenment, she leaves the Fowler home to secure a job, her will firm in its continuing dedication to resist Jane's fate, her pride comforted by fanciful images of Arthur Peyton's lifelong devotion. Just as well that she returns triumphant in the knowledge of a position secured with Madame Dinard, Millinerist, for chaos greets her. George has disappeared permanently with his ladylove; Archibald Fowler has on that day been declared bankrupt, and he collapses and dies before the next dawn. Amid the ruins of the Fowler prosperity, only the "impoverished family acres" in the South remain to provide bare support for George's mother.

At this point in a self-respecting Alger story, an "influential friend," incidentally a millionaire, ought to appear. And so he does for Gabriella. Judge Crowborough, poking among the packing-case confusion of the Fowler home, may be an ugly old roué attracted mainly to shapely females; he does have "the dignity of one who possesses an income of half a million dollars a year." True to form, he offers money, but although Gabriella refuses that, except in case of emergency, she accepts his offer of help in divorce proceedings with enthusiasm. Oddly enough, the idea of divorce causes her no qualms; her eagerness to have "her freedom" is most unladylike or at least un-Southern. Or would be if she weren't Gabriella. For, "being reasonable," she had absolved herself of responsibility to maintain her marriage on the afternoon of her sojourn to Madame Dinard's—even before she learns of George's desertion. "He had broken the tie between them," a tie that she now realized had been "humiliating bondage" at best, bondage to be borne only in the name of duty, and now George's behavior had released her of her duty.

Gabriella's "sweet reason" in this matter may well have evolved only from her circumstances—circumstances which allowed her to reinterpret honor, duty, and responsibility as Virginia Pendleton and even Susan Treadwell could not. These values were, after all, for Southerners most closely connected with "family," and Gabriella's family had been removed by distance, financial disasters, death, and disappearance from her and her two children as Virginia's and Susan's never were. That Gabriella was prepared to support her children then becomes only incidental. Most important, she could act as she did for herself and for them, and act honorably, because she was "free" to do so. This realization of freedom causes her almost joyous acceptance of the disasters that have fallen round her, nourishes her vision of the future as an adventure—a life in which "the imperative necessity was to keep to the last the ardent heart of the true adventurer" (281). Happy in what she rightly feels a rare chance to pattern her own destiny, Gabriella still protests too much that her position is not unique. It is doubtful if either she or Miss Glasgow sees the extent to which her "ardent heart" separates her from the "thousands of women living and fighting . . . far worse off than she" (275). Nor do they know or want to know, apparently, that Gabriella rejoices in a freedom that entails no real rejection of the old for the new. Vagaries of chance and circumstance permit her to accept adventure without denying the essential structure of the life she revolts against. Without those vagaries, Miss Glasgow's heroine might well have been faced with decisions neither she nor her creator wishes to consider. Meanwhile a heart made ardent by fortuitous escape from custom and ceremony into hardship is distinction enough to single out a Southern aspirant like Gabriella from the thousands of Carrie Meebers who are truly far worse off than she in their wistful longing to be enfolded by any parody of custom and ceremony chance may offer.

Gabriella's heart beats ardently throughout the modest, even commonplace adventures of a decade's career with Madame Dinard's in New York. She has before her constantly the option of succumbing to a flight to Richmond and the protecting arms of her family; constantly she rejects that option. Always it is her heritage of her father's "fighting spirit" that keeps the flame in her heart alive and her resolution firm. Indeed, "fighting spirit" becomes Miss Glasgow's emblazoned banner in this novel, the standard behind which one suspects the youth of the South are supposed to rise again, in orderly and well-directed ranks, of course, to rejoin, nay, remake the union. Even more, this spirit serves at once as the symbol of enduring Southern courage and the "true American" ideal—"optimism springing out of struggle." "Do you know," one of Gabriella's admirers sighs, "you have always made me think of the American spirit at its best—of its unquenchable youth, its gallantry, its self-reliance" (326).

In "fighting spirit," then, the best of the North and South are to meet and mingle. And so they do in *Life and Gabriella* when the heroine finally chases after and accepts the "improbable" Ben O'Hara ("the only [character] that conformed to an original model"[18]). Before that acceptance can take place, however, Gabriella must first be made aware of some of the limitations of her own revolt. Her acquaintance with the rather crude Mr. O'Hara and her rather irritated acknowledgment that he attracts her accomplishes this self-realization, slowly, grudgingly, but inevitably. She comes to see her past accomplishments as merely those of a Southern

---

[18] *Certain Measure*, p. 101.

woman living and working in the city, cultivating in herself, her children, her surroundings, the standards and ideals of her Richmond childhood, shutting herself away from the "multitudinous movements of life" around her.

For the first time, flowing like a current from the mind of the man beside her, there came to her an understanding of her own share in the common progress of life—for the first time she felt herself to be . . . an integral part of that city, one cell among closely packed millions of cells. Something of the responsibility she felt for her own children seemed to spread out and cover the city lying there in its dimness and mystery [470].

As her perceptions deepen and her sense of responsibility widens under O'Hara's tutelage, Gabriella must acknowledge his worth. Characteristically enough, she begins by lamenting his lack of grammar and his unfamiliarity with Shakespeare, by regretting that O'Hara was denied the university training wasted on George Fowler. Then, somewhat ungratefully recalling Judge Crowborough's "broadest culture" narrowed by the gleam in his "small, fishy eyes," she decides that if character and culture do not combine, character can best stand alone. From that decision, aided by O'Hara's good-natured tolerance of her objections to his speech, clothing, and furnishings, Gabriella proceeds easily to attribute "a kind of spiritual consciousness" to the "wild Irishman." His revelations of his rise from the gutter and a twenty-year loyalty to a drug-addicted wife complete her captivation. Of course Gabriella has reason to be captivated and humbled by the myth turned man that is Ben O'Hara. Nurtured in a society where the cult of family and the heritage of ideals are entwined, she sees him as a phenomenon: "Without friends, without knowledge, except the bitter knowledge of the streets, he had fought his fight, and had kept untarnished a certain hardy standard of honour" (457). And, having accepted his genius, she embraces his standards; Mr. O'Hara is wealthy; Gabriella decides for wealth as a measure of worth, helped along a bit, no doubt, in this traitorous view, by long experience with straitened unpleasantness. "Of course, I've passed the sentimental age," she declares. "If Mr. O'Hara had been poor, I suppose I should never have thought of him; but his money does make a difference. It stands for success, achievement, and ability, and I like all those qualities" (472–73).

One last barrier to accepting O'Hara remains invulnerable. He is not an "ideal." Nor, Gabriella realizes, is there ever any possibility that he will become one. Lacking the breeding, taste, restraint of a gentleman, lacking custom and tradition to order and discipline the violence of his virtues, those virtues, "like his personality, were large, flamboyant, and without gradations of colour" (479). Such enormity and gaudiness, even in noble deeds, ill fit the gentle attributes of Gabriella's visionary ideal, who behaves remarkably like her memories of Arthur Peyton. Responding like the practical woman that she is, Gabriella returns to Richmond to measure O'Hara against Arthur. Finding Richmond rather too much changed, too much addicted to the superficial benefits conferred by moneyed upstarts less sterling than O'Hara, Gabriella, perversely enough, finds Arthur Peyton too much the same. Now, despite his lovely behavior, she dethrones him as an ideal. Looking old, ineffectual, and acquiescent, Arthur has lost whatever "fighting spirit" he may have inherited. Despite the promise of his training, his intellect, his traditions, he has submitted to failure, distrust of life, negation. Afraid of risk, even of effort, Arthur, Gabriella judges, "had failed because he lacked the essential faith in the future" (515). Ben O'Hara, the incarnation of the fighting spirit and the hope of the future, wins her at last.

He embodied, she felt, the triumphs and the failures of American democracy—this democracy of ugly fact and of fine ideals, of crooked deeds and of straight feeling, of little codes and of large adventures, of puny lives and of heroic deaths—this democracy of the smoky present and the clear future. 'If this is our raw material today,' she thought hopefully, 'what will the finished and signed product of to-morrow be' [480]?

Ellen Glasgow continued to search for the promise of tomorrow in the products of an ever smoky present, but that promise reas-

sumed the image of her original Southern dream. The smoke grew
heavier, and never again did she allow herself to indulge in the
lighthearted audacity of optimism that permeates *Life and
Gabriella*. No more improbable Northern phenomena like Ben
O'Hara arose to embody the American dream for both North and
South. Her future heroes were all Southerners. And if they were of
the people, they were even more clearly above them. Always they
stood apart, solitary in their glory and their suffering—strong,
lonely leaders of men, lacking only someone to lead. The plight of
her future heroines was, if anything, even sadder. Most often the
ideal to which they might shape their dreams never materialized for
them to wed; indeed, women like Dorinda Oakley, Ada Fincastle,
and Roy Timberlake spent much of their effort remolding or
remaking an existence shattered by a George Fowler far less coop-
erative in his disappearance than Gabriella's first husband. Rarely
did ideal hero and heroine even appear in the same novel. When
they did meet and love, as in Miss Glasgow's next effort, *The
Builders* (1919), insurmountable obstacles kept them apart.

The obstacle permanently separating Caroline Meade and David
Blackburn, ideal leaders of the new South in *The Builders*, is
nothing less than David's wife, Angelica. Anna Jeannette Fitzhugh,
dubbed Angelica as a child because of her appearance, is the
personification of evil hiding beneath the lovely mannerisms of the
old South. Caroline and David, holding hard to courage and ideal
ism, masked in her by a quiet and rather colorless manner, in him by
a blunt, harsh exterior, go down to helpless defeat before Angelica's
externally gracious malice.

Ellen Glasgow omitted *The Builders* from her Virginia edition,
and she may well have done so merely because she realized that
Blackburn's naively conceived political monologues roared in a
vacuum. Not only are Blackburn's views on America's political
responsibility and role as leader of the world in the future (America
has at last entered World War I) detached from the structure of the
novel, they echo Miss Glasgow's more skillfully rendered position
in *The Battle-Ground* that war and its aftermath ought ideally to

serve as an awakening, a second chance to test and refine ideals. In *The Builders*, David Blackburn takes the position that the whole of America is to awaken from the evasive idealism that characterizes the manners and morals dominating the present government: "sentimental, evasive of realities, idealistic in speech, and materialistic in purpose and action."[19] Of course, an America emerging victorious from the war is obviously essential to Blackburn's vision of his country's political destiny and spiritual leadership in this novel, while a South defeated on the battlefield appeared equally important to the Southern awakening Miss Glasgow envisioned in the earlier work. But it is not difficult to see how the persisting confusions of post World War I America, like the illusions persisting in the South after the Civil War, caused Miss Glasgow in later years to view with chagrin if not despair a social scene she had once depicted as filled with hope and promise. In point of fact, the chaos and confusion characterizing Southern society after World War I became the controlling theme of almost all her later novels. As political prophecy, then, *The Builders* must have served the mature Ellen Glasgow chiefly as a mocking reminder of her political naiveté even as her tender treatment of the character of David Blackburn may well have stood as a mocking symbol of her naiveté in personal affairs.

I might add that while Miss Glasgow seems to me extraordinarily successful in banishing all naiveté from her treatment of characters in her later fiction, she was never successful in rendering convincing political leaders in terms of their politics. And she was least successful of all with David Blackburn whose political views are more abundantly set forth than those of Nick Burr (*The Voice of the People*, 1900) or Gideon Vetch (*One Man in His Time*, 1922). For the reason we have not far to seek: it is simply that, in fiction or out, Miss Glasgow, whatever her temporary enthusiasms, is totally apolitical in her perspective. What interests her is always individual character, never an individual's politics. A desire to conceive strong

---

[19] Ellen Glasgow, *The Builders* (Garden City, 1919), p. 22.

character in a position of authority rather than any abiding interest in political leadership as such explains her concentration on political leaders in three of her novels. It explains as well, even if it does not excuse, her failure to make these heroes aware of "the problems of the South" in any conventional sense. For, despite their own great sensitivity to their origins and their social position, none of Miss Glasgow's would-be political heroes conceives of his responsibility in terms of mitigating the differences between Southern social classes. In fact, Nick Burr and Gideon Vetch take pains to avoid serving the interests of the reform elements from which they arise, and David Blackburn shows himself the "black" Republican he is said to be chiefly by protesting against the political apathy of the New South arising from one-party domination.

None of the three is allowed to think in terms of the "sharecroppers" or "poor-white" problem or the "Negro question." This last omission is taken by several critics as particularly serious, especially in the case of David Blackburn. And, granted that Miss Glasgow might be allowed to justify the refusal of Nick Burr and Gideon Vetch to favor the interests of the groups that supported them on the grounds of principle or justice, this excuse certainly does not extend to David Blackburn. He appears unaware that there is a Negro question as well as unconscious that affiliation with any "progressive," and certainly any Republican, elements in the South confronts a Southerner directly with this question. (The entrenched reactionaries of the novel who represent the popular view, such as Angelica and her friend, Lucy Colfax, are quite aware of the connection; for them a Republican is "black" because he is particularly evil in his views on the Negro and, therefore, generally evil.)

McDowell is correct, I think, in his estimate of Blackburn's blindness on this point as one of the damaging features of the novel. But he goes on to say that Miss Glasgow must be considered in her condemnation of America for "evasive idealism" in foreign policy "similarly evasive in her presentation of the Virginia political scene" in this novel (although not in *Virginia*, where she recognizes the problem in Cyrus Treadwell's rejection of responsibility for and even blood ties with his own illegitimate colored son). It is the "similarly evasive" with which I would take issue. While it is quite true that Miss Glasgow, like her own Blackburn, fails to see the Negroes as an "unassimilated entity" not only in this novel, but in all her work, including *Virginia*, and while this is quite irritating in a hero who is drawn as a political leader, it is a perspective not at all comparable to the evasive idealism she so deplores. Truly enough, an evasive idealist would refuse, as Miss Glasgow does, to see the Negro as an unassimilated entity. For the entrenched Southerner of this evasive stamp, the Negro race as an entity has already been assimilated, has been given a place in the community or beneath the community in which it is expected to stay indefinitely without pain or disturbance to anyone. But for Miss Glasgow, the Negro is not an unassimilated entity since he is already viewed by the evasive idealists as having a definite if inferior place in the community; he is, if you like, only too well assimilated, only too much an entity and not a person. The problem is then to view him, as she views Parry Clay of *In This Our Life*, as an individual possessing his full share of emotions, capabilities, and aspirations, an individual who is entitled to fulfill himself not as a Negro with a designated sphere of activities in the community, but as a person who deserves full membership rights in any human community.

One might say, then, that David Blackburn, like Ellen Glasgow, refused to talk of the Negro or race problem because to him, as to her, such terminology belonged to the evasive idealists who would set the Negro as a race apart from the white community. To be sure this is an idealistic view intolerable in a politician, and it is one that belongs most clearly to the mature Ellen Glasgow of the last novels (surely not the Ellen Glasgow who conceived the stereotyped Big Abel of *The Battle-Ground*, for example). It seems, nonetheless, an admirable position when held by a Southerner, the only position that meets ultimate goals or dreams directly, at least to one like myself who with Mr. McDowell still thinks in terms of race problems and Negro entities.

But despite our contemporary anxiety to force upon Miss Glasgow an embarrassed recognition of the total failure of *The Builders* to confront political realities, it is more probable that her real rejection stemmed from an uneasy, half-conscious discomfort at the implications of the novel's allegorical structure. Not only must good submit to the demands of evil in *The Builders*, good is made to stand still while evil triumphs. What's more, there seems no chance for a good so bound by the dictates of the culture and tradition it strives to reaffirm.

This is not at all what Caroline Meade and David Blackburn are made to say or even to feel; it is only what happens. For Angelica wins her way by cold-hearted maneuvering amid the conventions of virtue. And dedicated as they are to well-mannered cultivation of honor and responsibility, the hero and heroine are totally without resources to expose unworthy intentions masked by superficial good manners. So Angelica, always solely motivated by her capricious desire of the moment, manages to ruin her sister-in-law's engagement, her husband's political chances, and to cast Caroline Meade out of her home as a conniver for her husband's affections. She does all this, moreover, almost before Caroline has really perceived that Angelica is not the ill-treated, virtuous wife of boorish David Blackburn, pitied by her community. In fact, Angelica has skillfully completed each move before even her husband or her housekeeper, who know her, foresee her intent. Even had they been able to foresee her purpose, it would have made little difference in their helpless state; Angelica never overstepped conventional propriety. Her virtue is the last decayed flowering of the Southern Eden of illusions—and the most dangerous flourishing. Virginia Pendleton possessed only innocent excess of virtue which drooped when opposed in weak, empty despair; Arthur Peyton and Gabriella's Berkeley relatives clung only to the virtue of graceful surrender to failure. But Angelica exercises

the kind of virtue that's no better than poison. It poisons everything that it touches because all the humanity has passed out of it, just like one of those lovely poisonous flowers that spring up now and then in a swamp. Nothing that's made of flesh and blood could live by it, and yet it flourishes as if it were as harmless as a lily [212].

Flourishes, no doubt, because Southern society is entirely unprepared to deal with lovely mannerisms that shield a venomous soul. And promises to remain unprepared. Caroline Meade and David Blackburn "behave well" with Angelica because their good manners, unlike hers, derive from generous ideals and delicately refined sensitivity to personal responsibility. Ironically enough, neither they nor apparently their creator can bear to imagine the "chronic malady of American life" as anything other than a "disease of manner." To the end they swear allegiance to the code that proclaims "there is no such thing as sound morals without sound manners, for manners are only the outer coating—the skin, if you like—of morals. Without unselfish consideration for others there can be no morality, and if you have unselfish consideration in your heart you will have good manners though you haven't a coat on your back [228–29]. So David Blackburn prepares to live out his life with Angelica in defense of this ideal while Caroline graciously fades away, allowing herself only the silent "scorn of the strong who is defeated for the weak who is victorious" (292). But as admirable and even as ideally "American" as we find their behavior, it is all too clear that Angelica has defeated them, and will continue to defeat the likes of them as long as she may live, whether or not they consent to recognize it.

The saga of Isabel Archer in James' *Portrait of a Lady* casts an interesting shadow on *The Builders*. Of course Isabel did not really aspire as David Blackburn did to lead her society to new heights of idealism. And she had in Gilbert Osmond a far more intelligent, subtle, and devious spouse than David's Angelica could presume to become. But in Isabel's decision to remain with Osmond and in the reflections with which she surrounds that decision, she expresses the same obliviousness of the consequences of her "defeat" as David enjoys in his surrender to Angelica. Miss Glasgow does not prepare us for Angelica's possible reaction to this attitude, but Osmond, as

James presents him, is certainly entitled to outrage. Never has devil's triumph been so snubbed as it is in Isabel's and David's positions. Whether it can be honorable, or even honest, to thus ignore the devil's due is quite a different question for each of the two novels. Yet it seems, at least, that for one like David Blackburn who proposes to remake America in his own mold, the faith that one can absorb evil by one's ideals is surely naive—a kind of deliberate blindness, not unlike old Mrs. Blake's in *The Deliverance*. Even the rude break with the past that Gabriella Carr achieved with her marriage to Ben O'Hara seems more promising.

Nonetheless, these Glasgow heroes and heroines have advanced far beyond Mrs. Blake in their attitudes toward the tradition of the old South. From Virginia Pendleton's tentative questionings and Oliver's guilty rejections to Gabriella's lighthearted defiance of proprieties is a long leap. And the crusading spirit of reform in David Blackburn that captivates Caroline Meade, although it accomplishes little else, testifies to a consuming desire to discriminate between what the South must preserve and what reject to achieve the American dream. Still, their experiences and their convictions are theirs alone; their communities pass them by all unheeding. And to those for whom community of feeling is the beginning and the end of all achievement, this is a sorely felt isolation. Ellen Glasgow needed heroes and heroines whose deeds might be seen and felt by their society, and to these she returned.

I BID YOU TO A ONE-MAN REVOLUTION — THE ONLY REVOLUTION THAT
IS COMING. — ROBERT FROST

During the period of Ellen Glasgow's concentration on novels dramatizing the awakening of Southern womanhood she also wrote a quartet of sagas of "social action." Each an attempt to bridge the chasm she saw between the old South and the new, these novels suffer considerably from the double-edged difficulty of a writer whose ideas are in transition trying to capture an even more determinedly transitional society. Only her abiding interest in character keeps these books from turning into sociological tracts. Her steadfast crusade in behalf of the Southern dream gives them a measure of importance.

Impatience with the way things were caused her to attempt portraits of young rebels and reformers in her earliest novels. Yet even in her youthful enthusiasm for the "new order" her hopes were hemmed by doubts. Michael Akershem, her first would-be emancipator, merely succeeded in destroying himself. Anthony Algarcife, her second rebel, arrived only at hypocritical frustration, and the hope of the people, the poor white Nick Burr, was killed before he might effect any significant change. Later novels suggested an even deeper despair and helplessness in the face of the growing chaos. Laura Wilde turned to the New York poor from the decayed remnants of Southern aristocracy in *The Wheel of Life* with only a faint hope that, unlike her former associates, slum dwellers might not be beyond help. And in *The Builders*, David Blackburn's glorious dreams of a resurrected South died aborning, undermined by the sweet malice of his wife, a perfect Southern gentlewoman.

It is not, then, particularly to be wondered at that Ellen Glasgow, having shown the old order repeatedly refusing to give way to anything save hypocrisy and continued self-deception, finally decides in favor of heroes who are given power to act. They act by casting off not their heritage but the distortions the present has visited upon that heritage. They must discard the fantasies of the past that encumber their world before they can recover that past at all.

The first of these "new men" appears in *The Ancient Law* (1908). Daniel Ordway has been a member of the New York expatriate aristocracy when we first meet him, but he has also been in jail for five years repenting his membership—specifically the "fever of speculation" that "consumed like disease the hereditary instincts, the sentiments of honour, which had barred its way"[1] and had allowed him to gamble and lose on the Stock Exchange funds belonging to his banking house. He begins his regeneration in a small town in rural Virginia as much through necessity as inspiration, for his father, having taken Daniel's wife and children into his Virginia home on the eve of Daniel's conviction, simultaneously forbade his son that home. But Ordway's bookkeeping in a tobacco warehouse is from the outset only a means of entering the community whereby he is able to undertake "good deeds." His activities range from deciding legal claims for indigent laborers to spading a vegetable garden for a thriftless, indolent family of former aristocracy. In his happy disguise as Daniel Smith, philanthropist extraordinary, he soon ingratiates himself with the community, further enhancing his popularity by Sabbath hillside sermons that earn him the title of "Ten Commandment" Smith and the additional admiration of a people well steeped in the tradition of oratory. Symmetrically surrounded half by kindred souls, half by contrasting horrible

[1] Ellen Glasgow, *The Ancient Law* (New York, 1908), p. 11. Page references to future quotations from this novel in Chap. 4 are given in parentheses or brackets after the quotations.

examples, Ordway divides his time between cultivating the like-minded and curing the wasterels. But while, as might be expected, his reforming magic works wonders on laboring drunkards, he is helpless to influence confirmed idle aristocrats like Beverly Brooke, who manages to exist on his ruined acres by dazzling the local clods with impenetrable charm and breeding.

Instead, Ordway aligns himself with Emily Brooke, Beverly's ambitious young sister, in an attempt to keep Beverly's family from starving, for Mrs. Brooke is as improvident and helpless as her spouse: "If her husband had dominated by his utter incapacity, she had found a smaller consolation in feeling that though she had been obliged to drudge she had never learned to do it well. To do it badly, indeed, had become at last the solitary proof that by right of birth she was entitled not to do it at all" (86). The elder Brookes, in fact, harbor all the ideals and mannerisms of Ordway's own family, and only the comparative affluence of the Ordways spare their pretentions the ridiculous illumination of the Brooke poverty. But in Emily Brooke, Daniel finds a more youthful embodiment of his own visions.

Was it some temperamental disgust for the hereditary idleness which had spurred her on to take issue with the worn-out traditions of her ancestors and to place herself among the labouring rather than the leisure class? . . . It seemed to Ordway, looking back at her from the end of his forty years, that he was brought face to face with the spirit of the future rising amid the decaying sentiment of the past [89].

Daniel's own attempt to become the spirit of the future by running for mayor of the town is thwarted when his past catches him up. Not only does confession of his guilt and jail sentence blight his status in his new world, but his father's death calls him back to his old life—a world in which he now finds himself lost, without acceptance or purpose. The Ordway relatives and his own wife and son are embarrassed by his presence rather because his old guilt is public knowledge than because it remains a felt evil. Even his daughter Alice, to whom he feels drawn by a kindred restlessness and dissatisfaction, plays upon his sympathies largely for her own selfish purposes. When he finally manages his escape from what has become the "larger prison" of the life into which he was born, the ignominious circumstances of his flight are overweighed by his great relief. The spendthrift Alice forges a check in her husband's name, for which act Ordway almost eagerly takes the blame, knowing that the society of the Ordways will unquestionably accept his guilt, since a man once violating their laws of life is never "safe" again. By her total inability to face the consequences of her final irresponsibility, Alice commits herself to the Ordway world for her father, an existence characterized chiefly by a large indifference to the effects of one's actions on others, actions justified only by strict attention to surface properties.

Momentarily startled by his absence of feeling at irrevocably cutting himself off from his family, Daniel soon realizes that his decision to do so, far from being heroic, was chiefly a matter of saving himself. " 'No, I did not do it for Alice, or for Alice's child,' he corrected quickly, with a piercing flash of insight. 'It was for something larger, stronger—something as inevitable as the law. I could not help it, it was for myself,' he added, after a minute' " (215). For himself and the possibility of creating a new life and a new Southern world. He begins this existence immediately by returning to the rural town in Virginia where he knows his real friends and his real purpose await him. On the very eve of his return he experiences the "great moment of his life" by averting a riot of the local mill workers. Ironically enough, he accomplishes this by using money inherited from his old life to purchase the mills, but if either he or his creator had paused to consider the source of his power, they would doubtless have insisted that only by such purchases could the real wealth of the South be restored.[2]

[2] Ellen Glasgow is here dramatizing the dream of Southern progress depicted by Cash in his chapter, "Of Quandary and the Birth of a Dream," a dream of power achieved by industrial wealth, power guided by the old aristocratic principles. It is, of course, the old aristocrats who now become the mill owners, for the purpose of reestablishing this genuine Southern ideal. The crusading religious spirit dominating attempts such as Ordway's to implement this dream is testified to by Broadus Mitchell in The Rise of Cotton Mills in the South (Baltimore, 1921) and Henry Savage, Jr., Seeds of Time: The Background of Southern Thinking (New York, 1959).

And Ordway feels that he has only begun as the snarls of the mill hands turn to cheers when he announces a new millennium under his jurisdiction:

He saw himself, not as Banks pictured him, living quietly in Tappahannock, but still struggling, still fighting, still falling to rise and go on again. His message was not for Tappahannock alone, but for all the places where there were men and women working and suffering and going into prison and coming out. He heard his voice speaking to them in the square of this town; then in many squares and in many towns. . . . He turned and stood for a moment looking back at the grass which showed fresh and green under the melting snow [484–85].

Clearly *The Ancient Law*, for all of Ellen Glasgow's ruthlessly "realistic" intentions is romantic fantasy in its own right. The novel is a new version of the Southern legend molded to fit modern circumstances; the hero is reincarnation of the paternalistic Southern gentleman meting out justice in a new sphere, autocratic arbiter of the wrongs of his lesser fellow men. His rejection of his past life and his family's standards is meant not as a repudiation of the hereditary role of the aristocracy, but as a return to that role—to the ancient laws of honor, responsibility, *noblesse oblige* as interpreted in the legends of his forefathers. But significant still is Ordway's sharp break with his old existence, a severing from family and associates more revolutionary in the community structure of the South than the break with the past almost expected of a comparable Northern hero. And equally promising is Ordway's discovery of the possibilities of the common man here—the standards and perceptions of the loyal and kindly mill manager and the young salesman, Banks, are compared very favorably to the principles and practices of the rigid, unseeing Ordways. To be sure, the old mill owner is but another Rainy-Day Jones in a position of more destructive power, and Ordway's only real "equal" is the wellborn Emily Brooke, but Ellen Glasgow's growing interest in the "average man of good will" emerges strongly here. Her next novel, *The Romance of a Plain Man* (1909), is dedicated to that "average Southerner."

Still a romance, as her title itself concedes, the saga of Ben Starr told in the first person seemed to Miss Glasgow in retrospect the "sad result of my youthful fondness for the heroes of romance." She had looked about her for the modern hero, speculating that if he existed anywhere it must be among the rising titans of Southern industry, a conclusion hardly unique except for the adjective. Yet the adjective is all-important in this novel. Ben Starr is not merely the average man "at last in the saddle" as Richmond in 1875 begins "the upward swing of recovery still bearing, one imagines, all the external signs of a devasted region."[3] He remains a member of the rising but firmly categorized "lower middle class," a son of long humble but long entrenched "Anglo-Saxon" stock descended from the English or Scottish pioneers who originally hewed down the Virginian wilderness.[4] And he is to the end overwhelmingly conscious of the deficiencies of his origin.

His sensitivity in this respect and many of his aspirations echo those of Nicholas Burr, and in fact their stories were intended as parallels: "Whereas, in the earlier story, I had dealt with the poorer class from the rural districts, in the present novel I followed the upward way of the working man in the city. The two books were meant to run a parallel course from the middle of the eighteen-seventies well into the first decade of the twentieth century."[5]

Ben Starr's career differs from Burr's, however, in two important ways: Ben gets both the money he wants and the lady he loves; his difficulty is paying proper attention to both. Nicholas never aspired to wealth as a means of achieving status, but Ben's desire for a fortune as proof of his worth stems from the confusion of a city boy who has struggled too long in poverty. And, of course, from the growing sentiment in favor of rising capitalists, the "Redeemers" of

---

[3] *Certain Measure,* p. 71.

[4] "Even if there were validity in the doctrine, prevalent among contemporary novelists, that the culture invented by the newest immigrants represents the only genuine American culture, there would still be no reason, in my opinion, for attempting to portray a confusion of strains with which I had few ties either of association or inheritance" (*ibid.,* p. 68).

[5] *Ibid.,* p. 66.

the South. These Redeemers, who "laid the lasting foundations in matters of race, politics, economics, and law for the modern South," according to C. Vann Woodward,[6] were indeed, as are Ben Starr and General Bolingbroke of this novel, principally devoted to railroad expansion as the chief means of realizing the industrial development of the South. There were also recruited among them men from the ranks of former plantation owners and Confederate soldier-heroes like General Bolingbroke who had the force and acumen to outwit or outlast the financial maneuvers of the carpet-bag regime. But since the number of Bolingbrokes equipped by temperament and the fortunes of war and Reconstruction to serve as successful Redeemers was necessarily small, that number was increasingly reinforced by rising members of the middle or lower middle class like Ben Starr.

That Ben Starrs could be and were accepted into the folds of even the most entrenched aristocracies with only the mild and ineffectual reservations shown by his wife's maiden aunts and the equally ineffectual scorn for their lack of social graces evidenced by the lost George Bolingbrokes of this novel is authentic enough. Woodward notes that as early as 1876 even such a conservative stronghold as Richmond showed a strongly favorable sentiment for the South's new middle class. For example, the *Richmond Whig and Advertiser* in that year actually argued, however condescendingly, that the "parvenuish" qualities of the upstart industrialists ought to be excused on the ground that they were, after all, the vanguard of a new way of life.[7]

But neither the possibility of the actual existence of such figures as Ben Starr nor the reality that they might be grudgingly accepted as necessary to sustain the dreams of the vanguard of the old way of life makes *The Romance of a Plain Man* a notable contribution to Miss Glasgow's social action sagas. As McDowell makes clear, Ellen Glasgow ignores almost entirely the economic and political realities which made careers such as Ben Starr's, as well as General Boling-

---

[6] *Origins of the New South*, p. 22.   [7] *Ibid.*, p. 151.

broke's, possible. What she does achieve by making Ben Starr a publicly unstained ideal representative of his kind is a dramatic, if still romantic, revelation that the most highly developed business ethics do not and cannot suffice in personal relationships or social regeneration. So there remains a sense in which Miss Glasgow's novel is the last word on the industrial dream of the new South. Perhaps by her very neglect of the roles that Northern capital, Northern capitalists, and politics played in developing the new South, she portrayed more accurately than she realized the blind faith that shaped the most compelling visions of the new Southerner. And, in *The Romance of a Plain Man* she was, after all, industriously engaged in pointing to imperfections in a vision that she, too, had seen, had hoped for, however briefly.

Appropriately enough, Ben Starr, as Miss Glasgow's representative of the vanguard of the new, takes as his hero from childhood up a member of the rear guard of the prewar South, General Bolingbroke, president of the South Midland and Atlantic Railroad, a dashing, daring nobleman of the old school, whose position is Ben's life-long dream. And Ben is early on his way to achieve that position, creating a fortune, losing it, rebuilding it once more in classic American fashion. Yet while it can be said of him as truly as of any man that he is indifferent to the money itself, or, more precisely, that he remains oblivious of the possibilities of pleasure its possession entails, he cherishes to the point of obsession the feelings of power and authority his mounting riches lend him. Cherishes them the more compulsively as the years of his marriage to Sally Mickleborough, a high-spirited young gentlewoman, serve only to strengthen "that odd, baffling sensation of struggling to break through an inflexible, yet invisible barrier," the barrier of class traditions by which he found himself "so hopelessly divided from all that to which Sally by right and by nature belonged."[8] Ben learns painfully and at long last the husband's amendment to the Walden

---

[8] Ellen Glasgow, *The Romance of a Plain Man* (New York, 1909), p. 322. Page references to future quotations from this novel in Chap. 4 are given in parentheses after the quotations.

maxim: A man may be rich in proportion to the things he can afford to let alone—but one of them is not his wife. The brief happiness he has known in the interlude of chance poverty between amassing fortunes promises to be restored when he finally renounces the presidency of the railroad for "daily and hourly care" of Sally.

A curiously naive, even amusing story in many ways, as Ellen Glasgow herself ruefully realized in her maturity, yet an interesting fable for all that. In the end, Ben Starr and his Sally cease to exist as individuals, become incarnated spirits of the best of the new and old South respectively.[9] Sally, with her long heritage of passionate principles and lovely manners, "her power of sustained sympathy, of sacrifice" (372), must rightfully belong to Ben to cherish in daily and hourly care, for only he in the modern world stands firmly enough for the big things—"courage and truth and strength and a clean honour toward men and women" (182). And, as Sally observes with a final wistfulness, "it is the big things, after all, that I've wanted most of my life" (464). Ben Starr alone possesses the intensity, the determination to act on these ideals, which the male representatives of the old South in this novel cherish mainly as sentiments. Even General Bolingbroke, though lionhearted and impeccably honorable in his business dealings, proves to have been heartless, even dishonorable, in his personal relationships; he broke the heart and finally the mind of Sally's Aunt Matoaca, whom he loved all his life, but not enough to acknowledge his responsibility for, let alone repent, the consequences of his affair with another woman.

Still, the General belongs to a fading generation whose strong determinations were at least as dominant as its weaknesses. His only descendant, young George Bolingbroke, Ben's contemporary, has a character more stainless only by virtue of its blankness of purpose.

---

[9] "If I invented Sally, she was, in a measure at least, a mingling of all those characteristics we used to think of as especially Virginian" (*Certain Measure*, p. 74). She also wrote: "As the part of the story-teller became thinner and vaguer, I felt that the picture of the changing world about him gathered reality, and that one heard through his consciousness the rapidly awakening tumult and confusion of the new South" (*ibid.*, p. 76).

Ben's impatient envy of George's effortlessly lovely manners, his solicitous attentions to Sally's smallest needs, his good horsemanship, emerges as merely the nagging and ultimately illuminating irritation an insignificant character may cause a large one. Ben Starr is capable of acquiring George's good qualities, if not of adorning them with George's grace in a single generation of effort. Indeed, as his career closes, Ben is on the point of doing so in the light of his new understanding of the necessity to moderate the claims of action and of love. But George has somehow, somewhere, lost his power to act. He is truly a representative of a charming, but irretrievably lost cause.

George's unflattering, ineffectual role is the only role accorded the aristocrat throughout Miss Glasgow's following venture in examination of the new force of an old class. *The Miller of Old Church* (1911), almost a sequel to *The Deliverance*, vindicates the wisdom of Lila Blake's marriage "beneath her" by celebrating the rising strength, the soundness, rather than the potential greatness of the rural hero.

Abel Revercomb, the young miller and Jim Weatherby's counterpart here, is no more a polished new leader of men than Ben Starr was.

A certain tenacity—a suggestion of stubbornness in the jaw, gave the final hint to his character, and revealed that temperamental intolerance of others which constitutes the strength as well as the weakness of the rustic who has risen out of his class. An opinion once embraced acquired the authority of a revelation; a passion once yielded to was transformed into a principle. Impulsive, generous, undisciplined, he represented, after all, but the reaction from the spirit of racial submission which . . . showed the disturbing effects of a freedom which had resulted from a too rapid change in economic conditions rather than from the more gradual evolution of class. When political responsibility was thrust on the plainer people instead of sought by them, it was but natural that the process of adjustment should appear rough rather than smooth.[10]

[10] Ellen Glasgow, *The Miller of Old Church* (Garden City, 1911), p. 47. Page references to future quotations from this novel in Chap. 4 are given in parentheses or brackets after the quotations.

Aside from the difficulty of discerning how Abel's political
ambitions are "thrust" upon him save by the dearth of interested
candidates among the surviving aristocracy at the turn of the
century, his is a convincing portrait. The sentence containing this
explanation of Abel's motivation is omitted from the passage in the
Virginia edition (37) in favor of emphasis on the possibility of and
incentive for "rising" that had been absent from the laborer's world
of Abel's parents and grandparents. As Shields McIlwaine points
out, this last emphasis is a "later-day adaptation of the abolitionist
formula" which assumed "first a certain capability in poor-whites
and, next, the desire to improve themselves in the New South."[11]
For McIlwaine such assumptions show that "Miss Glasgow told
particular, not general social truth," in her treatment of Abel
Revercomb. And he quite rightly remarks that none of Ellen
Glasgow's poor-white protagonists "have much 'class reality,' because they always rise out of their level." But in implying the
existence of a "level" for poor-whites from which Miss Glasgow
departed in her treatment of heroes of humble origin, McIlwaine
sometimes appears to come dangerously close to dividing Southerners into the two stereotyped classes of aristocrats and poor whites, a
longstanding Southern myth which he seems to feel Ellen Glasgow
shared. Actually, of course, McIlwaine is clearly not any more
guilty than Ellen Glasgow is of any such oversimplification, and his
criticism of her poor-white heroes as typical specimens of their class
remains sound.

The difficulty appears to be that Ellen Glasgow sacrificed sociological precision in treating a class in favor of attention to "fringe"
members of that class. Her poor-white heroes, like Abel Revercomb, have "yeoman" status usually based on both the community
position their ambition has earned them and some claim to hereditary superiority. For example, Abel's management of his mill plus
his inheritance of a strong character from his mother Sarah, a rigid,
dauntless Calvinist, allow him a background more promising for the

[11] McIlwaine, pp. 190–91.

purposes of "rising" than that enjoyed by a more firmly entrenched yeoman of long standing such as the good-natured, deferential Jim Weatherby, representative of the "good people" of the postwar generation in *The Deliverance*. And the dogged persistence with which Abel pursues his political career seems to create more distance between Abel and his brothers, the shiftless, irresponsible Archie and the morose, vengeful Abner, who do display qualities that stereotype poor whites, than could possibly be explained on the ground that Abel belonged to the second generation of postwar poor whites. The fact is that Miss Glasgow was interested only in one "type" of protagonist, and although she was actually equally concerned to discover this "type" among poor whites and "good people" as well as among aristocrats, we ought to expect that her Abel Revercombs and Nick Burrs will resemble in character and ambitions not only her Dorinda Oakleys and Ada Fincastles more closely than they do their own more "typical" families, but that both these "classes" of heroes and heroines, whether poor white or "good people," will be closer in perceptions and desires to Ellen Glasgow's well-meaning aristocrats such as Laura Wilde and General Archbald than are such fallen aristocrats as the Jonathan Gays or little Jenny Archbald.

McIlwaine graciously and perceptively terms Miss Glasgow a "spiritual propagandist" for her departures from "general social truth" in treating poor whites. He might have added that the important departure from the abolitionist formula which he notes in her novels, the omission of the poor-whites' relations with the Negro in favor of treating their position after the war as though it were still wholly determined by antebellum class lines, is an essential part of this spiritual propaganda, needed to reveal clearly that the change envisioned was a simple, direct transmission of values and responsibilities from planter to plebeian. I should add that Ellen Glasgow's preoccupation with the enduring dream of her society also makes clear the sense in which political responsibility in the Reconstruction period is "thrust" upon the Abel Revercombs. If the aristocrats no longer "take" their responsibility as a matter of course then, for Miss Glasgow, someone must be found who does. Perhaps, as McIlwaine gently implies, it was Miss Glasgow who thrust political responsibility upon Abel Revercomb, her ideal poor white. But even Mr. McIlwaine does not deny that there were Abel Revercombs, however particularized. This contrast is significant, for while Abel Revercombs and Jonathan Gays have appeared in earlier Glasgow novels and figure even more prominently in later ones, never before have the Revercombs been so dominant and the Gays so thoroughly weak.

Ellen Glasgow called *The Miller of Old Church* "the last of my books to be written in a fashion which I am obliged, however reluctantly, to call my earlier manner." She added, "I had not yet escaped entirely from the influence of [tradition's] emotional patterns. I was still feeling the backward pull of inherited tendencies."[12] This observation may well have derived from her consciousness that the really important new insight here is the pervading sense of horror with which she regards the total decline of her aristocrats. In the world of Jordan's Journey, there is no Laura Wilde or Daniel Ordway to enlighten the humble, and none promises to appear. Jonathan Gay, himself a voluntary expatriate, impatient to escape once more, is the best the old tradition offers; beside him stand only his mother and his aunt, both distorted products of the code of beautiful behavior. And the best that is said for Jonathan is that

all his life he had done the things he condemned, condemning himself because he did them. . . . He had lived above a continuous undercurrent of subterfuge . . . and yet all the time, he was conscious that his nature preferred the honorable and the candid course. His intentions were still honest, but long ago in his boyhood, when he had first committed himself to impulse, he had prepared the way for his subsequent failures. Today, with a weakened will, with an ever increasing sensitiveness of his nervous system, he knew that he should go on desiring the good while he compromised with the pleasanter aspect of evil [381].

One last hope for the survival of the "old way" figures importantly. An epidemic of interclass alliances occurs in this chronicle.

[12] *Certain Measure*, p. 129.

Jonathan marries a Revercomb daughter in secret, and Abel spends much effort in a long chase and final capture of the damsel of his dreams, herself the fair, though illegitimate, offspring of an alliance between Jonathan's uncle and his overseer's daughter. And though most of the deaths and disasters that take place are directly attributable to the difficulties of such "intermarriage," Ellen Glasgow sees the alliances as fraught with "symbolic implication." "Will the declining strain of the aristocracy be enriched or depleted by the mingling of social orders? Will the fresh infusion of blood save the old way of living? Or will it merely hasten the end of an incurable malady?"[13]

A decade later in the last of her novels of social action, *One Man in His Time* (1922), she still refused to decide these questions irrevocably. There is no doubt that the isolated survivals of the "declining strain of the aristocracy" exemplified by Stephen Culpepper and his Cousin Corinna are "enriched" by their mingling with the "lower orders" now in high places, but the degree of their old life salvageable or worthy of saving remains dubious.

At twenty-six, Stephen already feels that he has "watched the decay and dissolution of a hundred years."[14] By temperament a passive if critical observer, he appears a "stranger in an age which had degraded manners and enthroned commerce," surveying the present "from some inaccessible height of the past" (2). Yet beneath a conventional, almost priggishly old-fashioned manner, he buries "an inarticulate longing for heroic and splendid deeds," a longing only intensified by the disillusionment of his battleground experiences in World War I, experiences that left him with a "nervous malady" increasing "both his romantic dissatisfaction with his life and his inability to make a sustained effort to change it" (3).

Corinna Page, who has been the reigning beauty and wit of the Virginian Capitol society for a generation, also feels caught in the

[13] *Ibid.*, p. 128.
[14] Ellen Glasgow, *One Man in His Time* (Garden City, 1922), p. 1. Page references to quotations from this novel in Chap. 4 are given in parentheses or brackets after the quotations.

prison house of her day. An incarnated spirit of the best qualities of Virginia's tradition, Corinna has spent a lifetime "ruled not by passion but by law, by some clear moral discernment of things as they ought to be" (294). And, in her middle years, she concedes that her life has been a mean affair at best, filled chiefly with the shreds of damaged illusions. "Her beauty had brought her nothing that was not tawdry, nothing that was not a gaudy imitation of happiness. . . . The past, in spite of her many triumphs, had been worse than tragic; it had been comic—since it had left her beggared. Looking back upon it now she saw that it had lacked even the mournful dignity of a broken heart" (103). But she is even more determined than Stephen not to surrender to defeat, to search on for the illusive perfection her belief in things as they ought to be tells her must lie somewhere amid the chaos and confusion of her age. The heritage of "fighting blood" she shares with Stephen, although long thwarted, she refuses to give up.

Born into a society still feverishly devoted to what has become a caricature of past grandeur, Stephen and Corinna find their lonely souls fast enthralled by the personality of Gideon Vetch. But this powerful, fervent, and uncouth man newly elected governor of Virginia is "of the people" only in his origins; his convictions condemn him to a solitude even more precarious than that of Stephen and Corinna. For Gideon Vetch is intended as a man of action motivated by the human sympathy "that means imagination and insight." And insofar as imagination and insight are his guiding principles, they hold him to the impartial judgments that delight no faction and are protested as betrayals by his early supporters among the "common people." Indeed, Corinna and Stephen have scarcely resolved to pledge themselves to Vetch as the "redeeming principle" of the new "disorder" when he is killed attempting to mediate between the quarreling factions at a strikers' meeting. Stunned by what seems the irreparable loss of the only man she ever knew who gave promise of realizing her vision of perfection, Corinna gives way to despair. "Was death always like this—a victory of material and mechanical forces? An accident, an automatic gesture, and the complex power which stood for the soul of Gideon Vetch was dissolved—or released. . . . They had killed him, Corinna knew, because they could not understand him" (377)!

"They" are here the representatives of the new order, all who no longer abide by the traditions of the past. And "they," the plain people in a changing society to which Ellen Glasgow had so recently accorded a measure of allegiance, are severely dealt with in this novel. Stephen's original dissatisfactions stem from the conviction that his world had "all changed since his father's or his grandfather's day; it was all obvious and cheap, he thought; it was all ugly and naked and undistinguished—yet the tide of the new ideas was still rising. Democracy, relentless, disorderly, and strewn with the wreckage of finer things, had overwhelmed the world of established customs in which he lived" (2). And the "provoking inspiration" he finds initially in Patty Vetch, the Governor's spirited, almost hoydenish daughter, derives from his reluctant admiration for a young girl who "had already solved the problems which he had evaded or pushed aside," but solved them, he is sure, by some instinctive apprehension of "the secret of transition—a perpetual motion that went in circles and was never still." For in the beginning Patty is for him only a bright will-o'-the-wisp, fascinating because she has learned that "the only way to fit into the century was simply to keep moving in whirls of unintelligent unison; never to meditate, never to reason upon one's course; but to sweep onward, somewhere, anywhere as long as it was in a new direction" (97). Stephen's ambivalent feelings toward Patty are echoed in the contemptuous longing with which he regards the world that engulfs him outside his doorstep:

Elasticity, variability—were not these the indispensable qualities of the modern mind? The power to make quick decisions and the inability to cling to conventions; the nervous high pitch and the failure to sustain the triumphant note; energy without direction; success without stability; martyrdom without faith. And around, above, beneath, the pervading mediocrity, the apotheosis of the average. Was this the best that democracy had to offer mankind?

Was there no depth below the shallows? Was it impossible, even by the most patient search, to discover some justification of the formlessness of the age, of the crazy instinct for ugliness? He could forgive it all, he might eventually bring his mind to believe in it, if there were only some logical design informing the disorder. If he could find that it contained a single redeeming principle that was superior to the old order, he felt that he should be able to surrender his disbelief [98].

Yet before the Governor's death, Stephen thinks he has found that "redeeming principle" and the "spirit that comprehends, that reconciles and recreates" in the "human sympathy" motivating Vetch. Sympathy, he feels, is what his old hero, the aristocratic politician, John Benham, lacked—the quality that kept Benham a lifetime apart from the public he tried to lead. Having vindicated the modern mind, or at least having accepted the new leadership according to the sympathy of Vetch, Stephen immediately proceeds as promised to surrender his disbelief. This means, for him, a shaping vision of the future after his conception of a "logical design" to inform the disorder. He remarks to Corinna:

Both Vetch and John have failed, I think; Vetch for want of education, system, method, and John, because, having all this essential framework, he still lacked the blood and fibre of humanity. In its essence, I suppose it is a difference of principle, the old familiar struggle between the romantic and realistic temperament, which divides in politics into the progressive and conservative forces. . . . Irreconcilable, they call them, and yet I wonder. . . . It seems to me that the leader of the future, even in so small a community as this one, must be big enough to combine opposite elements; that he must take the good where he finds it; that he must vitalize tradition and discipline progress [321–22].

"You mean that he must accept both the past and the future?" Corinna's flat, toneless reply to Stephen's outburst is delivered with outward serenity, but not without inward irritation. Far from being inflamed by Stephen's enthusiastic conjectures, Corinna is chiefly made aware that when hearts like hers and Stephen's most crave the "substance of truth," they succeed only in benevolently dispensing platitudes. Her own very feminine solution for the ills of society lies very simply in "consideration" and good manners. "The whole trouble with life seemed to her to rise, not from mistaken theory, but from the lack of consideration with which human beings treated one another. Happiness, after all, depended so little upon opinions and so much upon manners" (323).

Corinna's solution, here exposed in its rather embarrassingly naked naiveté is, of course, the solution that has lain at the heart of Ellen Glasgow's social action novels. Her "discoveries" about the modern malady of her society have been in the main exposures of the deficiencies of consideration and manners in the survivors of the old Virginian aristocracy and the promise of these qualities in the rising leaders of the new South. It is Gideon Vetch's nobility of character rather than his convictions that captures Corinna's esteem, and it is ultimately his insistence on clinging to consideration unto death that vindicates her devotion to him as the personification of the ideal she has spent a lifetime seeking.

She beheld him suddenly as a man who was inspired by an exalted illusion—the illusion of human perfectibility. In the changing world about her, the breaking up and the renewing, the dissolution and readjustment of ideals; in the modern conflict between the spirit that accepts and the spirit that rejects; in this age of destiny—was not an unconquerable optimism, an invincible belief in life, the one secure hope for the future? It is the human touch that creates hope, she thought; and the power of Gideon Vetch was revealed to her as simply the human touch magnified into a force [327].

The force is not to suffice to secure Stephen the leadership of the future, for as he says of his own enthusiastic theory, "Haven't I felt this way a hundred times in the last six months, only to grow indifferent and even bored within the next few hours?" Rather, it is meant to confer upon Patty, Stephen, and Corinna the courage of Gideon Vetch's own illusion of human perfectibility. In Stephen's case the glow of Vetch's influence hardens into victory over the "struggle in his heart" between his inherited way of life and the world about him, a battle that Ellen Glasgow defines for him as "between tradition and life, between the knowledge of things as they are and the vision of things as they ought to be, between the conservative and the progressive principle in nature" (339). During a moment of awakening he determines for the "future" rather than the past—"not for philosophy, but for adventure—for the will to be and to dare." Moreover, Stephen's victory is only confirmed by his decision to marry Patty even after it is revealed that her heritage from the Governor is not the all-important tie of blood but merely that of association. For Patty proves to be the offspring of an unknown father and a circus performer mother, melodramatically rescued in infancy by Vetch as her mother is led away to stand trial for murder.

So it is that Patty, unveiled as a shatteringly modern young innocent, and Stephen, the transfigured last heir of the past, are to be joined in the afterglow of Gideon Vetch's reign. And in Stephen's heightened determination to marry Patty, despite her origins, Miss Glasgow at last recovers the nobility of the past that is to be symbolically united with the future. Corinna, conscious that such a marriage will violate "something sacred" to both her and Stephen in the tradition which they represent, is surprised by his firmness into admitting that she has misconceived Stephen's character, for if the possibility of his marriage belongs to his new convictions, his steadfast support of those convictions derives from his past.

She had forgotten that men of Stephen's nature . . . though they may not endure petty discomforts with fortitude, they are able, in moments of vivid experience to perform acts of conspicuous and splendid nobility. For the old order was not merely the outward form of the conservative principle, it was also the fruit of heroic tradition [363].

Thus Ellen Glasgow, even in the moment that she allows the old South to embrace the new, manages to reaffirm the best of tradition, and indeed, to define the "nobility" of the union in terms of that tradition. The sustained note on which the novel ends is one that combines the old optimism seen in the necessity of pursuing the unattainable with the new faith in progress toward fulfillment.

Corinna, too, is left in the light of Gideon Vetch's influence with a new world and a new life opened before her, yet only strengthened in her old convictions by his death. "Yes, youth was for the future, and for herself, she realized with a pang, were the things that she had never had in the past. Only the things that she had never had were really hers! Only the unfulfilled, she saw in that moment of illuminating insight, is the permanent" (378). The newly mingled world of the Culpeppers and the Vetches closes with the hopeful assessment of a wise, old soul. The Judge, Corinna's father, says of the Governor's career: "The merest ripple of change, perhaps, but it counts—it counts because in touching him we touched a humanity that is as rare as genius itself" (377). And with this final wisdom Ellen Glasgow's pursuit of public heroes halts. Her new dream of progress toward fulfillment by active devotion to unattainable ideals is, in the future, to be followed only by isolated, if very human, heroes.

THE SOUL, DOUBTLESS, IS IMMORTAL—WHERE A SOUL CAN BE DIS-
CERNED.—ROBERT BROWNING

Barren Ground (1925) is dedicated to the character of Dorinda
Oakley, a character that is Dorinda's fate. And Dorinda Oakley,
Ellen Glasgow insists, is truly a universal figure. "She exists wherever a human being has learned to live without joy, wherever the
spirit of fortitude has triumphed over the sense of futility."[1] But,
granting that joyless existences may be common enough, Dorinda's
triumph is a matter of overcoming a carefully particularized sense
of futility by means of a very precisely cultivated spirit of fortitude,
a triumph in which Miss Glasgow at times appears to stress the
Southern qualities too heavily. For although she suggests that this
novel is "the reversal of a classic situation"—the betrayed woman
emerging as victor rather than victim—this suggestion is, at best,
misleading. Dorinda is as far from the "classic" innocent as her
victory is distant from vengeance, or from anything we can immediately accept as victory, for that matter. Nor is Dorinda Oakley
acceptable even as the parochial American innocent betrayed by
parish or perishing visions in the manner of a Carrie Meeber, Clyde
Griffiths, or Jay Gatsby.

The heroine of *Barren Ground* has, as Miss Glasgow herself
emphasizes, a heritage almost unique in fiction. She and her family
belong to a "special rural class . . . a social unit which, though it
has been consistently ignored alike by Southern literature and

[1] *Certain Measure*, p. 154.

tradition has borne a liberal part in the making of Southern history."[2] This "class" of small, independent farmers and landowners still known in Virginia as "good people" (a label distinguishing them from aristocratic "good families") descended from English yeoman who conquered the Virginia frontier. And in the closing years of the nineteenth century, with which Miss Glasgow begins this novel, the "weakened progeny" of pioneer good people still held the freeholds that their ancestors "had won from the wilderness or the savannahs," still might look forward to standing as a "buffer class between opulent gentry and hired laborers." That these people of *Barren Ground* are, on the whole, to be considered merely ineffectual beside their battling forebears is beyond dispute; the reason for their weakening is all-important in determining what Miss Glasgow is trying to say in her saga of Dorinda Oakley, whose conquest of the soil we are made to feel as a return to the pioneer stance.

In one sense the decline of the good people, the "land-poor" Oakleys, Pedlars, Greylocks, and Ellgoods of *Barren Ground*, is only too clear. They "owned and had always owned, every foot of the impoverished soil which they tilled, or left untilled, on their farms." As the soil decayed, prosperity decayed, families decayed. And there was the great blight of the Civil War, a blight withering to both land and people.[3] But such decay suggests that both the class and the acres might be restored by a judicious distribution of fertilizer, seed money, and improved plumbing. This is a dangerous suggestion because it is a pat one, reducing the unhealed wounds of a withering culture to the nursed bruises of want. And as Allen Tate points out in "The New Provincialism," it was precisely this formula for recovery that plagued the Southern novel during its startling but often inadequate renascence between the two world

[2] *Ibid.*, p. 157.

[3] The conditions of Southern agriculture after the Civil War are examined by Allen W. Moger, *The Rebuilding of the Old Dominion*, pp. 43–63; C. Vann Woodward, *Origins of the New South*, pp. 175 ff., 406–16; Henry Savage, Jr., *Seeds of Time*, pp. 211 ff. For the Southern reaction to these conditions see W. J. Cash, *The Mind of the South*, pp. 153–75 and elsewhere.

wars. The "provincial" writing of this renascence, according to Tate, assumed that the South, "backward and illiberal, and controlled by white men who cherish a unique moral perversity,"[4] is unworthy to produce any literature except that of social agitation. The prescription for acceptable Southern literature consequently required that the writer must "ignore the historical background of his subject; and second, he must judge the subject strictly in terms of the material welfare of his characters and of the 'injustice' which keeps them from getting enough of it."[5]

Somewhat reluctantly Tate includes *Barren Ground* among the literary works written to this formula:

The novel that came nearest to real distinction was probably Miss Glasgow's *Barren Ground;* but even this excellent novel is written outside the subject, with the result that the frustration of her Virginia farmers is not examined as an instance of the decay of rural culture everywhere, but rather as a simple object-lesson in the lack of standard American 'advantages.'[6]

In answer to similar interpretations Miss Glasgow had previously replied that the novel was, after all, not about farming but about Dorinda. "The only thing that mattered was her triumph over circumstances. Even the reclamation of the farm, which a few critics have over-emphasized, was merely an episode. Systems of agriculture were unimportant beside this human drama of love and hatred, of passion and disillusionment."[7] Unfortunately the tone of shrill insistence predominates in Miss Glasgow's declaration, and obviously her reply hardly covers the charges. And the charges are important, for however timeless and individual she intended Dorinda Oakley to be, her heroine lived and moved as a representative of a very special class culture, was motivated as a restorer and preserver of a distinct and limited body of tradition, a tradition enfolding all the significance and justification of man's state for Ellen Glasgow. The questions remain: Are the "good people" of *Barren Ground* too distinctly Virginian and insufficiently repre-

[4] Allen Tate, *Man of Letters in the Modern World* (New York, 1955), p. 329.
[5] *Ibid.* [6] *Ibid.* [7] *Certain Measure*, pp. 160–61.

sentative of rural culture everywhere; and, perhaps more important, can their plight and Dorinda's individual victory over it be translated into the trivial assertion that while toil and poverty equal defeat, toil and money promise resurrection?

In contrast to the "good families" of Virginia, custodians of "custom, history, tradition, romantic fiction, and the Episcopal Church," the good people, Miss Glasgow comments, "according to the records of clergymen, which are the only surviving records, have preserved nothing except themselves."[8] For the inconspicuous social position they hold halfway between lower gentility and poor white is a social stratum encouraging the "useful rather than the ornamental public virtues." That she nonetheless considers these useful virtues as characteristic and as valid a part of the Southern tradition as the heritage of the aristocracy, she indicates with painstaking repetition. As in all her novels, she traces with loving care the ancestry of her protagonists, pointing out that Dorinda Oakley, on her mother's side at least, descends from good, sound stock. It is true that Miss Glasgow allows her a father who stemmed from the poor white class; but the Joshua Oakley who appealed to Dorinda's mother with the "eyes of a dumb poet and the head of a youthful John the Baptist" has nothing else to recommend him, and he shuffles out his life on the land he received at his marriage with the dogged, humble futility that stereotypes his class. And although Miss Glasgow insists that Dorinda, born of a union of opposites, possessed "the inherited conflict of types" that "kept her heart in arms against life,"[9] she allows her no discernible "Oakley" traits.

Dorinda is altogether an Abernethy, and much is to be made of this. Her great-grandfather, John Calvin Abernethy, retired missionary from India and Ceylon, "with a neat Scotch-Irish inheritance in his pocket" (7), first entered the lowlands of Queen Elizabeth County, Virginia, in the early nineteenth century from

[8] Ellen Glasgow, *Barren Ground* (Garden City, 1925), p. 5. Page references to future quotations from this novel in Chap. 5 are given in parentheses or brackets after the quotations.

[9] *Certain Measure,* p. 158.

the Shenandoah Valley, where "there was no canny bargain to be driven, at the moment." An eloquent preacher, he is also described as "a true explorer of the spirit as well, the last of those great Presbyterian romantics whose faith ventured on perilous metaphysical seas in the ark of the Solemn League and Covenant." But John Calvin was above all a practical man. Selling the slaves who accompanied the thousand acres he purchased and devoting the proceeds to redeeming black souls in the Congo, he thereby reconciled divine grace with an institution that he accepted because it existed. We are told to accept his piety within its narrow groove as deep and genuine, and his genius for its true worth: "He possessed sufficient integrity, firmness, and frugality to protect his descendants from decay for at least three generations" (8). For John Calvin knew, when his only grandchild, Dorinda's mother, "fell a victim to one of those natural instincts which Presbyterian theology has damned but never wholly exterminated" (9) and married Joshua Oakley, that, "after the manner of his class," Oakley would follow the destiny of all ineffectual spirits and proceed to "lose everything that was left." Knowing this, he devoted his last years to building up a decent inheritance for his great-grandchildren.

The first Virginian Abernethy seems authentic and acceptable as "good stock," perhaps partly because he was more than a little ridiculous but chiefly because he stands as a prototype of the generalized American pioneer whose rigid acquisitiveness we regard with a mixture of humor, shame, and awe, but whose achievements compose a myth we must cherish, for he represents almost all of the past almost all of us have. Northerners cannot really protest when this archetypal pioneer appears in the South, even in Virginia, although it seems a bit unfair, for while some Scotch-Irish Presbyterians undeniably settled there, Virginia has other, more celebrated myths of the past which the North is denied forever.

What is disturbing about Abernethy's behavior with his land, then, is not his method of acquiring it nor his ability to prosper on it but the assumption he shares with Ellen Glasgow that only the Abernethys of the South are constitutionally fit to achieve what he did. Or more precisely stated: Virginia is plagued with unique classes and conditions which intensify the difficulty of imposing on the land of their descendants the pattern of existence and achievement of the original Abernethys. Of the special encumbrance of black souls and white inferiors, Abernethy himself took account. And with disturbing frequency the novel reminds us that rural Virginia has been singled out for bleeding by the Civil War, the tenant system, the incurable prejudices of the farmers for the "old ways" of one-crop farming. (Jason Greylock, Dorinda's lover who betrays her and surrenders to life "through inherited weakness," foreshadows his defeat in his despair that "even generations of failure cannot teach the farmers about here that it is impossible to make bread out of straw" [112].) Even more ominous in the light of Dorinda's achievement is Jason's conviction that if he had only a little money he might reclaim his land; for although we are meant to see that Jason's congenital inability to act prohibits his success forever, Dorinda does reclaim her land with the help of a "little money" and a few borrowed books on agriculture.

Apparently, then, Dorinda Oakley's conquest of the land is to be magnified as the conquest of Virginian soil, a uniquely barren ground. But even if we cannot believe in the peculiarly Virginian aridity of her Old Farm, Five Oaks, and the surrounding acres, even if we protest that outworn soil and methods of farming are not exclusively Southern, even if poor whites portrayed as congenitally inferior individuals seem rather incredible to us, these flaws of exaggeration remain minor and even questionable as flaws. It may be truly said of them that, however they intrude, they are not what *Barren Ground* is all about. What we cannot allow is a Dorinda Oakley whose courage in borrowing two thousand dollars constitutes the sum of her achievement; a Dorinda who repeats her great-grandfather's canniness chiefly because of a second neat little investment.

Fortunately the heroine of *Barren Ground* emerges as a representative of much more than skillful manipulation of funds to replace one scraggly cow and a few rows of withered tobacco leaves with a sleek dairy herd and fertile fields. In fact money and "advantages" are meant to have remarkably little to do with her transformation of the land. Only her "approach to life" can explain the significance of her achievement, can ultimately justify the romantic pose in which her creator attempts to sustain her—Dorinda Oakley, an epic figure, silhouetted against the horizon, an earth goddess protector of the Virginia prairies. And that approach, the pattern of existence by which Dorinda molds her life and her land, is a matter of class and code long established and long enduring. The narrator of another novel, Allen Tate's *The Fathers*, speaks to this point when he is made to say:

Nobody in my youth discussed money; we never asked how much money people had; and it was a little different, I believe, from the ordinary good breeding that demands reticence about the cost of things. That too was never done; but the point of the other 'rule' was that it had grown out of long habit, out of a way of seeing men in society; it was less a rule than an actual habit of the mind. . . . The individual quality of a man was bound up with his kind and the 'places' where they lived; thinking of a man we could easily bring before the mind's eye all those subtly interwoven features of his position. 'Class' consisted solely in a certain code of behavior. Even years later I am always a little amazed to hear a man described as the coal man or the steel man or the plate-glass man, descriptions of people after the way they make their money, not after their manner of life.[10]

Individual status in the South was then a matter of "manner of life." The point seems deceptively simple and is, perhaps, deceptively irritating as an expressly Southern attribute. Nonetheless, while we may point to isolated and even recurring instances of an identical conception of class and code in regions north of the Mason-Dixon, we are hard put to find this ideal cherished so lovingly, so uniformly, for so long outside the South. At any rate, it is surely helpful in allowing us to appreciate that such labels as

[10] Allen Tate, *The Fathers* (New York: Putnam's & Coward-McCann, copyright 1938 by Allen Tate), pp. 134–35.

"poor white futility" are not merely categorical oversimplifications or half-baked race theories. It is more immediately useful in understanding the sensitivity a critic like Tate feels toward the horrors of a provincial literature "which sees in material welfare and legal justice the whole solution to the human problem."[11] His sensitivity perhaps causes him to minimize the comparable sensitivity to such a solution that Ellen Glasgow expresses in *Barren Ground*. Dorinda Oakley's performance in reference to this concept is above all symbolic of a "manner of life" that represents the ideal attainment of her class, an attainment which is literally meant to promise redemption for an order dilapidated and corrupt, to prefigure resurrection for the passionate believers.

If the resurrection seems to echo too loudly "of the South" and "in the South," it can only be suggested that Ellen Glasgow, in common with most mortals who look upon their little corner of the universe, shared the feeling of young Lacy Gore Buchan in *The Fathers* "that God was a Virginian who had created the world in his own image,"[12] or ought to have done so. The hollowness of the reality of Southern existence compared to the ideal Southern claims she laments constantly, but her outcry is only superficially directed against the sugared cruelty of maintaining an ideal where no ideal is realized. Her real point turns on what she, in common with her cloudy yet cohesive South, feels they believe in and desire and, above all, search to find embodied somewhere. All her novels can be viewed as efforts to give the ideal substance, but her special feeling for *Barren Ground*[13] may well derive from her unspoken, indeed, hardly conscious acknowledgment that of all her protagonists only Dorinda Oakley really allows her to project fully the "purpose" of the South. She meant Dorinda to exist against a background of unlimited space and time, "where the flatness created an illusion of immensity" and "over the immutable landscape human lives drifted

---

[11] *Man of Letters*, p. 330.   [12] *The Fathers*, p. 129.
[13] "The germ of the book had lain in my mind for many years; but when at last it had developed too vigorously to be ignored, I felt that I had broken away, even more sharply than in my earlier work, from well-established convention" (*Certain Measure*, p. 152).

and vanished like shadows."[14] The landscape of *Barren Ground* is larger and longer enduring than the salvation of Dorinda, which is bound up with it. But no landscape remains immutable, however strongly its viewers may wish it to do so.)

There was land to engage the souls of John Calvin Abernethy and his descendants unto the third generation, but the great transformation came and passed with Dorinda. The challenge of the land cannot be the same for her only spiritual descendant, her crippled step-son John Abner, for though we may believe in a Dorinda who never "despairs of contentment" with "the living communion with the earth under her feet . . . while the soil endured, while the seasons bloomed and dropped, while the ancient, beneficent ritual of sowing and reaping moved in the fields" (509–10), we cannot accept the enduring reality of the "ancient, beneficent ritual" even for John Abner, much less the kindred souls who are landless. Nor is the difference we discern a matter of the vast Oakley acres having acquired tractors and milking machines to remove the heart of man from the heart of the land. It is merely that the "immutable landscape" does not go on serving the souls of countless generations, will not be tamed and retamed, time out of mind, by those who must find some solid ground in which to embody that deathless but specter-thin ideal. If all this is only to say that all things change, very well.

Ellen Glasgow's concentration on the fate of the tradition in the hands of the "city-pent" in all of her subsequent novels indicates that she realized well enough not only the inevitable mutability of the landscape, but the clear probability of a tradition not only mutated but lost once separated from the soil upon which it arose. To the extent that she was aware of this danger even in writing *Barren Ground*, I think we do both this novel and her work as a whole an injustice if we insist on the primary importance of what has been called the "mystique of the land" celebrated in *Barren Ground*. And although we may discount her later attempts to deny

[14] *Ibid.*, p. 158.

the importance of land and the life of the soil in shaping Dorinda's destiny as simply inaccurate in view of the importance given to both land and landscape in the novel, the injustice remains.

Of course, my discomfort at finding the phrase "mystique of the land" applied to *Barren Ground* may arise simply because I cannot share fully the feeling pointed to by the phrase, but neither, I think, could Ellen Glasgow, despite *Barren Ground*.[15] Even had Ellen Glasgow shared the sense of identification with the soil that presumably characterizes some agrarians within the Southern tradition, she did not wish to allow herself the simple, charming, impossible stand of the group called the Southern Agrarians; this much is evident from her protests that land and agriculture are unimportant to Dorinda's triumph. Her reason for denying herself this stand, whether consciously articulated or not, seems clear. Although one may grant that the best, the "easiest," the surest way to preserve a tradition and a code undistorted lies in following the manner of life that originated that code as Dorinda does, the problem of how to preserve any code when its origins have become impossible or unreal for the majority must persist. And certainly did persist for one haunted, as Ellen Glasgow was haunted, by the need to show that traditional ideals could and must survive, indeed, must extend themselves, not only cut off from their native ground but in alien surroundings.

There is a distinction here between soil and surroundings that must be made, and was made by Miss Glasgow. I think one might argue convincingly that for Dorinda (and even for the Agrarians) the soil itself, even the rural way of life, is not essential; undeniably it is most impressive to grapple bare-handed with one's destiny, perhaps simply because the ground is tangible, but it is not essential. It is possible, as John and Ada Fincastle of *Vein of Iron* and, for that matter, the city dwellers of the Queenborough trilogy discover, to

[15] Compare Miss Glasgow's novel with Elizabeth Madox Roberts' *The Time of Man* (New York, 1926), a contemporary work in which there is created a genuine mystique of the land, a sense of something far more deeply interfused between the land and those who live on it than we ever find in Miss Glasgow's work.

possess a common heritage rooted not in the soil but in one's surroundings, not in the land but in the landscape—in the sense of holding in common what Robert Penn Warren has called "the shared place." It appears to me that Dorinda's "communion," like that of Christopher Blake of *The Deliverance*, is with her surroundings, lies in her feelings for the "shared place" of her ancestors and not with the soil or even what has always been referred to so vaguely as nature or natural scenes. It might be argued that this sense of communion with the shared place, which for most Southerners was in fact a rural landscape, is all that has ever been meant by such phrases as "mystique of the land"—at least as applied to the Southern scene. But if so, then the phrase is inexcusably misleading.

The important questions of defining the boundaries of the "place" that can be shared and the boundaries of the sharing remain. If it is to have limits more precise than the generalized common past of the South, how precise must those limits be for the sharing to continue? If the family acres or the rural community, the Old Farm, or Pedlar's Mill of *Barren Ground* restrict the "shared place" too much in space, let alone in time, does not the rapidly changing Queenborough of Miss Glasgow's trilogy make a mockery of the entire concept?

Much has been written of the Southern feeling for "place," of the care and precision Southern literary figures exercise to capture it alive. One senses that this emphasis is important not merely because it is the only means for making vivid, let alone clear, the props that particularize any heaven or hell (and in the particularizing, of course make generalizing and, hopefully universalizing, possible), but for the very fundamental reason that in the place must be found the all-important if not always tangible things to be shared.

Ellen Glasgow acknowledges that in her early work she spent time and effort to transcribe the "places" of her novels with complete fidelity to the original models. In her later work she came to realize that fidelity to the "atmosphere" was more important than fidelity to the particulars of the landscape. Despite or, perhaps, because of this later qualification, several critics have praised her precision. The point I wish to make is that if in the beginning of her career Miss Glasgow mistook the landscape (she never mistook the land) as a part of the heritage to be shared rather than the mere frame within which the heritage to be shared must be sought out, she soon ceased to make this mistake. As her quest for the means of sharing and transmitting a heritage grew sharper, area became less important or, more accurately, less usable for her, although time obviously did not. She did appear to assume that aristocrats too long sheltered from the necessity to grapple with the unpleasant realities of life were in greater danger as candidates to continue anything than rising yeomen or poor whites who had not been so sheltered. But shelter or lack of it did not depend on urban or rural background or even on class origin, but on the measure to which her characters had distorted what she assumed to be a common heritage. Yet if a particular South became less credible to Miss Glasgow as a necessary background to sharing and keeping alive this common heritage, she had to render something transmittible in order to make sense of her own dream.

She chose finally the family background—standards and principles of behavior and conduct which she assumed all Southerners of the best sort of whatever station in life had bred in blood and bone as well as drummed in ears from birth. In fact, she sometimes went so far as to deny that these standards and principles had ever had anything to do with a common past or place and asserted that they were the principles and standards of civilized men everywhere and always would be. Of course this seemed a cruel disinheritance of the thin little Southern baby that remained the heart of her work even after she had torn away so much of the tattered legend that covered him. Fortunately she only discarded his coverings. The baby was small, even scrawny, and it wasn't too clear how he would continue to live so nakedly. But he was alive, and he was Southern.

What has this baby introduced into the discussion, let alone all the discussion of the vanishing shared places and the impossible, shared "mystique of the land" to do with Dorinda and *Barren*

Ground? Probably if Dorinda's child had been allowed to live, *Barren Ground* would have seemed a less powerful novel. Certainly its power would be diffused if Dorinda had had to raise a son, to reclaim him for the future along with Old Farm—as Ada Fincastle of *Vein of Iron* had to raise her illegitimate son Ranny apart from the Old Manse in order to reclaim it for him, and as Roy Timberlake planned to raise her illegitimate child in the projected novel called "Beyond Defeat." A child on the scene, interfering in a struggle with the land that derives much of its power from Dorinda's isolation and solitude, does not sound promising, but neither is Dorinda's solitude promising for Miss Glasgow's dream, however dramatically effective it may be.

If Dorinda is supposed to have or to share a mystique of the land, she transmits it to no one, including the reader. But if, as I think fairer, we oblige her to show only a devotion to a way of life, to a shared place that is capable of extension in space and time beyond Pedlar's Mill and even, ideally, beyond a rural environment, she transmits this feeling to no one except the reader. Hers is a truly impressive personal victory, but it is hers alone. And an isolated victory is a defeat for Miss Glasgow's dream by her own definition; for if she can insist that an apparent defeat such as that suffered by Asa Timberlake of *In This Our Life* is really victory so long as he keeps his vision alive not only for himself but for his daughter, then she must concede that a vision Dorinda keeps alive for herself alone is a vision that dies with her. I have suggested that the only "shared place" that really continued to be available to Miss Glasgow for the perpetuation of her dream was the family. Dorinda, it is true, has Nathan Pedlar and his children for her adopted family. And if she had really "shared" her vision with Nathan or, more precisely, learned to feel before it was too late that he possessed a vision to share with her, she might really have adopted his family to perpetuate her dream. But with the denial of emotion, of feeling for any human being, she destroys any possibility of transmitting her vision or Nathan's. Little wonder his club-footed son John Abner grows to maturity bitter and morose at his lot. John Abner has been "crossed in love" more fully than Ellen Glasgow dares acknowledge. The ground of the dream remains barren in this novel.

Meanwhile, the ideal lives on in the disembodied daydreams of the wistful, "over-civilized," city-pent heroes of Ellen Glasgow's later novels—and there is Dorinda.

The way I've been obliged to see it is this: our ideas and instincts work upon our memory of these people who have lived before us, and so they take on some clarity of outline. It's not to our credit to think we began today, and it's not to our glory to think we end today. All through time we keep coming in to the shore like waves —like waves. You stick to your blood, son; there's a certain fierceness in blood that can bind you up with a long community of life.[16]

This advice of a Southern gentleman to his son at the outbreak of the Civil War in Stark Young's *So Red the Rose* helps us to realize how Ellen Glasgow obliges us to see Dorinda. Young's aristocrat had descended from another John Calvin Abernethy, who maintained his slaves, apparently with considerable material benefit and equally considerable anguish of responsibility for his descendants. But the "blood" and the responsibility, not the presence or absence of slaves, are the qualities that identify good families and good people here. The special "fierceness of blood" Dorinda Oakley inherited from her Abernethy forebear is as important as it is vague, but her heritage of "responsibility" we see must be felt and realized in *Barren Ground*. John Calvin, we must remember, had devoted his declining years to accumulating a comfortable inheritance for his descendants, however his prime of life had been dedicated to achieving his own needs.

At twenty Dorinda Oakley is endowed with an April charm and a vital, romantic spirit. Vividly alive to the possibilities of "adventure in the silver-blue of the distance" (12), her imagination nourishes the smothered fire of her "inner life," although her outer world is monotonously unterrible in the worst sense. In her youthful vigor and in the energy of her dreams, Dorinda, looking out upon the bleak landscape of Queen Elizabeth County from the

[16] Stark Young, *So Red the Rose* (New York, 1934), pp. 150–51.

window of Pedlar's store where she stands wrapped in a flaming orange shawl, is very like her Northern sister, young Carol Milford from Blodgett College, who stands on a hill by the Mississippi leaning against the winds of the wheat lands as her taffeta skirt bells about her. The whole of life blossoms out for Dorinda "like a flower in the sun" at the attentions of young Jason Greylock, dutifully returned from the "city" to attend his father and take over the "scattered rural calls of a profession that father was too drunk to pursue" (12). Carol Milford's love of her healer, Dr. Will Kennicott of Gopher Prairie, was nourished on the departed glory of the Bohemian life, but both girls reached toward life with the expectant arms of the eternally young who feel only emptiness around them. Neither the absence of sophomoric aspiration for a Bohemian existence nor the melodrama of her subsequent desertion by Jason really separates Dorinda's story from Carol's.

Dorinda's real distinction lies in what Ellen Glasgow chooses to call her heritage of "an incurably Presbyterian conscience," a conscience which she generally rendered in terms of allegiance to the Episcopalian establishment if the conscience stricken happened to be of good family rather than good people. The strength of Dorinda's conscience is early prefigured in the episode of the blue dress chosen by her at the cost of rejecting a red cow much needed at Old Farm. Jason had said that she ought to wear blue; Jason was the center of her universe; she had a blue dress made. But her money, earned at Pedlar's store, had been saved and promised, had been intended for the red cow. And while her parents attempted to reassure her in her choice, her father with kindly humility, her mother with "the dry tolerance of disillusionment," while "she wore the blue dress gaily enough," she did not doubt that it was the "symbol of selfishness" (96). Ellen Glasgow wants us to see Dorinda's choice as one she "knew" to be essentially a matter of "abstract morality," as, no doubt, the determination of the first Abernethy to labor that his descendants might enjoy the fruits of his toil is to be viewed. Despite this terminology it is difficult to see what is meant other than a very concrete and personal interpretation of and commitment to traditional values.

Nonetheless, this clarity of decision about right and wrong is, however simply based on an inherited sense of values, quite helpful. Helpful because unshakable, or if you prefer Ellen Glasgow's terminology, incurable—a quality that promises to hold out through the strongest emotional turmoil, the longest assault by change or circumstance. Some of our more celebrated American innocents —Carrie Meeber, Clyde Griffiths, Jay Gatsby—have been disturbingly deficient in this respect, but others like Huck Finn, Isabel Archer, and Newland Archer have shared with Dorinda Oakley the unbending certainty of conscience which is the source of both their glory and their anguish. A characteristic comprehensive enough to include a Huck Finn who expects to live in hell because of his decision to free Nigger Jim and an Isabel Archer who does live in hell because she decided to live there when hell seemed heaven may not appear very meaningful. And to claim further that this characteristic is one that distinguishes a special class of American innocents is very likely to appear ridiculous. The Clarissa complex, American style; "know how" for the damned innocents. It is temptingly easy to caricature the qualities that unite these figures, most of whom serve as examples illustrating the best way to turn your lot in hell, if you must buy one, into a garden of Eden with snakes or a very acceptable little purgatory. For apparently the American rules in these matters, if they are held to strictly, prohibit both a graceful death and a prolonged withering. The rules are almost always so interpreted, perhaps merely because the tragic, final surrender lacks appeal as a Pyrrhic and somehow un-American victory, but more probably because the creators of these innocents who lose their innocence and preserve it for their triumph as well, however they differ in other respects, are united in their conviction that there is yet something left for their innocents to do or, at least, to stand for.

Dorinda's innocence, like that of her counterparts, is of course the special innocence bred of particular custom and ceremony, not the absence of these attributes that produces a Silas Lapham, Carrie Meeber, or Jay Gatsby. The distinctive quality of her victory involves a generous submission of self to principle, a renunciation so "old-fashioned" that it raises the modern eyebrow of skepticism. Is it, after all, possible to give up so much of oneself, one's personal aspirations, to a kind of communal salvation and still exist meaningfully as a person? A quizzical eyebrow is in order here, for although Dorinda's achievement symbolizes the ideal of her "class," she is and remains very much an individual, suffering for herself. Her tears and her bruises are hers alone. Furthermore, a small, if select, crowd of other fictional characters, mostly British females, have refined the renunciation principle that is a compromise between self and ceremony. Most of them surrendered quite self-consciously some portion of their ambition and dream, but almost all got their man at last, or a man, at any rate. If Dorinda is only another addition to the Diana Warwicks, Clara Middletons, and Dorothea Brookes, her sole distinction becomes that of working out her destiny in terms of the soil, compromising on land rather than on a husband.

But as important as reclaiming, indeed redeeming, the land is to the Dorinda, who is a symbolic figure, restorer of her generation to its rightful traditional status, the Dorinda who is merely a suffering individual behaves in a quite believable manner during the process. A young girl bewildered and hurt by the forces of chance and circumstance that have left her abandoned and pregnant with Jason Greylock's child, she reacts blindly, instinctively. Her attempt to shoot Jason on the eve of his return to his father's house with the bride he has married out of weakness may be melodramatic; it is surely sincere. And her failure to shoot because "something stronger than her conscious will, stronger than her hate, held her motionless" (164) is a personal, not an inherited failure. Indeed, the "nameless force within the chaos of her being" that prevents her from hot-blooded murder, nothing but "a physical inability to bring her muscles beneath the control of her will," if it signifies anything more than hysteria, signifies rather a dimming of her hereditary "fierceness of blood" under the pleasures of "civilization" than a return to her symbolic status as preserver. Neither at this moment of failure to achieve immediate revenge nor in her later return to Old Farm does Dorinda appear conscious of choosing a traditional destiny. Never as an individual does she pose as the girl with the hoe, aware of her mission on earth, and her personal ambition to revive Old Farm seems just as fortuitous and rather less contrived than the series of accidents that allow her to miscarry her child and find employment and helpful friends in New York.

Nonetheless, however convincing and instinctive Dorinda's behavior during her personal crisis may be, we, too, are obliged to see with the Southern gentleman of *So Red the Rose* "ideas and instincts" working upon her memory of her great-grandfather, until John Calvin Abernethy takes on some meaning, some clarity of outline for Dorinda. She "understands" him for the first time on the night Jason's treachery is revealed to her, and a phrase of his that her mother had recalled to her, a phrase that allowed her to see him immediately and initially as a human being, runs through her thoughts again and again: *"He never came to Christ till he had 'thirsted for blood'"* (163).

The first Abernethy, then, had his Christ and his land, however belatedly acquired, to channel the fierceness of his blood. Dorinda, even in her desperation, knows that a religious "salvation" can never be hers. Returning to her home in the moonlit night after her encounter with Jason, numbed by the feeling that there is nothing she can say or do, she finds her family "waiting prayers" for her. To her mother's insistence that "it might make your head better to hear a chapter of the Bible," she replies shortly, "No, it won't. I'm not coming. I'm never coming to prayers again" (167). Hers is not the pitifully defiant gesture of one who forsakes God because he feels God has forsaken him. Despite the denominational character of Dorinda's conscience, she knows immediately that the God of her great-grandfather and her mother is not and cannot be meaningful to her. Although she had earlier mystified Jason by repeating her mother's religious "habits of speech," and though, as Miss Glasgow points out, "habit rather than belief" is, after all, "the ruling principle of conduct" (84), Dorinda is incurably nondogmatic if not nonreligious. Perhaps her familiarity with the futility of her mother's religious mania separates her forever from the Abernethy

Christ; more immediately probable, the religious orthodoxy of her region has impressed her modern soul with its absurdity in the death of Rose-Emily, the wife of Nathan Pedlar, the storekeeper. Earlier when Mrs. Oakley had remarked, "There ain't but one thing that keeps you going and keeps a farm going, and this is religion. If you ain't got religion to lean back on, you'd just as well give up trying to live in the country." Dorinda had merely replied obstinately, "I don't feel that way about religion. . . . I want to be happy" (101). And so she was until Jason's betrayal deprived her forever, she felt instinctively, of youth, hope, and love. Life she had still and wanted, even as she lay on the rain-sodden moss by the roadside, peering from behind the brambles at the buggy that carried Jason and his bride. She was to rediscover much more than life, though hers was always to remain a secular salvation.

The Dorinda who loves Jason Greylock is for Ellen Glasgow not only a transformed but an "unreal" Dorinda, whose "natural" self survives only in "momentary sparkles of energy" (107). The disillusioned Dorinda of New York, however efficient, is similarly unreal, deprived of "life" not because she has been deprived of love but rather because having rejected passion, dreams, romance, and her love for Jason as attempts to "make life over into something it was not" (182), her "essential self" without roots in an alien soil is benumbed. Her memories of the April fields, blooming orchards, and singing pines of Old Farm, even her reluctant thoughts of the broomsedge, flower of desolation, hateful because "too much alive," too much a symbol of renewed suffering, persist, growing slowly into a compelling vision. Dramatically released amid the soaring harmonies of a concert hall symphony, the vision demands recognition, demands the courage of acknowledgment—and returns her to life.

She saw it with an intensity, an eagerness that was breathless;— the fields, the road, the white gate, the long, low house, the lamp shining in the front window. For the first time she could think of Old Farm without invoking the image of Jason. For the first time since she had left home, she felt that earlier and deeper associations

were reaching out to her, that they were groping after her like
the tendrils of vines, through the darkness and violence of her later
memories. Earlier and deeper associations, rooted there in the earth,
were drawing her back across time and space and forgetfulness.
Passion stirred again in her heart; but it was passion transfigured,
recoiling from the personal to the impersonal object. It seemed to
her, walking there in the blue twilight, that the music had released
some imprisoned force in the depths of her being, and that this force
was spreading out over the world, that it was growing wider and
thinner until it covered all the desolate country at Old Farm. With
a shock of joy, she realized that she was no longer benumbed, that
she had come to life again. She had come to life again, but how dif-
ferently [238–39]!

Dorinda's recoil from the personal to the impersonal, her persisting rejection of romantic love that she may dedicate her "real" self
to transfiguring the desolate land of her fathers maintains her in a
dangerous pose—dangerous because suggestive of a strained
artificiality, of extra-human behavior, or to the modern sensibility,
of a burgeoning case of neuroses. One simply is not allowed to say
of love, as Dorinda does, "But I don't need it. I am through with all
that" (233). As her New York friend and employer, Dr. Faraday,
tells her firmly, this attitude is merely "nervous revulsion." It dries
up one's "life force," and whatever that may mean, it is bad. Yet
while the heroine of *Barren Ground* remains "through with all that"
to the last, she is saved from an epic posture her height cannot
sustain by her steadfast admission that she has not found the
"completeness, the fulfillment that she had expected of life" (345).
She knows often a feeling, indestructible if fleeting, that she has
missed something bright and beautiful, and she has always a sustained awareness that the "monotony of contentment" (378) she
achieves, if different and perhaps even better than her youthful
ecstasy, is totally unlike anything she called happiness then. But
over against these vague regrets there returns to her always a "blind
sense of a purpose in existence which had evaded her search," a
sense at which "the encompassing dullness would melt like a cloud,
and she would grasp a meaning beneath the deceptions and the

cruelties of the past" (248). This sense of purpose is as fugitive as her sense of loss, yet it is also as indestructible, and, meanwhile, there is always a long day's work to be done.

Dorinda Oakley is, then, as incurably human as she is incurably endowed with a Presbyterian conscience. It is impossible to see her return to Old Farm as a deliberate renunciation of a life of love. After all Jason deserted her, not she him; there happened to be about her no other young men who appealed either in New York or in Pedlar's Mill; there were always with her those "earlier and deeper associations" reaching out to her. In the meantime, as her vision of the land awakened in New York, her father lay dying on Old Farm, and they needed her there. As Dorinda felt, "after all, the decision had been taken out of her hands" (248). Only the strength of her desire to reclaim the land and to find a meaningful pattern of life separated her from other dutiful young things, and these strengths, after all, were matters of heritage.

That "meaningful pattern of life" is symbolically rendered in *Barren Ground* by the three stages of Dorinda's career entitled "Broomsedge," "Pine," and "Life-Everlasting." In her youth the slender, waving broomsedge that dominated the untilled acres of Old Farm was the "one growth in the landscape" that thrived on "barrenness; the solitary life that possessed within itself an inexhaustible source of vitality" (124). Fighting the broomsedge was to Dorinda's people "like fighting the wild, free principle in nature." And yet "they had always fought it. They had spent their force for generations in the futile endeavour to uproot it from the soil, as they had striven to uproot all that was wild and free in the spirit of man" (125). There is, we are made to see, in Dorinda's youthful, passionate devotion to Jason Greylock a comparable untamed freedom of spirit, at least in part a product of inherited frailty. Two of her great-grandfather's sisters, her mother tells her, were for a time demented victims of love, though one, fished from a millstream where she had thrown herself in a suicide attempt, dried off, "sobered down and married somebody else and was as sensible as anybody until the day of her death." The other recovered from her disappointment in an asylum and "went as a missionary overseas" (102). Apparently the great-aunts shared with Dorinda the unconquerable vitality of the wild, free spirit that needs only the ordered tranquility of a patterned existence to surmount defeat.

Dorinda fights and conquers the wild freedom of the broomsedge with the same passionate vitality with which she loved Jason in her youth, for though the force of her youthful spirit is in her maturity tame and ordered, that spirit has not weakened. She comes to recognize finally in the winter nights of her contentment as she lives over her "romantic folly" and "thwarted aims":

that the strong impulses which had once wrecked her happiness were the forces that had enabled her to rebuild her life out of the ruins. The reckless courage that had started her on the dubious enterprise of her life had hardened at last into a fortitude with which she had triumphed over the unprofitable end of her adventure [460].

The years of "Pine" following her return and her parents' death are the years of restoration, years when Dorinda feels that her past life must be ignored for the "moment in which she is living." Her memory of the singing pine, ever green and bronze against the sky, sacred to her vision of the land, must be protected against her "secret terror" that memories of past sorrow, anguish at recollections of her love for Jason, will overwhelm her and leave her helpless. Like the harp-shaped pine that shelters the graves of her family, Dorinda guards her heritage with unbending vigilance. The pine remains dominant, silhouetted against the evening sky, surrounded by ever-growing fields of green, for Dorinda's deepest instincts are committed to the land and in the land she conquers. "The farm belonged to her, and the knowledge aroused a fierce sense of possession. To protect, to lift up, rebuild and restore, these impulses formed the deepest obligation her nature could feel" (341). These are years of work during which Dorinda's fierce sense of possession becomes almost a mania as the land prospers, the dairy herd grows, and the green fields lengthen. She acknowledges neither abiding love nor hatred for Jason, but although she tacitly concurs with Bob Ellgood's charitable concession that Jason's decline into the drunken inertia of his father is a matter of "blood," laziness "bred in the bone," the "mental malaria" of the country, she is obsessed with a desire to possess Five Oaks, the land Jason inherited from his father. At length, during her encounter with Jason as she purchases his land, she realizes his total indifference to her as a figure of the past, and she surrenders forever the Dorinda of her youth. From her secure, middle-aged vantage point of "triumphant independence," she can begin to assess the worth of her achievement.

Flowers of life-everlasting bloom and dry in the fields without losing form or color. As the slow years drift by, it often seems to Dorinda that her soul has bloomed and withered on the land. The heady glory of power, command, achievement, she has known, but such intoxication is momentary and all glory is transient. Her inmost strength, her invulnerable spirit, the virtue of the pioneers "who had triumphed over life," the quality with which she had triumphed over the land made her hard, at times too hard—hard-bitten, even hardhearted. She knew moments when the "permanence of material things, the inexorable triumph of fact over emotion, appeared to be the only reality" (336). Such moments were always disturbing, for she remained aware that her parents, denied the material prosperity she had achieved, "possessed a spiritual luxury which she herself had never attained."

She had inherited, she realized, the religious habit of mind without the religious heart, for the instinct of piety had worn too thin to cover the generations. Conviction! That, at least, they had never surrendered. The glow of religious certitude had never faded for them into the pallor of moral necessity. For them, the hard, round words in her great-grandfather's books were not as hollow as globes [410].

But Dorinda's "religious habit of mind" wears well, never really fades. Each new acquisition, each added luxury on Old Farm brings her uneasiness. Thick carpets and shining machinery are sources of consternation and embarrassment, somehow annoyances attributed on the surface to the "visionary gleam" of the husband of her middle years, Nathan Pedlar, but soliciting always from Dorinda anxious thoughts of the primary importance of labor and the fruits of the land. Her "pallor of moral necessity" seems and is meant to appear the glowing flush of a twentieth-century devotee whose faith, however secular, produces out of barren ground, a mental harvest rich and fertile. "Firmness of purpose, independence of character, courage of living, these attributes, if they were not hers by inheritance, she had gleaned from those heavy furrows of her great-grandfather's sowing. 'Once a Presbyterian, always a Presbyterian,' her mother had said when she was dying" (411). As the vanguard of the secular Presbyterians, Dorinda Oakley does well, never surrendering her purpose.

Hours had come and gone when she had felt that there was no permanent design beneath the fragile tissue of experience; but the moral fibre that had stiffened the necks of martyrs lay deeply embedded in her character if not her opinions. She was saved from the aridness of infidelity by that robust common sense which had preserved her from the sloppiness of indiscriminate belief. After all, it was not religion; it was not philosophy; it was nothing outside of her own being that had delivered her from evil. The vein of iron which had supported her through adversity was merely the instinct older than herself, stronger than circumstances, deeper than the shifting surface of emotion; that instinct that had said, 'I will not be broken.' Though the words of the covenant had altered, the ancient mettle still infused its spirit [459–60].

   Although the martyr that is Dorinda Oakley has altered until her victory is no longer a martyrdom nor meant to be, she shares with past martyrs not only moral fibre but the stiff-necked attitude that so often accompanies it. And Dorinda's attitude toward her marriage to Nathan Pedlar frequently appears just as comic as the rigid postures of the original martyrs. During the years of her mania to possess the land, it is driven home to her that she needs a man around the farm. There is too much to be done alone, and reliable hired help is scarce. In addition, the appeal of the solitary life dims in the shadow of middle age. And so she yields to Nathan's urging, for "without him she would never become anything more than a farmer who was extraordinary chiefly in being a woman as well; and this provoking disadvantage was a continual annoyance" (364). One suspects that Dorinda's decision to overcome the provoking annoyance of being without a man is chiefly Ellen Glasgow's reluctant and derisive acknowledgment that her heroine is after all playing a man's role. And since, unfortunately enough, it is not likely that the salvation of the south can be achieved solely by female tidying up, she must permit the men to share her heroine's destiny. Males of Dorinda's stature are rare enough, but females are even rarer—alas! Dorinda's marriage is then, in part, a product of her creator's concession to proportion and the way things are.

Miss Glasgow is not willing, however, that Dorinda should surrender any of her dominant role or epic stature to a man, and so she permits Dorinda to deny Nathan any such liberty as "lovemaking" and to maintain him as a tractable hired hand. As might be expected, this relationship serves rather to reduce Dorinda to the comic level on which Nathan exists than to elevate her beyond him. Yet it is useful in allowing us to see more clearly that Nathan Pedlar is really the comic counterpart of Dorinda Oakley. With his "flat clownish features, bleached grass mustache, and hair like motheaten fur" hiding a noble, even "visionary" soul, he is the very prototype of the unlovely hope of the South. And if his concentration on "modern improvements" makes him seem on one level much closer to the Southerner of Tate's complaint who needs only standard "advantages" to "get ahead," his dedication to principle awards him the melodramatic death of a hero much more conventionally acceptable than Dorinda can ever hope to be. Killed in the flaming ruins of a wrecked train while saving women and children, Nathan has a monument erected to his memory. Dorinda is left to concur with the popular opinion of Pedlar's Mill that "there was more in Nathan than anyone ever suspected" (443).

Ellen Glasgow adds to Dorinda's sentiment at Nathan's victorious death, a death that "filled the aching void in her heart": "Where the human being had failed her, the heroic legend had satisfied" (456). No more appropriate comment can, I think, be made of Miss Glasgow's conception of Dorinda and her destiny in *Barren Ground.*

EVERYWHERE IN THE WORLD OUTSIDE OLD CULTURES WERE BREAKING UP, CODES WERE LOOSENING, MORALS WERE DECLINING, AND MANNERS, ANOTHER ASPECT OF MORALITY, WERE SLIPPING AWAY. . . . AN INCREASED MOMENTUM, A SHRILLER VEHEMENCE, A WILDER RESTLESSNESS — THESE WERE THE VISIBLE MANIFESTATIONS OF A DECAYED AND DISSOLVING SOCIAL ORDER. — ELLEN GLASGOW

After long enchantment with Dorinda, Ellen Glasgow found herself anxious for the perspective of comic detachment. And if in the Queenborough trilogy of tragicomedies her point of view is still at least as anxious as detached, she has achieved in the biting Olympian mood that controls these novels a mature and effective rendering of her society. All three books are dominated by the well-defined and well-limited horizons of the fading Richmond aristocracy, the Southern perspective she knew best. The really interesting accomplishment in the Queenborough trilogy, however, is the progressive development through each book of Ellen Glasgow's view of the definitions and limitations of that aristocratic horizon.

Lightest in vein, the first novel of the trilogy, *The Romantic Comedians* (1926), has as its hero Judge Gamaliel Bland Honeywell, distilled essence of the aging Virginia gentleman, who "for thirty-six years . . . had endured the double-edged bliss of a perfect marriage."[1] Now a widower and approaching sixty-six, the Judge is outwardly still the perfect gentleman of a lifetime's cultivation: "An upright, even a religious man, with a rich Episcopal flavour of temperament, he was disposed to encourage liberty of thought as long as he was convinced that it would not lead to liberal views" (3). In keeping with the character he has preserved is

---

[1] Ellen Glasgow, *The Romantic Comedians* (Garden City, 1926), p. 1. Page references to future quotations from this novel in Chap. 6 are given in parentheses or brackets after the quotations.

Queenborough's expectation that he will sweeten the dignity of his last years by marrying the love of his youth, Amanda Lightfoot. A belle of the eighties and, as the Judge often reminds himself, his ideal among women, Amanda at fifty-eight has matured in the "patience, sweetness, serenity, all the Victorian virtues" including the crowning "queenly pride" most admired by the Judge, since it "had left him as free to follow his later fancies as if she had not been the one great love of his life" (14). For in the proud aftermath of a youthful lovers' quarrel, Amanda had sailed off to Europe, and the Judge, who had delayed his chase, found on his pursuing ship several months later more versatility in his emotions than he expected: he had promptly become "entangled" with another woman and "almost automatically" engaged and married to her, the Cordelia of his thirty-six years' bliss. Rejecting numerous other suitors, Amanda had remained at once true to the ideal love of her girlhood and a "safe" ideal for the Judge—a confirmed "womanly woman" incapable of "the slightest gesture of allurement." Before the birth of his first child, the Judge, still caught up in his passion for Amanda, had begged her to run away with him but as the years confirmed his comfort, they strengthened his relief that the ideals of virtue and devotion to duty that made Amanda's refusal as predictable as her rejection of other suitors had kept them both from disaster.

Now, thirty-seven years have passed, and while the Judge, in rare moments of poignant longing, still cherishes the memories of his one great passion, it is the Amanda of his youth who is incarnated as his lifelong love, never "the well-preserved Amanda of the tarnishing years." He finds himself obstinately resisting Queenborough's attempts to push him toward the present Amanda, "A wonderful woman, but, with her silver-grey hair and her fifty-eight years, she must have put the thought of love outside her life" (15). For all unknowing the Judge has been caught by the spirit of the twenties where

The upheaval of the post-war decade had disturbed the steady stream of experience, and from the shaken depths embryonic fragments of impulse had floated to the surface of consciousness.

Everything was becoming—or so it seemed at the moment—nothing was finished, except the Great War and the great tradition. There was no immunity from discontent.[2]

Confused and not a little shocked as his own embryonic fragments of impulse overflow into desire for Annabel Upchurch, a twenty-three-year-old poor relation of the lost Cordelia, Judge Honeywell discovers his traditional scruples unavailing in the April world around him. Far from immunizing his discontent, they prove to lend themselves with ridiculous ease to the support of his renascence of vitality. While his reason warns him of the absurdity of falling in love with a young girl, his "principles" adjust themselves to his awakened yearning to live intensely, to experience "the secret of life" he feels he has missed.

And this yearning to be kind, to give happiness, to fondle gently, included not only all the soft little things in the room, but the whole world as well, with the possible exception of handsome spinsters who had kept—by Heaven knows what sacrifices!—their late Victorian figures. To confer happiness! Surely this was the highest privilege that money could bring! The power to give happiness to others, to restore wounded spirits, especially young and innocent spirits—what could be nobler than this [60–61]?

And so, scruples covered over by the delusions of desire, blanketed by the comforting myth that young women disillusioned by tragic experience prefer "the older men who have learned to be kind without being exacting," Judge Honeywell asks for and is awarded Annabel's hand.

Annabel's "tragic experience" of being thrown over by her fiancé, Angus Blount, who took her at her word and married someone else, has affected her chiefly with a desire for revenge. Unlike Amanda, who after her similar lover's quarrel of the eighties chose to perpetuate romance by rejecting all other possible suitors and remaining true to her "ideal" in queenly Victorian fashion, Annabel, lacking other outlets for quick revenge, announces herself

[2] *Certain Measure*, pp. 218–19.

through with romance and young men forever. And as she grows increasingly irritated in her dissatisfied state with the deprivations of the genteel poverty in which she and her widowed mother live, she decides that marriage to the wealthy Judge wouldn't be so bad after all. Of course Annabel has her own twentieth-century ideals of fair play; so, knowing of the old romance between Amanda and the Judge, she goes first to Amanda to ask her whether she would like to be married to the Judge. True to her standards of "perfect behaviour," Amanda denies her feelings. Annabel feels the last obstacle to her marriage removed. For, although she suspects Amanda's evasiveness, she fails completely to understand it. She has told everyone of her troubles with Angus; reticence for Annabel only throws suspicion on the intensity of one's feelings.

The inevitable disaster in this generation-crossed marriage appears with comic promptness. After Annabel has dragged the increasingly weary and dyspeptic Judge around Europe for three months, nostalgia for his familiar fireside almost overbalances his growing desolation as his visions of happiness prove more illusive than ever. But on their return to Queenborough, Annabel not only tries to rearrange his furniture, but while the Judge nods by his altered fireside, swiftly falls in love with another young man. She runs away with him just as swiftly, and the Judge, pursuing and confronting her, finds himself not only agreeing to divorce her but generously promising to support her and her lover. For exhausted by what he feels as the final defeat of his hopes for happiness, he is suddenly transfigured by an almost mystical impulse of benevolence, a radiant, though fleeting "sense of divinity." The radiance of his vision, his moment of pure and selfless ecstasy, soon fades. But recovering from his exertions in his familiar bed, he is comforted by his satisfaction at having "done the best he could" all his life. And comforted, he begins to listen once again to the whisperings of the tender little leaves of a second April. The novel closes as the Judge dreamily lets his vagrant thoughts drift from the shapely young nurse who attends him to the possibility of winning "supreme happiness" when the prime of life is well past. Yet, half-secure in his new half-wisdom is the promise that his response to a second spring will include marriage to the ever-faithful Amanda.

Amanda, Annabel, and Judge Honeywell are, of course, the romantic comedians of the novel. Indeed, since this is a comedy, their characters are close to caricatures, even as the respective "forms" of social behavior they represent are reduced to somewhat oversimplified formulas. But they are also the "happiness hunters" in what Ellen Glasgow recognized as a "morality play." She would like to think of the play as one in which "although the setting is Virginian, the characters belong to no particular age or place,"[3] are rather drifting figures in a scene and a situation which were as fluent as time." In this conception of her morality play, Amanda embodies "submission to the awful power" of duty; Annabel is "youth in arms against life" demanding beauty and joy as its right; and the Judge, "not the pattern of declining gentility, but the universal hunger for a reality that is timeless," a man come to disaster less because of an "individual revolt against nature than as a part of the universal striving to break through the stale crust of experience into some intenser reality than life had afforded" (277). Although the novel as a comedy may be susceptible to this interpretation, its "morality" is not. Miss Glasgow's very eagerness to promote its "universal" framework despite her usual attention to rendering time and place argues more desire for than achievement of disinterestedness. She herself qualifies her insistence that her characters drift in time by remarking: "Yet none of them moved in a vacuum; all were linked together not only with one another, but with the dramatic unities which they observed and obeyed."[4] The point is that the dramatic unities here, if admittedly not exclusively Southern, are observed always from the Virginian viewpoint.

Behind Amanda Lightfoot's lifelong immolation to "ideal love" lie not only the generalized precepts of the Victorian twilight but the carefully sustained and peculiarly Southern heritage of Virginia Pendleton. For Amanda is merely an older Virginia. Her life, filled

---

[3] *Ibid.*, p. 223.   [4] *Ibid.*, p. 219.

with nieces, nephews, canaries, and the poor has, if anything, strained her evasive idealism less than the actualities of marriage burdened Virginia's. The possibility of change eludes Amanda even more thoroughly than it eluded Virginia. For Amanda's Queenborough unites in encouraging her pose as Dinwiddie cultivated Virginia's, and no vulgar, commonplace association such as Virginia's daily intimacy with Oliver ever shadows Amanda's ideal. She continues to wear the blue and lavender of the Judge's youthful preference, all unsuspecting that he now prefers the bold reds and greens of the twenties. His marriage to Annabel forces her to face actuality for the first time in almost forty years, and with her ideal love brutally torn away, she can only crumple and fade. Not even Virginia's fumbling, futile efforts to save her ideal of marriage are open to Amanda, and, of course, unmarried Amandas never have a son to comfort their betrayed faith.

Ellen Glasgow has called this novel a tragicomedy. From the perspective that is comic, it is conceivable that Amanda can and even probably will consent to bolster the Judge's declining years and illusions, as well as her own, by marrying him after all. Certainly the resilience and sheer impenetrability characteristic of their evasive idealism gives strong promise of such an outcome. But their situation seen as tragic, or rather pathetic, which is what Ellen Glasgow really meant, makes unthinkable the fulfillment of the happiness they have hunted for a lifetime. The Judge's marriage to Annabel forced upon both him and Amanda at least intermittent acknowledgment of the chasm that separates the dreams they cherish and the often haunting nightmares of the actual. Never again can either return permanently to their long twilight sleep where their world "like the Garden of Eden, was unaware of its own innocence" (180).

Of course there is good in their new half-knowledge. They have learned, not that the Garden of Eden on earth is a myth, never that un-American heresy, even for Annabel, but merely that the ancestral Southern barriers against snakes do not provide complete immunity. Amanda is left with the knowledge that her realized "happiness" is and ever has been a "mixture of fortitude and hypocrisy" (304), a hypocrisy so devious that it deceived her altogether. Judge Honeywell cannot help being chastened by his memory of the ludicrous ease with which he mistook the voice of a serpent for the call of human destiny. Yet their error has been only innocent blindness to the imperfections of their own principles; and if the naiveté that assumes human perfectibility to be possible providing one holds strictly to the tradition-tested moral axioms of the Virginia of the eighties is rather terrible in its simplicity, it yet makes possible the vision of Southern heaven that Ellen Glasgow cannot bear to let go. Amanda and the Judge will never be wholly satisfied with less than ideal perfection. Their only happiness, like that of Corinna in *One Man in His Time*, must lie in continued devotion to that unattainable perfection; their only reward must be found in rare moments of almost inhuman selflessness, moments that come and pass in an instant; yet moments that bring, so the Judge feels, a vision of divinity—perhaps a scene in the Garden of Southern Eden in which the visionary sees himself strolling pleasantly with other Virginian angels.

The modern innocent, Annabel Upchurch, is pathetic not because she mistakes her vision of happiness but rather because she has discarded all such visions. For Annabel the attitudes and behavior of her elders lead only to "shams," and since shams don't work, they are clearly immoral. The ease and thoroughness with which she has cut herself off from the "great tradition" continue to disturb Ellen Glasgow, despite her efforts to explain Annabel's alienation as a product of youth's rebellion combined with the upheaval of the Great War. They continue to disturb Miss Glasgow because she feels that Annabel is yet worth saving. Annabel herself says, "I haven't any moral sense, but I have a heart" (93). And so she does, a heart and the unconquerable iron determination to achieve fulfillment that Miss Glasgow has always found such a valuable characteristic. Indeed, Annabel is the American dreamer incarnate, with nothing behind her except expectation and nothing before her but her outstretched hands. And such grasping expectation is so terribly un-Southern, so completely devoid of a sense of obligation, a true responsibility to the necessary forms and formulas of achieving one's visions that Annabel can say of her suffering to the Judge, "It isn't my fault. . . . I don't believe anything is anybody's fault" (111). Bemused though he is and well perfected in a lifetime of imperfect perception of faults, he is at least sure that such a doctrine or lack of it is "dangerous in theory and fatal in practice" to all visionary Edens. And the practice for visionary Edens is always ultimately the real point in Ellen Glasgow's novels.

Even the two characters in *The Romantic Comedians* who give context to the ideals of the happiness hunters by their own limited desires support the Judge's view, however inadvertently. His twin sister, Edmonia Bredalbane, might be a caricature of Annabel grown old. For she, too, overthrew Queenborough conventions in her youth when she refused to be ruined by an affair, and, aided by her forthright hedonism and the Atlantic Ocean, managed to return in triumph two generations and four husbands later. Now, to her delight and the Judge's horror, the rising generation not only accepts but appears to enjoy Edmonia, treating her scarlet letter "less as a badge of shame than as some foreign decoration for distinguished service" (84). Having long since dismissed Victorian conventions as the product of Methodist and Baptist pleasure-baiters, Edmonia still lives for the pleasures of the moment, narrowed by her age to the savors of good food and drink. She has, she tells the Judge, had a "good deal of fun" from her life by managing to make a little happiness go a long way. For, as she says, "I never approved of the sour kind of duty you pretend to enjoy. . . . I've always believed that happiness, any kind of happiness that does not make someone else miserable, is meritorious" (227). Annabel would doubtless applaud this declaration, and even the Judge is shaken by it sufficiently to ponder the possibility of a "leak, after all, in his inherited system of prudential morality" (229). But the question written large over the lives of both Edmonia and Annabel remains the doubt that their pragmatic approach to happiness can ever lead to the happiness the Judge and Amanda have in mind, let alone avoid a full portion of misery.

Mrs. Upchurch, Annabel's mother, provides a more conclusive

answer to this question that Edmonia is capable of giving either by precept or example. A woman of "invincible good sense," Mrs. Upchurch, like Edmonia, abides by the convictions of long experience rather than those encouraged by the prolonged innocence of the happiness hunters. Repeated disappointments have caused her to renounce interest in the possibility of romantic happiness; she wants only comfort and peace, and to that end encourages the Judge's interest in Annabel, though she is amazed at his gullibility. Nevertheless, Annabel's hysteria over the short-lived frustration of her love for Dabney Birdsong causes Mrs. Upchurch, "in spite of her disillusioned intelligence, to wonder about the past and to speculate, even more darkly, over the ways of the present."[5] She muses over Annabel's charge that her elders pretend that they are being noble by doing their duty when they are only afraid of life.

Was it true, she asked herself, in sudden depression, that not duty, but the fear of living, had held back youth in the past? In the earlier generation, how many girls had married men old enough to be their fathers or grandfathers, and yet nothing disastrous had come of it, nothing, at least, with which husbands, aided by duty or the fear of living, had not been able to deal. Women had known then how to live without love, just as they had known how to live without beauty or happiness; but she realized now, watching Annabel's bleak despair, that it had been because they had something else to put in its place. Something abstract and ultimate! Something as unalterable and as everlasting as the Rock of Ages! Even if duty were merely a symbol—well, a symbol, Mrs. Upchurch decided is better than an abyss to fall back upon. A quiver of weakness attacked her elbows and knees. It seemed to her that there were no longer any moral properties left in the world. Experience was reduced to the sum of pure egoism [300].

But although Annabel's flight might well have confirmed Mrs. Upchurch in her despair over the irrecoverable loss of the "moral properties," it does no such thing. A wise and comparatively impartial observer of the generations that adjoin her own, she is yet committed by her cheerful "good sense" to the conviction that the

[5] *Ibid.*

"consecrated beliefs" of the Judge's generation have not only meaning for but continuity with Annabel's world. So she decides to take the "brave and noble" course—to rejoice for the deserving Amanda, at last to be confronted with the possibility of her deserving reward, while she mourns for the pain she is convinced Annabel must yet suffer in learning the consequences of betrayal. In the end Mrs. Upchurch takes everything that has happened as proof of "how mistaken people were when they denied the law of compensation in life" (341).

They Stooped to Folly (1929), the second book in the trilogy of tragicomedies, is predicated on Mrs. Upchurch's rather precarious latter-day transcendentalism. Nonetheless, Ellen Glasgow succeeds remarkably well in this novel in giving substance and direction to her affirmation of the continuity of the "sacred beliefs." She achieves this by much delicate and not a little sharp probing beneath the various disguises used by the various generations to perpetuate these beliefs.

In *A Certain Measure* she observed that this story grew from a consideration of the "two preeminent woman myths which have exerted a benign or evil influence over the English novel" (227): the myth of woman as an inspiration born with Clarissa, and the modern myth of woman as an impediment, an obstacle to all man's higher activities, which Ellen Glasgow interprets as a cultural acquisition of the brave young men returned from World War I, an acquisition "born of the irregular union between democracy and disenchantment." She had intended her comedy to revolve around the "ruined woman" of three different generations. A subject rich in ironic possibilities, the "almost forgotten" myth of the ruined woman embodied chivalry, moral tradition, sentiment, and a well-honored invention of man—in short, all the favorite Glasgow ingredients. But although the fable of the ruined woman persisted as the "recurring motif," the novel begun as a satire unfolded as "a serious study, with ironic overtones, it is true, of contemporary society." Contemporary society was again the Queenborough of the twenties living in the light of a victory "won at the cost of a few lives and many illusions." This is the Queenborough, "essence of all Virginia cities," where

the foundations of the old aristocratic order, overthrown two generations before by nearer conquest, had never safely settled back on their corner-stone of tradition. The superstructure of faith was no longer invulnerable. To the dispassionate or cynical observer, it appeared doubtful whether the recently fallen standards, which had once so gallantly withstood material destruction, would ever rise again over the lost provinces of the spirit.[6]

But Ellen Glasgow was never dispassionate or cynical when probing either standards or spirits, and she probes both in *They Stooped to Folly*.

The leading spirit of this novel is another well-to-do Virginia gentleman and lawyer, one Virginius Curle Littlepage. Combining the roles of Judge Honeywell and Mrs. Upchurch, he is both participant and spectator in the modern dilemma. A middle-aged urbane humanist confirmed in respect for convention and deference to tradition, Virginius, like the Judge, can look back upon a lifetime of comfortable achievement, sober pleasure, and perfect marriage; and he too finds all these woefully inadequate when placed beside his youthful dreams of happiness. Rather more reflective by nature than the Judge, he cannot decide whether his melancholy is a result of middle age, the general inadequacy of human experience, disappointed idealism, or unwilling nostalgia for the war's excitement. Although the last possibility horrifies him, he is sufficiently fairminded to acknowledge that "nothing else could be compared in vehemence with that witches' sabbath of released desire." The war, he knows, revealed the natural man and woman, perhaps particularly the woman:

We were trying to be too superior, and it was a relief, even to the women, especially to the women, when the savage hunger broke through the thin crust we call civilization. It was a relief to us all, no doubt, to be able to think murder and call it idealism. But the war wasn't the worst thing. . . . The worst thing is this

[6] *Ibid.*, p. 237.

sense of having lost our way in the universe. The worst thing is that war has made peace seem so futile. It is just as if the bottom dropped out of idealism.[7]

In his more sanguine moods, however, Mr. Littlepage is less certain of the defects of a bottomless idealism. The new standards, however ignoble they might seem in the light of old traditions, were undermining those traditions. Even Southern gentlemen now suspected "that the ruined woman is an invention of man." And even he may now begin to inquire "fearfully but hopefully" whether something was wrong with the past.

Deeper than law, sharper than logic, the corroding doubt penetrated his mind. Was there a fatal flaw even in the Episcopal Church? Was the ideal of pure womanhood infested with moth and decay? Beneath these derisive questions, it seemed to him that the stern but noble features of the categorical imperative had been battered beyond recognition. How often in his youth had he heard his father lament somebody's 'loss of faith,' as if such a deprivation were a calamity. Yet he himself had found that a world without earnest conviction could be far from uncomfortable. It afforded, among other luxuries, ample leisure to regret all the pleasant opportunities that one had missed in the past [20–27].

Foremost among the missed pleasures lurks his memory of an abortive affair with his opulent neighbor, Amy Dalrymple. An Edmonia Bredelbane of Virginius' own generation, Amy's European conquests had embraced only a single husband, who ungallantly died in five years' time, leaving her to flit airly between Paris and Queenborough in what was for Virginius the fascinating atmosphere of old scandal. Fifteen years earlier, moved by her youth and velvet brown eyes, Virginius had overcome his repugnance for the divorce court and consented to act as her counsel when her first husband, discovering her lover, in accordance with the "style of the period, had promptly transfixed her by a divorce" (16). Since her lover just as promptly married a lady of impeccable

[7] Ellen Glasgow, *They Stooped to Folly* (Garden City, 1929), p. 5. Page references to future quotations from this novel in Chap. 6 are given in parentheses or brackets after the quotations.

conduct, Amy was left alone, supported only by Virginius and his noble wife, Victoria. And on one of her summer flights to Queenborough after Peter Dalrymple's death in Paris, Virginius "was tempted to become more than a friend though, perhaps, a little less than an advocate." He had taken pleasure in a stolen embrace one evening, but the next day he had taken only righteous satisfaction in disappointing the waiting Mrs. Dalrymple by giving her up and writing a long letter to Victoria, then in Europe on an art pilgrimage with the children. Many years had passed since that August evening, but still the "memory vibrated in his steady nerves"; and though honestly prejudiced in favor of strictly virtuous women in his unromantic moments, Virginius, under the spell of modern doubt, grew more relaxed in principle and began to "sweeten disapproval with tenderness when he thought of Amy Dalrymple's frailty" (21).

He is kept from testing his tenderness with action, however, by the very doubts and indecisions over past and present judgments that promote his tenderness. Literally surrounded by pure and ruined women of three generations, Mr. Littlepage is constantly hard beset not only to keep his own mind and heart agreed upon the proper labeling of the respective ladies, but to keep the respective ladies securely classified by behavior. Among the ruined women his poor Aunt Agatha of the generation preceding his own gives him least trouble. Her virtue irretrievably lost forty years before, poor Agatha had meekly, even trustingly, ever since "observed the superstitions as thoroughly as she had discarded the moral principle of the Victorian age" (109). Defenseless in her betrayal, she had submitted to lifelong banishment in her family's third-story back bedroom, her ill-gotten child whisked away while her family deplored the "temporary derangement" that had permitted her ruin. Although her heart had been broken, her life spoiled, and her value permanently impaired, Agatha's settled convictions remained unruffled; her simple faith in the Protestant Episcopal Church, even her maidenly faith in men, endured. And though Mr. Littlepage is aware that poor Agatha is and always has been featherbrained,

although he knows that in place of "temporary derangement" the
twenties would have chosen for her waywardness merely the crude
term "over-sexed," or at best, "nymphomaniac," although he acknowledges that the contemporary view of poor Agatha is tolerant
amusement for a curious relic of the sentimental tradition, even
pride at being able to point to a classic antique, he still feels that
there is much to be said for a code of manners "so influential that its
authority was exerted over the frail and fallen" (110). In his own
generation Mrs. Dalrymple, for all her velvet eyes, light heart, and
rebounding spirit, had acted only as a romantic, never an intellectual
rebel against this code. Never in her long addiction to improprieties
had she thought of disputing the merit of the double standard
anymore than Agatha had ever considered questioning the authority of Pauline views upon "feminine deportment." And Mr. Littlepage is convinced that their suffering "had been alleviated by
reverence for the powers that afflicted them" (109).

His secretary Milly Burden, a ruined young lady of the twenties,
has no such reverence; indeed, to Virginius she seems to have
nothing to fall back upon at all. Her apparent rejection of the
"moral law and the expert testimony of experience" in the name of
the right to live her own life both shocks him and fills him with
compassion. For the defiant courage with which, in the face of the
loss of her virtue, Milly insists upon mourning only the loss of her
lover appears to him the desperate experimentalism of modern
youth. He cannot think her bad; she is so young, so vulnerable, so
filled with determined vitality, in short, so appealing that she forces
him to consider the startling possibility "that a woman can be noble
without goodness or good without virtue." And, he reflects finally,
the saddest thing about Milly's past is not her pitiably small crop of
wild oats but rather the ease with which she has been able to discard
her heritage.

So although he recognizes, however reluctantly, his duty to
discharge Milly for the sake of his wife, his other secretary, and his
reputation, he postpones this moral obligation indefinitely. Instead
he tries to help Milly locate her errant lover, Martin Welding, who

returned to France after the war, unaware of the birth of their child and its immediate death, because Milly chose suffering silence despite the withering blight of her mother's moral sense. For his pains of kindliness Mr. Littlepage finds himself embroiled in a grotesque and intolerable muddle. His agent in the search for Martin has been his daughter Mary Victoria, the "romance of his life," and a sterling young woman bent on recovering the postwar world by doing her independent duty in the Balkan kingdoms. Mary Victoria's interpretation of duty often seems to Mr. Littlepage a demand, from pure motives, no doubt, for the "right of moral encroachment on the life of others." But despite his apprehension that his daughter's conception of duty is a mere "label for unbridled impulse" far removed from the duty of his youth that had meant violence to appetite, he is aghast to discover that she has not only tracked Martin to his foreign hospital bed but married him as well in the name of that duty.

Overwhelmed by a feeling of futility, Mr. Littlepage finds his confusion amid modern standards further confounded. He had always been sure that his daughter represented the finest transplantation of pure womanhood into the modern chaos. "That Mary Victoria, his own daughter, his noble, earnest, high-minded daughter, so eager to sacrifice herself in [what now appeared to him as an inaccurate and abominable phrase], world service—that Mary Victoria should have been involved in this moral catastrophe" (49)! Nor will his principles, however undermined by modern circumstance, really allow him to exonerate her as a victim of the trickery of fate any more than they permit him to discharge Milly of responsibility for her folly. He knows that Mary Victoria must have at least suspected the "truth," and her conviction that she married Martin to save his life, or at least to save him from himself, seems at best a pernicious form of self-deception, encouraged by her share of contemporary youth's outrageous demand for the right to its own life.

Neither the events that follow this marriage nor the attitudes of any of the individuals whose lives touch Mr. Littlepage's own existence help him to resolve his confusion. Martin Welding proves to be all that Mr. Littlepage has feared: "a white-livered mooncalf, who wrote unwholesome books that nobody bought, and had lived long enough in Paris to lose the last shreds of American idealism" (264). Before the year is out Martin has found Mary Victoria's attempts to improve and save him intolerable, and leaving her pregnant, has escaped to longed-for loneliness in the high Himalayas. That Mary Victoria should be comforted in her desolation by the words Mr. Littlepage utters about her duty to bring a happy child into the world appeals to his emotions as at least right and proper—although he feels vaguely that he is echoing something.

But Milly's reaction to Martin's flight only startles him anew. He had watched her grow tight-lipped and silent after Martin's return as Mary Victoria's husband, and his heart had quivered for her hopeless suffering even as it cowered at the thought of the future pain Mary Victoria must surely suffer from such a weakling as Martin. When he reluctantly accompanies Mary Victoria to discover from Milly where Martin has fled, he recovers his lost adoration for his daughter as, broken but undefeated, she surrenders Martin verbally to Milly and happiness. But his pity for Milly and for his daughter's classic gesture of sacrifice is roughly trampled upon by that intrepid young lady, who declares with what he interprets as the "hard little laugh . . . of youth that is lost in its own selfish concerns" (348), that she doesn't want Martin any more and hasn't since his return. What she does want is not the serene and forbearing pose of woman betrayed that Mr. Littlepage admires so much but, shockingly, to renew her "insatiable appetite for disaster." For Milly says firmly that she is off to New York to find "something worth loving" this time.

Virginius Littlepage is left as he began, confirmed if confused in the tradition that nurtured him. His hope of discovering missed delights by surrendering anew to Mrs. Dalrymple's charms, a desire encouraged by the demands of the youth around him, is thwarted by the strength of his heritage. In the rosy enchantment of her seductive presence he finds temptation too brazen to be tempting, the demands of guilty passion too exacting.

> Though he still desired Mrs. Dalrymple, he was content, at least for the present, to desire her less as a happy lover than as a disappointed idealist. For in common with the best masculine taste of the great tradition, he preferred sin on the stage and elsewhere when it was treated in the grand manner, with an orchestral accompaniment. Without musical or at least dramatic support, he felt that it left one entirely too much at the mercy of one's appetites; and appetites, though useful in evolution, are superfluous in the finished product of the Southern gentleman [298–99].

Or, at least, superfluous in a Southern gentleman molded in the influence of his wife's inspiration.

For Virginius, after thirty years of marriage, still sees Victoria Littlepage as one endowed "with every charm except the thrilling touch of human frailty" (13). And Victoria's perfection, though it has always discouraged the pleasure of love, has never ceased to bolster Mr. Littlepage's youthful ideal of chivalry. An ideal so long bolstered becomes a habit, and even as Virginius bends to embrace Mrs. Dalrymple, a sardonic spectator in his mind warns that his natural bents will never be strong enough to overcome that habit.

No more than Virginius can Victoria violate the role in which she is molded. The surprising thing is that she contemplates such violation, for she lives and dies a Southern gentlewoman, voicing every platitude possible to each situation that confronts her. Yet at fifty-five she wistfully yearns to forget herself and her duty to others, dreams of the swooning ecstasy of delight her youthful fantasies compelled at the approach of the young Lochinvar of her mind. But instead of young Lochinvar, she had married Virginius and acknowledged that there were no Lochinvars outside of legend. Still, she is tired of fuss and confusion, of too many demands for her moral influence and maternal infallibility.

Burdened to the breaking point by the weight of her daughter's difficulties and the effort to keep her own approaching death from her family, Victoria feels that she can no longer endure the strain "of sparing people, of persuading them to do right, of being an inspiration for good" (196). The moral prop of the accepted superiority of wives and mothers taken away from her by the twenties, it seems to her that she must give way. Not only are her children growing beyond her reach, but even Virginius is showing signs of resistance, and unwholesome cynicism at the thought of being offered up unto the third generation to come. Although her role as inspiration interferes increasingly with her own fulfillment, Victoria never surrenders until she drifts quietly into her longed for rest of death. Indeed, she emerges from her struggle a Virginian Mrs. Moore merely enfolded in the mannerisms of a Southern lady. Never to be mistaken for an advanced or intellectual woman, not even to be counted particularly intelligent except by a very young and infatuated Virginius bewitched with her smiles over the more obscure passages of Browning. Victoria has spent a lifetime without failure in any difficulty to perceive and accomplish the right thing, the kindly, generous, even daring gesture, given propriety by her infallible if absentminded accompaniment of action with platitude.

And like E. M. Forster's Mrs. Moore, she is celebrated chiefly in death. Virginius, rising at least to Southern heights of mysticism by calling forth all his subverted emotion, enshrines Victoria in her grave with all the attributes of a "tutelary divinity." "For this Victoria in heaven, who resembled the actual Victoria as little as a star resembles a glowworm, had won at last his unalterable fidelity" (320). Her embittered and discontented elder son Duncan emerges from apathy into frantic celebration of her incomparable virtues, and her second son Curle, modern optimist supreme, whose favorite slogan is either "Boost, Don't Knock" or "Don't Knock, Boost," (his father can never remember which), translates his sincere love for his mother into increased speed and production in his business affairs. Perhaps Victoria would have been most gratified, however, by Mary Victoria's unconscious tribute to her training when she resolves to dedicate herself as a power for good in the life of her

child. Surely in her daughter at least, there lives on the role of
woman as inspiration to which Victoria devoted her existence,
although Martin Welding has already found that role an intolerable
impediment to his own desires. But remembering Victoria's own
regrets, one can never be sure that she would not be as much
saddened as uplifted by Mary Victoria's continued dedication in a
world without props. On the other hand, Victoria Littlepage as a
woman whose perceptions can always be counted on, whatever
position real or legendary she feels she must maintain, might well
discern at last Miss Glasgow's hopes that the moral props, no matter
how they seem to be ignored or ridiculed by the young in years or
heart (all Southerners and most Americans) still stand, and above all
still support, even their most enthusiastic detractors.

Yes, even Milly Burden, even perhaps ultimately Martin Welding. Certainly Milly Burden would not call her ideals "moral," and
most certainly they are not taken from any strictly Southern
morality. Nonetheless, they might be counted all the closer to the
Northern version of the American dream for their very failure to
rely on a Virginian Eden. Milly's determination to win her second
chance, to seek once more "something worth loving" is predicated
not only on a heritage that insists this "something" must exist in the
here and now of her lifetime, but on the defiant daring, hard work,
and resourcefulness that is her path to fulfillment as an American, if
not as a Southerner. So it is that Ellen Glasgow's partial reassurance
to those like herself who fear the final loss of the great tradition
becomes the retort that all is not lost. Instead, the best of Virginia's
youth, at least, have merely merged with or reemerged as the leaders
of the perpetual chase after the American dream. For Milly is meant
to be numbered among the best, despite both her past and her
apparent lack of sensitivity about it. She takes her place in contemporary literature with the growing and versatile group of Burdens
bent to the task of carrying the past into the present. After all, she
has inherited in plenty the iron determination Miss Glasgow likes to
think of as always accompanying the best Virginian chromosomes;
she has as well endured a thorough training in the most severe and

depressing strictures of the Virginian heritage at the hands and tongue of her mother, a training that has attempted to smother her behind the background so many Northern innocents lack. Truly enough, it is doubtful whether anyone would choose Mrs. Burden, who caricatures Southern middle-class morality with a will, for one's portion of tradition; still Milly's mother is very definitely there, holding on—although reduced to lecturing unwed mothers in Queenborough's Home for Unfortunates, renamed House of Hope under the pressures of modern laxity.

In *They Stooped to Folly*, then, Ellen Glasgow reluctantly, tentatively lets the old manners go, for the young at least, lets them go in the name of moral continuity. The morality is one that finds as always the charm that soothes melancholy in the dream of an Eden on earth, even if it is not maintained exclusively by Virginians; and it includes an art that allows the guilty, if not to wash their guilt away, certainly to lift their heads again with iron determination to earn a second chance at that Eden. She lets the old manners go, but not as far away as Martin Welding would wish them. Although he too might be excused as but a frantic seeker after Eden, she cannot permit his back-door tactics. He is written off as "a member of that vocal generation which, if ever it were lost in fact, was in contemporary fiction but too easily regained,"[8] a sufferer from the fatal Glasgow malady, "congenital weakness of fibre." And the final irony of her attitude toward Martin is implicit in her insistence that she found him "appealing and likable," a victim of a successful war and a booming mechanistic society. For she sees Martin as one whose disordered sensibility and frail moral stamina might well have been sheltered if not cured under the serene sense of infallibility possessed by the Old South.

Indeed, young Duncan Littlepage seems merely a Martin moored, despite his skepticism, by the Littlepage family regime or routine. And Marmaduke Littlepage, Virginius' older brother, bachelor artist and rake, might well be a Martin Welding matured

[8] *Certain Measure*, p. 241.

in the comfortable security of Queenborough's disapproval. Virginius looks upon Marmaduke with disapproving envy as one who has refused to compromise with life and has become shabby, untidy, disreputable, but a free spirit. What Virginius cannot see, of course, is that Marmaduke is a free spirit within Queenborough—and this, Marmaduke himself might sardonically observe, makes all the difference. As it is he knows himself blessed with the double vision of an insider outside the pale. To Virginius' complaint that he holds no sentiment above ridicule, Marmaduke replies almost wistfully, "If you complained that I hold no age above ridicule, you would be nearer the truth. I am, I hope, a citizen of eternity" (132). A citizen of eternity, yet residing in Queenborough, Marmaduke is a caricature of Ellen Glasgow's "civilized man in despair of civilization"; indeed, he is condemned by it and his own disillusioned romanticism to a protective buffoonery. For his romantic idealism, though sorely tried by his society's war and peacetime attitudes, still survives, centered now in his hopeless love for Louisa Goddard, Victoria's friend and intelligent saint. As Marmaduke expresses his feeling, "I have got into the habit of unattainable desire. It is the only permanent force left in the perpetual flux of my universe" (129).

Marmaduke is saved by his habit as are Virginius, Victoria, and Louisa, who has buried her lifelong love for Virginius beneath beautiful behavior. And so, too, are saved those of the younger generation who have inherited some of the qualities adhering to the habit, despite their scorn for habit's possible deprivations. Mary Victoria's pride, Milly's stubborn sense of fair play, even Curle Littlepage's irritatingly easy acceptance of his inherited code promise to keep them safe. But the code was meant to secure the dream for the dreamers, not to save them from themselves. Here it is shown failing consistently in its purpose, leaving only the compensation of the habits it cultivates. A more precarious compensation is difficult to conceive, for among these terrifyingly innocent Edenites, the idea that end and means are separable, that one does not necessarily provide the other, is an idea that seldom arrives before they are old and grey. And even then, even then for the Judge Honeywells and Virginius Littlepages, its acceptance is painful, difficult, and slow.

Surely the danger is then much greater for the true Queenborough innocents: those successfully sheltered from all possible barriers of experience in their patterned path to Eden.

In *They Stooped to Folly*, even the young were forced to face those barriers as part of their price for the new freedom of the twenties. But in the sunlit autumn world of *The Sheltered Life* (1932), the Queenborough of 1914, pre-lapsarian innocence still prevails. True enough, of the old country families who had clung together in Washington Street since the War between the States, knit by ties of kinship and tradition to resist change, adversity, and progress, only the Archbalds and the Birdsongs remain to fill "the breach between the old and new order." The rest have been driven away by the evil smell of chemicals that rises from the industrial section in the hollow.

Even old General David Archbald, though unaware that his era is dying, feels that both he and his age are drifting, "not aimlessly like dust, but somewhere to an end."[9] Still, General Archbald has always been aware that he was not made for his time, and at seventy-five still wonders at his own endurance, an endurance that enabled him to sacrifice "his youth, his middle age, his dreams, his imagination, all the vital instincts that make a man, to the moral earnestness of tradition" (33). Born different, he had been called a milksop in his childhood because "he saw visions in the night and wanted to be a poet" (138). The General's early isolation of sensitivity in a society that had combined its moral infallibility with manners that were "a perpetual celebration of being alive" had cultivated in him a lifelong pity for the helpless and lost. He can still recall seeing as a child a buck at bay pulled down by the hounds of his exultant grandfather, who was secure in the enjoyment of his conviction that the Lord's generosity had given unto Virginians not only Negroes for servants but animals for sport.

At first, watching the death, he had felt nothing. Then in a spasm, the retch of physical nausea. For the eyes of the hunted had looked

[9] Ellen Glasgow, *The Sheltered Life* (Garden City, 1932), p. 378. Page references to future quotations from this novel in Chap. 6 are given in parentheses or brackets after the quotations.

into his at the end; and that look was to return to him again and
again, as the childish fear of the dark returns to the grown
man when his nerves are unstrung. In how many faces of men,
women, children, and animals, all over the world, had he seen that
look of the hunted reflected? A look of bewilderment, of doubt,
of agony, of wondering despair; but most of all a look that is seeking some God who might, but does not, show mercy [142].

Though all his life David Archbald had admired that robust and
virile grandfather, indeed, dedicated himself to perpetuate his heritage, he had remained "a civilized man in a world that is not
civilized." Kept by his too abundant compassion from living
selfishly, he had deferred always to the needs of those around him.
Only once in his life had he loved a woman passionately, and this
woman he had loved and lost in his youth without ever wholly
possessing her. Now in his old age he suspects that even the haunting
memory of his thwarted love has endured because it was rooted not
in desire but in pity for the hunted bewilderment of his beloved. His
wife of thirty years he had proposed to as a stranger because he had
compromised her with an accidental, overnight sleigh ride. To save
appearances they had married, and saving appearances, had lived
amicably together, more in duty than in passion bringing three
"well-appearing children into the world." At her death in his
seventy-first year, he had felt regret but hoped also to marry once
more "to find a little happiness at the end." Instead, put off by his
daughters' expectations and the needs of his son's widow and his
granddaughter, he had first postponed and then abandoned his plan
to remarry, for he found himself finally incapable of disrupting
their comfort.

He has enjoyed life, survived even being a good citizen, successful lawyer, faithful husband, and indulgent father, being, "indeed,
everything but himself." For after the loss of the love of his youth
and the news of her suicide, he knew that the poet within him and
the "living torment" of his pity had died; he felt his spirit
crippled—"a twisted root, an ugly scar, at the source of his being"
(164). Toughened by his despair he found his youthful distress at

the hunted buck, the driven slave, men killed and killing in battle, hardened into annoyance. And he found as well, to his amazement, that much pleasure could come after one had "ceased to expect happiness." But he never found the second chance of a Dorinda Oakley or even a Milly Burden. For the mark of Ellen Glasgow's truly civilized man is that he has nowhere to go and nothing really to which he may turn. Old Uncle Tucker is permitted to admire the birds and flowers; Roger Adams is allowed his editorship and Marmaduke his paintings; Corinna may keep her shop and the General his lawbooks—all of them may fall into the right pattern, but always they must find with David Archbald that "the centre of the pattern was missing" (164). In the end, after all, their lives have been lived entirely "upon the shifting surface of facts." The all-important ecstasy of standing within the gates of Eden, the fleeting ecstasy of a Dorinda surveying her waving fields, they have lost without possessing.

General Archbald, at least, even in his eighty-third year, has not abandoned hope. He takes vicarious pleasure in the happiness of his elder daughter, Isabella, who has defied propriety and married out of her class, even as he cannot look upon his younger daughter, Ella, without pain. Ella, condemned to a life of loneliness and defeat by her homely features and sickly constitution, confronts him daily with the defeated side of his own nature. While Isabella, ignoring her fiancé and refusing the chastened manner Queenborough considers appropriate to a mild indiscretion she has committed, runs off with the family carpenter, Ella sits at home indulging her frustration with hypochondria and petty malice.

The General can only sigh with hope for Isabella and regret for Ella, sigh and reflect that "it was useless to deny that all the Archbalds were subject to intermittent flashes of nature." His own sister Margaret had eloped with an Italian musician, although that had turned out badly when the musician was discovered to have a wife in Europe. His brother Rodney had been called crazy because he had committed suicide at twenty-nine, leaving a scrawl that said, "Shadows are not enough." And long ago, in the early years of

Virginia, his great-aunt Sabina had publicly defied God and escaped the witches' stake only by her ties with all the best blood of the colony. The General might have forgotten all this long ago if Isabella's features had not been "a living memorial" to his great-aunt. Then when he had become reconciled to Isabella's countenance, his memories were renewed by his willful granddaughter, Jenny Blair Archbald, who, even at ten, mingled Sabina's doubts with Rodney's eyebrows and the sharp tongue of his own dead wife. And just as the Archbald heritage was revealed once more in Jenny Blair's willfulness, so it was repeated in her sheltered upbringing after the pattern for whose center the General has searched so long. For no Archbald, even the General, questions the worth of the pattern; it is only that given the Archbald flashes of nature, there is always some risk in the individual search for the center.

Isabella found it by her escape into the fulfillment of a happy marriage, but his sister Margaret had not, Ella could not hope to, the General himself after his youthful despair and long disappointment was still looking, and Rodney had disastrously stopped trying. As for Jenny Blair, secure in the sheltered existence that preserves her innocence from both the contamination of experience and the realization of her own nature, she is as unaware at eighteen as she was at ten that the patterned life may impose limitations on her desires. She sees life only as what she "would wish it to be" even as the General can see it only "as it is."[10] Through these two conflicting points of view Ellen Glasgow attempts to "interpret reality." As the story unfolds it becomes increasingly evident that although they arise from the same pattern, Jenny Blair's selfish innocence sure of its ability to conquer experience and the General's compassionate experience uncertain of its capacity to discover meaning beneath the complex surface of existence nowhere touch.

At ten Jenny Blair is enchanted by her feeling of daring all perils as she skates down the forbidden Canal Street in the poorest section of Queenborough. The excitement that causes her to stumble and

[10] *Certain Measure*, p. 201.

hurt herself before the house belonging to Memoria, the mulatto woman who does the Birdsongs' laundry, is only enhanced when taken within, she discovers Mr. Birdsong himself bending over her, beautifully attentive as she eats a brandied peach to help her pain. But if her adventure enchants her, she is intoxicated by Mr. Birdsong's suggestion that they keep everything that has happened a secret between them, intoxicated by his manner, enraptured by his confidence and praise.

In exactly the same spirit she falls in love with him at eighteen–after provoking him to a passionate, impersonal kiss. Falls in love and precipitates a tragedy that has been twenty years in the making. It isn't her fault, Jenny Blair tells herself; she loves living and wants to be happy; being with George Birdsong is such a joy, it can't be wrong. John Welsh, the Birdsongs' young ward, has insultingly called her attitude toward happiness a "sparrow vision," but Jenny reflects, "there was nothing she could do about it. If attending to your own happiness meant the sparrow vision of life, that vision seemed to her to have its advantages" (299).

George Birdsong's years of surreptitious but hardly secret pleasure-seeking testify to the advantages he too finds in the sparrow vision. Nonetheless, George's is a shamefaced testimonial to his felt sense of inadequacy to sustain his perfect marriage. Eva Birdsong had been a celebrated belle of the 1890s when he married her, so striking in beauty that she not only delayed wedding processions but was rumored to have once delayed a funeral merely by passing by. Twenty years ago, her sudden, surprising elopement with George, who was charming and well favored, but otherwise the least eligible of her many suitors, was justified by Queenborough as the inevitable outcome of a great passion. Eva herself encouraged this view. Convinced that she had sacrificed world fame by surrendering a career in grand opera to her great love, without children, she feels a constant need to acquit her choice to herself and her world. Only a perfect love, a perfect marriage can satisfy her; the grandeur of that love must make her and George sufficient unto themselves, all other interests overshadowed by their happiness with one another. George, loving her deeply and admiring her sincerely, finds himself repeatedly incapable of trying to live up to Eva's standards, or, at least, quite uncomfortable in any sustained effort to do so. In consequence, he is repeatedly unfaithful and repentant.

Not that George doesn't try to live up to Eva. In her most severe illness he refuses to touch cigarettes and whiskey, appropriate symbols of his too human weakness, until Eva is out of danger. And he does attempt to discourage Jenny Blair's persistent chasing after him. "Whether you know it or not," he flares in angry confusion at her constant tempting, "innocence when it lives to be eighteen is wicked" (354). But how wicked, how genuinely evil Jenny Blair's cultivated blindness becomes not even George is prepared to accept. Nonetheless, it is acceptance of this conquering evil that Ellen Glasgow finally achieves in *The Sheltered Life*, an acceptance she refused to permit in the first two books of her trilogy of tragicomedies, an acceptance she was at pains to deny in *The Builders*, her fullest early treatment of the possibilities of evil sheltered behind the Southern code. Sheltered innocence precipitates evil violently, even melodramatically in *The Sheltered Life*, precipitates disaster with entirely convincing ease.

For twenty years the Eva Birdsong whom Jenny adores and would not hurt for the world, except that she cannot help preferring George for herself, for twenty years this Eva of perfect beauty and behavior has struggled to maintain that perfection in her marriage. The strain accompanied by inevitable disappointment has always been too great; even Jenny Blair perceives that behind her lovely, artificial smile, Eva never seems real. Finally, burdened intolerably by her illness, Eva finds her ideals shattered beyond repair. Too weak and ill to combat the nightmare visions of reality that overwhelm her, she knows only the terror of the cornered deer who, attempting to flee, finds himself surrounded. In her calmer moments Eva knows that there can be no escape for her—either forward into reality or backward into her long cherished illusions. All that she is or will ever be has been dedicated to something that "Never really existed." Or so she confesses tonelessly to Jenny

Blair. But even as she does so her terror mounts, and with growing hysteria she insists: "Women are like that. What they value most is something that doesn't exist. Nowhere. Not in any part of the world. Not in the universe" (367–68). Of course Jenny Blair completely fails to understand Eva's meaning, and though she feels her "very bones" dissolving in pity, can only hope that Mrs. Birdsong knows nothing about her and George.

Yet if the irony in this scene seems heavy, it reaches violence in the final denouement. Looking into her garden from her library window at twilight, the distraught Eva discovers George with Jenny Blair in his arms. Completely unbalanced by this final shock, Eva preserves her shell of public decorum to the end. Smiling vacantly, speaking vacantly, "George, I want you," she disappears into the twilight gloom of their house. When George, obedient as always to her request, follows after her, she kills him with a shot from his hunting rifle. John Welsh, the young civilized man, discovering what has happened, hastily summons his counterpart, the General, to concur that the shooting was an accident, while Jenny Blair, failing to thrust the horrors that confront her "into the nightmare of things that could not have happened," screams with the shrill hysteria of a trapped animal. As John, in anger more human than civilized, seizes her to shake her into silence, the General intercedes with his longer disciplined pity, remarking almost absently, "Don't be brutal, John. The shock has unnerved her. Remember how young she is, and how innocent." And Jenny Blair flies to accustomed refuge in the General's arms crying, "Oh, Grandfather, I didn't mean anything. . . . I didn't mean anything in the world" (395)!

So it is that swiftly, almost savagely Ellen Glasgow shatters forever the heroic mold of her great tradition in the haunting last scenes of this novel. And the evil odor that finally overwhelms the last of the old families of Washington Street rises from their own inner decay to mingle with the stench of chemicals from Queenborough's growing industry. Still, no other Glasgow novel, within or without her trilogy, better deserves its designation as tragi-

comedy. For as always, her final irony is reserved for the defeat that
is victory, and since her abiding rule promises that the strength of
the defeat shall indicate that of the victory, victory here is compelling. Or at least tenacious. Who wins or even what survives is,
of course, the perplexing question.

The General in the calm of old age that is always for Ellen
Glasgow "strangely like happiness" muses on the future of the
drifting age, the flattening world around him:

Beauty, like passion, would decline to the level of mediocrity. With
the lost sense of glory, the power of personality would change
and decay. It was possible, it was even probable, he thought, that
the individual would return to the tribe from which it had so lately
emerged. Better so, perhaps. . . . Of one thing alone he was sure,
—life would never again melt and mingle into the radiance that
was Eva Birdsong. . . . To go onward, civilization must fold
back, must recoil from individualism and seek some fairer design
[377–78].

That the particular sense of glory which so long sustained Eva
Birdsong and the General in their surrender of self has been lost
forever seems undeniable. Yet, however firm the General's conviction of the irrevocable departure of the old glory that created the
radiant Eva, he never doubts that civilization will go onward to a
"fairer" design. And just as "civilization" entails much more for the
General and his creator than "society," so the fairer design of that
projected civilization must allow that whatever is to be more fair
must be not only more just but, somehow, more glorious; for surely
without the glory there can be no dream. The design of the old
glory, after all, permitted all along the possibility of Jenny Blairs,
neglected the possibility of the Ellas, as the history of the Archbald
"nature" testifies. And in the beginning as in the end, there were
always the George Birdsongs—always finally uncovered despite all
the stretching of the pattern. Eva Birdsong and the General, born
sensitive, born civilized, if you will, knew instinctively that the
pattern was for the glory, that glory must be patterned or it cannot
live; they believed as well, almost to the end, in the final superiority

of their own native design for happiness, more noble surely, more promising than grand opera or an international affair. And nobly they await the glory. Nobly because they knew that all those round them either forgot the pattern in the pursuit or kept the pattern and forgot the glory. The Virginian design for happiness had seemed to them always wonderfully well wrought, but it had faded; it had not worn well. Above all, however securely they had been enfolded by the pattern, they had never felt clothed in glory. Yet only once in the weakness of terror does Eva confess her fear that lifelong devotion to a glorious myth has destroyed her. In the end, it is George who must die for his final, intolerable betrayal of that myth. Eva, of course, is mad when she finally shoots George—and as pathetically ludicrous in her madness as any Lady Hamlet who has lived too long in Virginia is likely to be.

But the General agrees with Eva—or at least he feels that civilization will have to get itself a new myth, one easier on most people because obviously most people find the old myth too strenuous. Furthermore, he is sorry because he admired the old, strenuous myth, admired the Evas who fought for it. And while he is very old, he is terribly sane. Although his long years of loyalty to the pattern have not been lived as a Hamlet might have lived them, they have kept him from the role of a Southern Prufrock. So he knows that Eva's meticulous devotion to the most obscure motifs in the old design for glory has required constant high courage, particularly since even the brilliantly emblazoned emblems in that design have faded beyond recognition for the young. Indeed, did not Jenny Blair, wrapped so closely by the fabric of Queenborough life, fail to perceive any design at all? The General knows this is true, but for Jenny Blair he cannot quite accept it; after all, she is so young, she has been so much protected, she needs only a little time to look and see. Meanwhile the General acknowledges that Jenny Blair, although a vivid little thing, like most of her generation gives no promise of measuring up to the Evas.

His last illusion, Eva possesses forever for the General something he quaintly calls "personality," or even more oddly, "individualism." He means, of course, that familiar iron determination to realize the communal Eden for which Ellen Glasgow shares his enthusiasm; but applied to Eva "personality" and "individualism" are singularly appropriate, if unfamiliar. Eva has no land, no family upon which to perpetuate her heritage; she can celebrate it only in herself. But this she does to the fullest until her whole self and soul are given over to an expression of traditional ideals. In the process, of course, her self and soul, the self and soul so sacred to modern individualism and personality, are sacrificed to her heritage. Nonetheless, to the General, this deliberate sacrifice of self seems the highest individualism possible.[11] And this sense justifies his terminology, also justifies his reluctant admission that such sacrifice cannot succeed because it always has been, is, and will continue to be too rare. For surely that which is most rare in human behavior is most individual. And most precious. And most impossible.

The old design has failed then, and the failure is final this time. To fail its vision of glory must ultimately doom any design, but to fail itself brings immediate fatality. Any victory left cannot be for the old pattern. But a victory wrought by the downfall of the design that failed is another matter. To those who have long assumed a design for living necessary to achieve the fabric of one's dreams, a fading moth-infested pattern that is no more than a tattered mockery of a once splendid carpet indicates merely the necessity for a new and better design. It is no more than one's obligation to point out the threadbare patches of the old. It is vital to admit that so many worn-out places in the original demand mending, even a new weave, however difficult, even treacherous such admission may seem to those taught that their old design was guaranteed for a world's time. And the recognition of such necessity is a victory. But giving up the carpet is not even a possibility—not when you know

[11] The General's use of "individualism" to describe Eva's special attributes is also advocated by John Crowe Ransom when he observes: "There must then, really be two kinds of individualism; one is greedy and bogus, amounting only to egoism; the other is contemplative, genuine, and philosophic. The function of a code of manners is to make us capable of something better than the stupidity of an appetitive or economic life" (*The World's Body* [New York, 1938], p. 34).

that all paths to glory must have patterned carpets. One pattern that you thought a very good pattern, and your very own besides, must be discarded, and in the discarding is the loss that is victory. But the design for living must be reworked or the victory remains only loss.[12]

General Archbald is aware that such reworking is a specialty of young men, particularly young American innocents like John Welsh. The part of him that is old and tired and worldly wise can only distrust John's fervent faith in the new design for eradicating social ills, particularly as John's projected Utopia is to be reached by grouping poverty and injustice with communicable disease and by wiping out the entire class "scientifically." But the General is an American, too, an old innocent and Virginian, and so there remains part of him committed to that "fairer design" of his dreams, alien to his long compassion for "those who cannot be blended into a design" (263). And it is his believing self which finally triumphs over his doubting self, convinces that weary skeptic to rest content that both the heritage and the vision of glory have been entrusted to the John Welshes.

After all, the General concedes, John Welsh, though shockingly crude in his outspoken references to the state of Eva Birdsong's kidneys, is still Virginian enough to worship Eva. And even if, as the General suspects, John's love embraces only the personal and not the symbolic Eva, whose sacrifices infuriate him, "he is honest, anyway, and he has the rare gift of moral indignation." In his last years the General has come to feel more and more uneasy about the weakness of such "sober indignation" in his world. Now, he notices

---

[12] General Archbald's attitude in acknowledging the defeat of the old design for living may be illuminated by William Alexander Percy's similar stand: "Should I therefore teach deceit, dishonor, ruthlessness, bestial force to the children in order that they survive? Better that they perish. It is sophistry to speak of two sets of virtues, there is but one: virtue is an end in itself; the survival virtues are means, not ends. Honor and honesty, compassion and truth are good even if they kill you, for they alone give life its dignity and worth. . . . Love and compassion, beauty and innocence will return. It is better to have breathed them an instant than to have supported iniquity a millennium" (*Lanterns on the Levee: Recollections of a Planter's Son* [New York, 1941], p. 313).

wryly, John has become a good deal happier since he has found things to blame. "What the world needed, it appeared, was the lost emblem of evil" (373). But the General finds the problem of evil as perplexing and difficult as John feels it certain and intolerable. It is the old terror of hidden snakes in Eden. His generation thought they had proscribed the existence of all snakes, that snakes provided for ceased to be dangerous, but the snakes were there, most powerful than ever. Now John's generation was confident of the strength of its quick, scientific extermination. Still, even with success, and success was always so difficult, there was always fear; "and the look of driven fear is not, he told himself, unlike malevolence."

Yet, sitting in the sunshine of the garden, the General is visited by "a sense of fulfillment"; dreaming of Eva Birdsong, his last illusion, he feels the vague presence of contentment. "After all," he found himself repeating aloud, "character may survive failure. Fortitude may be the last thing to go" (379). Ironically enough his contentment swells just as Jenny Blair departs the garden to precipitate the Birdsongs' tragedy. Still, the General dreams on in the peaceful mood that permits him to reflect that while his own generation "felt about social injustice . . . John's generation talks about social injustice; and, perhaps, who knows, the next generation, or the generation after the next, may begin to act about social injustice" (270).

FROM THE BEGINNING, I HAD KNOWN THAT I WAS ENGAGED UPON
A FAMILY CHRONICLE, THAT I WAS STUDYING, NOT A SINGLE
CHARACTER OR GROUP OF CHARACTERS ALONE, BUT THE VITAL PRIN-
CIPLE OF SURVIVAL, WHICH HAS ENABLED RACES AND INDIVIDUALS TO
WITHSTAND THE DESTRUCTIVE FORCES OF NATURE AND CIVILIZATION.
—ELLEN GLASGOW

Ellen Glasgow's comment on the genesis of *Vein of Iron* (1935)
serves as well to illuminate her purpose in her last published novel,
In This Our Life (1941). In the light of her Southern dreams her
continued preoccupation with the "vital principle of survival" was
predictable. After recognition as painful as it was final in *The
Sheltered Life* that the South's traditional design for living had
worn out in too many places, she characteristically turned her
attention to the parts of the pattern still durable, and, above all, to
those in whom the pattern still endured. Since she felt that so many
of the modern city dwellers of her beloved Richmond and the
surrounding Tidewater had succumbed to the "disintegrating
forces in the modern world," forces that perversely denied the
necessity of any design for life, she looked first in *Vein of Iron* to
the mountain-dwellers for survival by design. More precisely, she
chose to focus on the descendants of the Scotch-Irish pioneers, her
father's "forbears" who had settled the "upper valley of the James
River and the fertile wilderness between the Blue Ridge and the
Alleghenies."[1] The Fincastle descendants of her fictional family
chronicle were still there when the twentieth century opened, still
lived on in the old family manse, although both family and manse
had been altered considerably since their beginnings. Nevertheless,

---

[1] *Certain Measure*, p. 165.

as Ellen Glasgow says, "They had always lived under that roof."[2]
It is this circumstance that really distinguishes the Fincastles from
their Northern counterparts in the pioneer tradition.

The Fincastle destiny had always been manifest in their own
Shut-in Valley. To be sure, Miss Glasgow decorates the background of the Fincastle chronicle with ancestors, male and female
alike, battling Indians, and the elements so that the "Presbyterian
spirit and the Presbyterian theology" may be predestined to victory
in the Valley of Virginia, at any rate. But all this is immediately
recognizable as standard scenery for any American pioneer; it is the
durability of that "spirit" and "theology" that counts in *Vein of
Iron* after Indians and elements have been overcome. Or, perhaps,
because they have been overcome. In most American versions of the
pastoral idyll the pioneer conquerors of the soil diminish in stature
with each succeeding generation, diminish, of course, in direct
proportion to the shrinking of their battlegrounds. Once the wilderness and the Indians are gone, so, too, are the pioneers. And most
often the land remains only as a growing city block, or, as in Miss
Glasgow's earlier version of the Southern pastoral, only barren
ground.

---

[2] *Ibid.* p. 172. Ellen Glasgow herself knew and cherished family memories of
such a roof, although she had never lived under it. In a letter to Allen Tate
written from Richmond on September 30, 1933, she says: "I have just returned from
a wonderful trip to Rockbridge, where my father's people of the Glasgow name
settled on the old plantation of Green Forest (Glasgow means Green Forest in
Gaelic) when the country west of the Blue Ridge was still scarcely more than a
wilderness. The fine old house (1780) is still standing, with immense pillars. It
was burned once [in] 1820 and rebuilt on the original foundation, with the
original columns and the old brass locks and some of the old woodwork. What a
spirit those pioneers had!" (*Letters of Ellen Glasgow*, ed. Blair Rouse [New York:
Harcourt, Brace & World, 1958], pp. 145–46).
    The Glasgow roof, unlike the Fincastle roof, ceased to provide protection for
the family in Ellen Glasgow's generation. In the appendix of genealogical notes
on her ancestors in *The Woman Within*, Miss Glasgow remarks that the ravages
of the Civil War forced her parents to surrender the Green Forest house permanently: "After the War Between the States, they tried to restore the old place
at Green Forest: but an invasion had passed over it, and the family fortunes were
irretrievably ruined. In the end, the old homestead passed out of the family, and
my parents spent the rest of their lives in Botetourt County, and in Richmond"
(p. 299).

Vein of Iron is not, however, another *Barren Ground*, though in many ways the later novel is a reworking of the earlier chronicle and Ada Fincastle but a latter-day Dorinda Oakley. If *Barren Ground* is Miss Glasgow's version of the modern South's pastoral dream, *Vein of Iron* is her modern pastoral reality—or at least a much more tough-minded blueprint of the dream. Yet the surface similarities between the two books are numerous. Both Fincastles and Oakleys must be classified as "good people" rather than "good families," although the Fincastle claim to goodness descends directly through an unbroken male line of "stouthearted" Presbyterian ministers and the Oakleys had to rely on Dorinda's maternal great-grandfather, the Presbyterian missionary, John Calvin Abernethy, for their sturdy genes. But both derive their heritage from "intrepid Scottish metaphysicians, who had placed freedom to believe above freedom to doubt, and had valued immaterial safety more than material comfort." Moreover, that heritage has become secular rather than sectarian in the minds and hearts of Dorinda Oakley and Ada Fincastle, a religion in and of this world rather than beyond it; but it is a religion that endures, however its tenets have been converted.[3] These two heroines whose youthful dreams are matured rather than blighted by bearing illegitimate children, proceed in triumph to adapt their heritage to conquer the destruction of "nature and civilization" and to preserve the world around them. True enough, the world around them is hardly larger than their families, but the worlds of the South always begin and end with the family.

Yet the beginnings and endings of the two novels differ surprisingly. Ellen Glasgow repeatedly complained that *Barren Ground*

---

[3] Marshall Fishwick testifies to the durability of the Presbyterian code and, incidentally, to the excellence for Ellen Glasgow's purposes of her chosen material, when he says: "But whatever the limitations of Calvinistic ethic, it is morally strong. This is why it withstood the wear and tear of pioneering. The Ulsterman's God was not a thing of sweetness and light, but a strong, fullblown, sinewy God. His people should not expect an easy time of it. So they wove and spun, provided for their own, and set table with the food grown by their own toil. The limestone streets of their villages looked hard. So did their red brick houses with severe stone trimmings and plain white pillars" (*The Virginia Tradition*, pp. 60–61).

was misinterpreted as being a novel about "cultivation of land"; she was equally irritated to find *Vein of Iron* described as "a novel of the depression." But however justified her protests that such labels distorted her intentions, she does use land and depression in the respective novels as materials for salvation. And very different materials they are. Indeed, in *Vein of Iron*, tilling the soil never presents itself as a way of life; the land itself has no more than symbolic value as the place where the Fincastle heritage originated. Ada's father, the fourth John Fincastle, hoes in the garden occasionally because hoeing quiets his nerves if not his mind, but this is the extent to which the modern Fincastles are sustained by the land. Both Ada and her father accept the divergence of their lives and their land with scarcely a qualm, for it is not so much a matter of changing times as of changing Fincastles. They are not the lengthened shadows of their forebears; no true Fincastle has ever been a shadow of anyone, and they no more think of serving the land to support their bodies than they contemplate serving Presbyterian orthodoxy to support their souls. And when admiration for the labors or convictions of their ancestors inflames their memories, it is never nourished by nostalgia. It is as if they were past all that forever.

So, in fact, they are. Not only has the present John Fincastle never possessed the practical talents of a John Calvin Abernethy or of his own parents, for that matter, he can scarcely remember when he has possessed their faith. Truth, for John Fincastle and Ada, is always to be discovered; for their forebears truth had been revealed. And, Miss Glasgow seems to suggest, only revealed truth allows time for cultivating land, for unquestioning dedication to family and community living.

No man who has to provide for a family, John Fincastle thought, has a right to search after truth. Perhaps not anywhere in the world. Certainly not in America. But were the Renaissance and the nineteenth century in Europe the only ages when men believed that they could discover truth as they discovered a gold mine? When men believed that the search alone was worthy of the sacrifice?

Missionaries, Mary Evelyn declared, sacrificed their families all the time, but his mother insisted there was a difference when people were sacrificed to a truth that had been revealed.[4]

John Fincastle didn't care to recognize this difference. His "religious education," he imagined was, ironically enough, responsible for his indifference. At least his convictions or lack of them which arose from that education had led to his trial for heresy and schism and finally to his being deposed by the Presbytery. Now in his middle years he perceives the error of his youth: he had believed that knowledge would bring him the means to defend the doctrines of his inherited church. Instead it had brought him only awareness of a "multitude of gods" men had invented—"and all to be reconciled, one with another, before they could be vindicated" (49). Although he was dispossessed of doctrines, however, his religious zeal did not waver; he would reconcile; he might even vindicate, and meanwhile he wanted a charge among the "dispossessed of the earth." Or so he thought when his scholarships in London and Germany ran out. Then, back in Virginia, he had been prepared to decline a call from the largest Presbyterian church in Queenborough when he met Mary Evelyn. That meeting had, he thought, "swept away his vocation" among the conventionally dispossessed. Later John Fincastle was ever unable to decide whether strength or weakness had guided his decision to accept the Queenborough church in order to marry Mary Evelyn. His dilemma was real, "for he had been born with an other worldliness of the mind." As a solitary scholar among the poor he would have been scarcely afflicted by the ostracism of his church; as it was, his family had been forced to share both that ostracism and the poverty that accompanied it.

The ostracism itself was inevitable. The fourth John Fincastle could no more surrender the convictions he published throughout his life in his many-volumed history of religious thought, *God as*

<hr>

[4] Ellen Glasgow, *Vein of Iron* (New York, 1935), p. 48. Page references to future quotations from this novel in Chap. 7 are given in parentheses or brackets after the quotations.

Idea, than his ancestors might have betrayed the beliefs that brought them to the Valley of Virginia. The qualities of his inherited faith remained to him undiminished, but his idea of God had altered too much for any established Presbyterian community to tolerate.[5] So it was that he first found himself forced to resign the pulpit of the Queenborough establishment, and finally, with the publication of the second volume of his history, banished from pulpits altogether with the loss of his charge in the old stone church built by his great-great-grandfather.

The lifelong outcast status of John Fincastle, whose unorthodoxy, despite Miss Glasgow's youthful enthusiasm for Darwin, spurns alike traditional and "scientific" views of God, is surely an accurate rendering of the persisting conditions under which steps forward in Southern fundamentalism had to be taken. Ellen Glasgow deals squarely with the all-important problem of how the strength of such steps is to make itself felt. Fincastle should not be taken as an entirely isolated thinker, as Francis Butler Simkins makes clear when he refers to the almost prohibitively high educational requirements set down for ministerial candidates among the Scotch-Irish Presbyterians.[6] Apparently the later-day John Calvin Abernethys of the South were much better equipped intellectually

[5] At least one established Glasgow critic finds John Fincastle's idea of God as intolerable as the Presbyterians did. McDowell asserts that the novel fails because John Fincastle's speculations "lack a firm basis and a precise definition" (p. 209). I would say rather that John Fincastle's speculations lack a firm basis and a precise definition in established philosophical terms. He is, after all, a theologian, despite both Miss Glasgow's and McDowell's use of the label "philosopher," but even if his theological commitments do not exempt his ideas from the obligation to be firmly based and precisely defined, surely his symbolic status in the novel prevents his failures in this regard from assuming any great importance.

And if we allow for the limiting strengths of Fincastle's heritage and isolation (which are, of course, Miss Glasgow's as well), Fincastle emerges as a quite convincing Southern intellectual, perhaps because of rather than despite the inadequate formulation and defense of ideas he displays in the novel. His importance lies in his ability to question and refine his moral heritage without discarding it and, above all, to transmit that heritage to his daughter, accomplishments that are seen by Miss Glasgow as capable of fulfillment only through actions in the society of men, never merely through conceptions confined to the world of ideas.

[6] *A History of the South,* pp. 157–58.

to defend their creed than John Calvin Abernethy found necessary. Yet, as W. J. Cash has asserted, the tragedy of the modern South is not that it lacks intellectuals, but that the intellectuals cannot communicate with the people. Ellen Glasgow has resolved this dilemma in *Vein of Iron* through the nonintellectual Ada Fincastle, who translates both her father's principles and her heritage of the Presbyterian conscience into domestic triumphs, as effective as they are modern.

Through all this John Fincastle emerges as protector and defender of the true Southern heritage in modern times. And modern times are kind to both him and his family, for they challenge them with plentiful adversities. That is, the Fincastles find themselves constantly in circumstances which demand that they struggle to preserve their convictions and often their existence. Such circumstances Ellen Glasgow has always presented as invigorating for ideals, even necessary for their survival. Indeed she appears to distinguish between suffering and adversity by making the former a negative state in which the soul withers through inability to act and the latter a positive condition which allows the soul to flourish because mind and body have plenty to do. Adversity becomes, then, the means whereby the Fincastles can renew the pioneer spirit of their ancestors. But, most important, adversity is the means of sustaining the iron-veined qualities that make the pioneer heritage worth preserving. For within the serene shelter of Shut-in Valley, hereditary forms have already become formulas deprived of meaning. As John Fincastle phrases it, the trouble with the village of Ironside is that of any community where "all likes and dislikes are inbred until they become like the half-wit families over in Panther's Gap" (73).

Still, even John Fincastle's tested views and actions are not sufficient to reveal the vein of iron heritage to its fullest—"that instinct for survival we used to call 'the soul of man,' "[7] according to Miss Glasgow. His deficiency, as he himself is constantly aware, is one of temperament: "all the outward aspects of living seemed to

[7] *Certain Measure*, p. 168.

him fragmentary, unreal, and fugitive. He had not willed this; he had struggled against the sense of exile that divided him from the thought of his time, from his dearest, his nearest. Nevertheless, it was there. His inner life alone, the secret life of the soul, was vital and intimate and secure" (50). And the inner life, as both John Fincastle and his creator know, is not enough to sustain a living heritage. The principles of a John Fincastle who believes "that a man may be free to do anything he pleases if only he will accept the responsibility for whatever he does" might serve as foundations for a new Jerusalem in any green and pleasant Virginian valley; the practices of a Grandmother Fincastle who believes as her husband did, "If you flosh the water, you will have scum without fish" (75), are vital to the building of any Jerusalem anywhere.

So it is that Grandmother Fincastle takes her place in the family chronicle as preserver of convictions, of memories, of food. As impatient as she is bewildered over her son's heretical views, she can never understand how he or any man who denies the Virgin Birth can have such a fine face. Yet all her life she has been dedicated to an ideal her husband preached from the pulpit, an ideal very like that which motivates her son: "Life will yield up its hidden sweetness . . . only when it is being sacrificed to something beyond life" (40). But to Grandmother Fincastle this ideal evokes memories of rebuilding homesteads, congregations, communities, from the ruins of disasters wrought by Indians, disease, drought; rebuilding, renewing her convictions, and through everything, enjoying her experiences, enjoying the feeling of being alive, robust, and at work with and for her family.

Her daughter Meggie, John Fincastle's sister, is but an extension of Grandmother Fincastle into the next generation. But Meggie is an important extension, for she embodies proof that they also survive who only serve and wait. Thirty-three when *Vein of Iron* opens, Meggie already feels older, and with the shortage of men in the Valley is as destined to remain unmarried as she is assured election to salvation for her perfect convictions. Yet Meggie's enjoyment of life is as robust and steadfast as her mother's has ever been. One believes Meggie when she reflects that she has never "had any sentiment (for her life was too full of useful activities and her heart was too full of her family)"; one sees in the serene Meggie whose background presence sustains so well, the sincerity of her outlook: "If the Lord had appointed her to marriage, He would have arranged it all in His own good time. As it was, she had put her hope in little things, and she had been happy. She was the only member of the family who was never low-spirited, not even in the long winters, when sometimes they were snowed in for a week" (60).

John's wife, Mary Evelyn, is really the outsider in the Fincastle family. Often she seems to cling to her frail hold on life so that she may be nurtured and sustained by the Fincastles, and almost always she appears more symbolic than real. Gentle, lovely, sensitive, Mary Evelyn is Ellen Glasgow's last emblematic Virginian lady. Bred in "the Tidewater," she languishes there an orphan whose once wealthy relatives are now elderly, unkind, decaying, until John Fincastle rescues her with his love. To Grandmother Fincastle, Mary Evelyn always made the "heartbreaking appeal of the dying or the poverty-stricken. Though she was happy, her happiness, like her beauty, was too ardent to seem natural" (43). And even the Fincastles can give Mary Evelyn only intermittent fulfillment, a life pierced by flashes of ecstasy and balanced with tragic interludes, but a life never dull, never meaningless. They cannot sustain her, for she represents a way of life not only alien to their own, but past forever. Mary Evelyn, despite her happiness, weakens daily, wastes away slowly in the shadow of the mountains. She dies in Ada's young girlhood.

Ada herself is the heroine of the family chronicle. She never stands alone on Dorinda Oakley's heights; nor are the elements of the Fincastle tradition embodied in her necessarily superior to those of the rest of the family. Rather, she becomes the heroine of *Vein of Iron* because she carries her heritage successfully into the essentially alien modern world, here represented as the city of Queenborough after World War I. Ada, like Dorinda Oakley, presented as the child of a "mixed" marriage who has inherited the "conflict of types," seems to emerge as the exclusive product of the stronger branch. Like the rest of the Fincastles, she worships and serves her gentle mother as one of the dispossessed the Fincastles always seem to love instinctively and long to solace; there is nothing of Mary Evelyn in her makeup. Even her brief surrender to emotion with Ralph McBride hardly resembles her mother's lifelong impulsiveness, her faith in the supremacy of feelings. For she sees in her flight with Ralph a "dream coming true," even as John Fincastle saw such a dream in his first vision of Mary Evelyn. But her romantic heresy is tempered as is her father's romanticism and heresy by the conviction that any individual must be prepared to accept responsibility for his actions. So in the midst of emotion, she says to Ralph, "I try to stop thinking. But I can't. . . . I'm happy. I'm not afraid. Not even if I have to pay for happiness with all the rest of my life" (208). And the "mute supplication" in her "unconscious being" is to her grandmother's Redeemer: "Don't punish us, God. We aren't hurting anyone. Don't punish us, God" (212).

Later, after their child is born while Ralph fights on in Europe, Ada sees her grandmother fail and die, and she accepts responsibility for that death because she refused to repent of her affair with Ralph. Ada's first battle with life has been a revolt like her father's from the doctrines of her inherited faith. And although her revolt is practical, almost domestic, while John Fincastle's was based on principle and an abiding idealism, Miss Glasgow suggests that Ada is the more thoroughgoing revolutionary. Certainly she defies community decision as her father, who seemed to expect and even agree with his outcast status, never did. Indeed, Ada rejects the community of Ironside altogether, once she feels that it has cast her out, and from that time looks to a new frontier to conquer. She urges her father and Meggie to leave with her for Queenborough to await Ralph's return. Her postwar dream is to "build a home in the wilderness of the machines as their forefathers had cleared the ground and built a home in the wilderness of the trees" (278). For if the city seems without morality, without even individuals who possess the precious identity she calls "soul," her village seems to her committed to the sacrifice of souls in the name of a pernicious morality.

Ada's rebellion began when Ironside forced Ralph McBride to marry the village flirt, Janet Rowan. "In trouble," Janet took advantage of a quarrel between Ada and Ralph at a village dance to lure Ralph to her room in classic fashion and then to expose him as her lover by screaming at a nonexistent mouse. And though the villagers, even Janet's parents, certainly John Fincastle, may doubt Ralph's guilt, they are committed to upholding the appearances of morality and custom, to demand that Ralph, as the man named, marry Janet. When Ada protests with the strongest appeal she knows, that it isn't "right," John Fincastle says only, "I know, my child, but we cannot alter a rule of conduct. No matter how wrong or absurd it may be, it is stronger than we are" (147). Or, stronger, at least, than he can be. In the face of Ada's frantic pleas he can only confess that no one would listen to him; no one ever has; he has chosen retreat from life; he cannot deal with circumstances.

Ralph, too, succumbs, telling Ada bitterly that he is a "trapped" fool. No more than Ada and her father is Ralph a believer in the code to which he surrenders; yet Ellen Glasgow sees him as a victim of the "curdled religion" of his mother, the "agonized conscience" which has broken his will. Ada reflects about his decision: "It was Ralph who had said he couldn't accuse Janet. He had sacrificed himself, and her also, to a last rag of chivalry, to a tradition in which he did not even believe" (166). But surely the chivalry of Ralph's agonized conscience is a peculiar chivalry at best—the bitter chivalry of unwilling acceptance of a guilt he denies. Peculiar, but understandable, and less chivalry than despised habit. What Ralph seems to accept is that he must be punished for being in Janet's room; he is guilty because he was there. No matter that nothing "happened"; no matter that no one believes anything happened; no matter that he doesn't feel guilt; he was there and guilt and its consequences follow from this fact.

Ralph McBride never really recovers from the bitterness and cynicism his trapped surrender brings. Or perhaps it would be closer to Ellen Glasgow's intent to say that he is never able to mend a will broken by the agonized conscience of Ironside tradition. For in *Vein of Iron* once again she has given an instance of evil wrought by the outworn pattern of the tradition she defends. But this time her sympathies are not divided; this time her sympathies are wholly with the young who break the code. Break the code, to be sure, in order to uphold the qualities in the tradition that code was formulated to preserve, but break it nonetheless. Ellen Glasgow has come a long way since her stand in *The Builders*, where she insisted both that manners and morality were essentially one and that beautiful behavior might conceal evil ends. In *Vein of Iron* she no longer concerns herself with beautiful behavior—never, of course, a primary characteristic of the frontier tradition. She is concerned with morality; not the morality of convention but of the iron-veined heritage, which in this novel breaks with tradition that tradition may conquer.

The sole conqueror is Ada Fincastle, for Ralph McBride is saved only as a member of her family, her world, one of the dispossessed the Fincastles sustain. Ellen Glasgow said of her purpose in this novel: "What I wished to do was to test the resistance of this vein of iron to outward pressure, and to measure the exact degree of its strength."[8] In Ralph the strength failed; as his mother's religion had curdled and broken his will, so the iron in his veins had grown brittle and snapped under pressure. Miss Glasgow suggests, as she will, that the quality of the McBride iron had never been really first-rate owing to Irish adulteration, but except for her questionable commitment to adulteration by racial origin, she is merely signifying that some individuals are weaker than others. Ada is of the strong. And with all her strength, she strives to build a home in the machine wilderness of Queenborough for herself and her family.

At first the family thrives. Aunt Meggie grows serenely confident that there must be room for everyone, even scholars like her father, in a postwar world made safe for democracy. John Fincastle himself takes heart, for he finds work teaching again in a fashionable

[8] *Ibid.*, p. 173.

Queenborough girls' school. Not that he has ever liked teaching, but when his Ironside pupils filtered away after his pacifist views became known, he had felt intensely his loss of responsibility, and now he can complete the last volume of his work and wait for the "good end he could never miss." As for Ada, she becomes stronger daily, feeding on the promise of the future, her love for Ralph, her plans for her family, which she hopes can return in triumph to Ironside a few years hence after conquering the city. Even the infant Ranny flourishes, with all the impudence of a modern illegitimate child, before his father's return to marry Ada.

So in the beginning it appears that Ada's defiance has restored all that Ironside's hollow morality distorted. Then Ralph returns, his dark moodiness unchanged. His bitter cynicism has only been deepened by his war experiences and six quarreling years with Janet, six years of waiting for her to find a richer man and divorce him, only to have the divorce arrive with prompt mockery just too late to allow him to marry Ada before sailing for Europe. He is eager to share in the postwar prosperity, to sell unlimited numbers of automobiles for Ada and his son; but his faith in life, in the purpose of existence, in the goals and standards that make living meaningful for the Fincastles, seems gone forever. And after seven years of comparative prosperity and content in Queenborough, he still feels about life as he did on the day he agreed to marry Janet: "Everything flattened out and went dead on me. But I get a lot out of life as long as I take it on the surface. It's only when I punch through the surface that the world seems to go rotten" (308).

Soon afterward the surface of life is punched through for him. Not only is Ralph badly injured and temporarily paralyzed while demonstrating an automobile to a flirtatious, teen-aged neighbor; the depression descends before he recovers. Ada, who as her father reflects, will always "carry her way of life with her as the pioneers had carried their Bibles beside their flintlocks and shot pouches" (301), reacts to Ralph's accident by providentially returning to her old work in a department store before the depression hits. She is even able to find a "new kind of happiness" in Ralph's and Ranny's renewed dependence upon her. Yet she is herself surprised at the distance between her newly experienced contentment and her youthful ideas of happiness, even as Dorinda Oakley reflected with amazement on the difference between the dreams of her youth and the realized satisfactions of her maturity.

But if Ada is quick to find advantages in disaster, the other members of her family need time to rise above discouragement and depression. Ralph, convinced that he will now fail in the world that has failed him, broods in prolonged convalescence. Even the resolutely cheerful Aunt Meggie explains to Ada that she understands why the wild and irresponsible young like jazz—"It seems to let out something that's stopped up inside of you. . . . There's mightly little to cling to when you've lost your convictions. And even convictions don't fill up your time somehow" (326). As for John Fincastle, even before Ralph's accident his observations of urban life in postwar Queenborough had filled him with dismay.

Had it been like this in his youth? He tried to look back, but the view was too far and too faint. Still, it seemed to him that his generation had held, however loosely, to some standard of living. Nobility of motive had not then become a lost issue. . . . Everything, from the aimless speeding of automobiles down to the electric dust in the sunlight, appeared to whirl on deliriously, without a pattern, without a code, without even a center. . . . All this, he reminded himself, was merely the foam of transition, and would disappear as it came. But would the perpetual flux and reflux of individualism reduce all personality to the level of mass consciousness? Would American culture remain neither bourgeois nor proletarian, but infantile? Would the moron, instead of the meek, inherit democracy [293–94]?

Yet curiously enough, as the situation worsens the meek in the Queenborough world, at least, emerge as a steadying force. It is they who give purpose to the Fincastles' struggle to restore values to existence. The Mulberry Street community of neighbors is a community composed almost exclusively of humble foreigners, in that they are foreign to the modern city and its ways whether they were born in Europe, in the Valley of Virginia, like the Fincastles, or merely in another age and another way of life. When the depression deepens and lengthens, when reduced prosperity gives way to a real struggle to survive without starving, the Fincastles begin to look beyond their own troubles to help their community. Ada and Aunt Meggie are kept busy continually feeding the starving, sympathizing with the destitute, mourning the lost. Ralph, with reckless Irish generosity, gives away most of his sporadic earnings. His teaching job lost because of his age, John Fincastle devotes himself to the desperate around him as he had longed to do in his youth, as he had never been able to do before. He even indulges in wry self-congratulation at his practicality as he introduces an old and starving neighbor to the bread line and donates the suit saved for his burial to enable a young man to accept a teaching offer. And when he feels his death near, he immediately sets out by bus to die in Ironside, almost gloating over the funeral costs his journey will save.

So it is that John Fincastle the dreamer returns his family to Shut-In Valley. The strength of his last dream he bequeaths to Ada, of whom Ralph says, "It is queer that a dreamer should be a rock to lean on" (461). Of course Ada had always dreamed of returning when "they had prospered and saved, and all the children in Ironside had grown up" (290). And at last it appears that the Fincastle convictions have prospered and been saved by their sojourn in Queenborough, and Ada and Ralph, if not the children of Ironside, are mature. To Ralph's protest that if they stay they will be only peasants without land, Ada rejoins, "Nothing can make peasants of us but ourselves." Besides, she insists, they have much less to do in restoring the old manse than the first Fincastles did in hewing it out of the wilderness. The stench that permeates the deserted and overgrown garden is an alien smell, one left by camping gypsies or an animal, a stench that care will quickly eradicate. There is always someone in a village who will cultivate a garden; Ralph can sell automobiles in the Valley; Ada can do "a little dressmaking"; Ranny can spend his summers away from school at the manse, and "when he gets on in the world, he may like to have this place for his children." Ada's dream, a dream she has felt from the beginning of her days, is complete, the last detail painted in. She has never been more sure.

She had a sense, more a feeling than a vision, of the dead generations behind her. They had come to life there in the past; they were lending her their fortitude; they were reaching out to her in adversity. This was the heritage they had left. She could lean back on their strength; she could recover that lost certainty of a continuing tradition [461].

In *Vein of Iron* it was the Fincastles alone who continued tradition; even Ironside, certainly the city, seemed hostile to their heritage. With her final novel, *In This Our Life* (1941), Ellen Glasgow returns to the city and its hostility. But although her affirmations in this final work often appear dusty, even battered beyond recognition, she insists that she intended them to stand for the certainty of victory. Victory for what, by what, through what? Presumably victory for tradition, sometimes called plain "civilization" in Miss Glasgow's later writings, by character, through fortitude. "My major theme," she says of the novel, "is the conflict of human beings with human nature, of civilization with biology. In this constant warfare tragedy lies, not in defeat, but in surrender."[9] Character, an individual's moral heritage, alone can defy surrender, and the neglect of this definition of character is responsible for modern chaos in Miss Glasgow's view: "We have refused to acknowledge that the disintegration of character is the beginning, not the end, of defeat, or that this weakening moral fibre is first revealed in the quick or slow decline of human relationships, and in the abrupt conversion to a triumphant materialism."[10]

As *In This Our Life* unfolds, it is soon apparent that however strong the author's intentions at the outset to embrace the "interior life" of a whole community, she has at her disposal not even a family but only a father and daughter who retain any interior life or character worth examining. The old pattern of life in Queenborough is gone; the Southern community is now indistinguishable

[9] *Ibid.*, p. 250.   [10] *Ibid.*, p. 252.

from the urban industrial North. Money can confer position where once, as Miss Glasgow would have it, only position conferred position—and duty and responsibility. Position now means power to the "modern temper," power presumably to find happiness; but that final goal of every man seems to have grown more elusive than ever. "The modern temper, as it pressed round me, in a single community, appeared confused, vacillating, uncertain, and distracted from permanent values."[11]

Old William Fitzroy, "the last great Southern captain of industry," controls the disintegrating Timberlake family upon which the novel focuses. Himself dying of cancer in his "plethoric eighties," William has never been able to buy any happiness more lasting than platinum blondes, but he goes on trying. Indeed, the "sudden avuncular weakness" of his old age for the younger of the Timberlake daughters, his grand-niece Stanley, however seemly and benevolent its appearance, is merely William's last effort to buy the approval of one last shapely blonde. He has long tried to command at least the obligation of all the Timberlakes by providing funds for their luxuries—his niece Lavinia's marriage-long hypochondria and his grand-nieces' pretty clothes.

For Asa Timberlake, Lavinia's husband, will always be a failure by prevailing standards. He belongs as his father did before him to the old way of life, abruptly cut off for the Timberlakes by the "robber barons" who swallowed up the Timberlake Tobacco Factory, destroyed his father, and undermined his values. Now, at fifty-nine, Asa works for the new Standard Tobacco Company and waits for the day when he will be turned away without compensation, a faceless, forgotten number, waits in galling dependence on another robber baron but will not be destroyed, for he has a sustaining dream. Oddly enough the dream depends for its fulfillment on William Fitzroy's money, but then Asa never really expects to realize his dream. He only wishes that a Lavinia made wealthy by William Fitzroy's death will no longer want him around; a not implausible speculation, for he and his wife have nourished a genteel

[11] *Ibid.*, p. 249.

contempt for one another since their marriage. And if Lavinia doesn't want him, he will have slipped his obligation both to her and to Uncle William. Then he can go to Hunter's Fare on the James River and live out his days with Kate, widow of a dead friend and companion on whose farm and in whose woods he has spent his only happy days. Asa's is a love affair with a way of life, and in his dream the hunting dogs figure as importantly as the placid Kate. But although Asa actually visits his earthly paradise on occasional Sundays, he cannot believe that he will be allowed to enter it to stay. Even if Lavinia and Uncle William no longer remain as obligations, there will be responsibilities to his children.

The Timberlake children provide most of the active consternation in the novel. Asa's only son Andrew does nothing positive or negative worth mention, but as a perfect product of modern society, an unquestioning, "well-adjusted" young man, his mobile, materialistic standards fill Asa with sadness, even disgust. Asa's daughters are another matter. His youngest child Stanley, a hollow little egoist with the appearance and demeanor of a sweet Southern innocent, is personified evil loose in a society that has lost the means to resist her.

In an attempt to correct the impressions of "careless" readers who appeared to regard Stanley as the "core" of the novel, Miss Glasgow insisted: "She is not evil; she is insufficient. She is not hard; she is on the contrary, so soft in fibre that she is ruled or swayed by sensation."[12] Miss Glasgow's wish to reassert Stanley's "insufficiency" is justifiable. Stanley is hollow; she is weak with the total weakness of the self-centered who demands and receives pity; even Asa and Roy, his older daughter, pity her, for she is so completely without resources outside her own desires. In truth she is only a latter-day Jenny Archbald in a Queenborough that shelters her without the excuse of a patterned purpose. But there remains a sense in which those careless readers who so irritated Miss Glasgow by finding Stanley vivid and important are also right. Not because, as they may have judged, Stanley has the vividness and force of any

[12] *Ibid.*, p. 259.

single-sided figure in a novel whose main characters are distinguished by many-sided emotional and even intellectual reactions.

Stanley is important because if she herself is not sufficiently
conscious of her motives to be called evil, she nonetheless represents
the evil force with whom Asa and Roy must deal in defending the
pattern of their dreams. And while they do deal with her according
to their pattern, they cannot contain her within or by that pattern.
She is evil not, of course, because like Angelica Blackburn she
perverts the pattern by scrupulously following its form and ignoring its substance, not even because, like Jenny Archbald, she does
not understand that there is a pattern, but because no one with
whom she involves herself except Asa and Roy any longer acknowledge a pattern at all.

She is pretty, clinging, defenseless, and a woman. She appeals; so
she is defended. But no one except Asa, not even Roy, considers
anything beyond Stanley's appeal in protecting her. The question
of the purpose and end of their protection does not extend further
than her appeal. Since this is the case, she represents the evil that
Roy and Asa cannot defeat, indeed, the evil that defeats their dream.
For their victories, real as they are meant to be, are not realized
outside themselves. There can be no lasting internal victory for a
communal dream.

Stanley begins her destruction by running off on the eve of her
own wedding with her sister's husband, continues it by driving him
to suicide, climaxes her havoc by allowing a Negro youth to be
jailed for her crime of running over and killing a small child and
then abandoning her automobile, and ends, after a forced confession
and easy pardon, by evoking only pity and renewed love from the
suitor she originally intended to wed, now promised to her sister.

With Stanley's initial flight and its consequences, Asa awakens to
the disturbed realization that each member of his family is lost in
isolation. To Roy he laments, "The hardest thing for me to believe
is that family feeling no longer means anything, for better or worse.
It has done harm enough, I know, but at least it held things together

when the world rocked. Anyway, the family as a unit now seems to be only another habit that has played out."[13] But Roy, his cherished hope for the future whom he believes "stronger than any of us and finer in many ways," answers shortly that she fails to see her obligation to love an enemy because that enemy chances to be her sister. Besides, Roy is committed to the "new gallantry." Her husband, she believes, is entitled to his freedom at any time, in any way he wants it. It is beneath her to try to hold him; her business is to arrange for a divorce and to go on as though nothing has happened. In this stand Asa knows there is hypocrisy at least as deep and far more dangerous than the attitudes considered proper by the past order to which he belongs. Of course, the code of Asa's father would have demanded righteous killing of the man in the case, and, Asa reflects sardonically, no matter how much he may regret the passing of such quick finality of authority, he is certain that he would lose any physical or moral duel he attempted with Roy's husband. So he can only watch Roy suffer through a modern bout of the "miserable sinner feeling" she is so scornful of in him and his ancestors.

Ellen Glasgow's rendering of Roy's "modern sensibility" in her reaction to her sister's perfidy and her husband's desertion is both penetrating and convincing. It stands along with her treatment of Milly Burden and Ralph McBride as strong evidence that she understood and appreciated the "modern temper," at least as it displayed itself among those who had inherited the "Presbyterian conscience," far better than is indicated by her rather too sweeping condemnations of the modern generation in her autobiography and critical works as a race of soft, sentimental sensation-seekers.

Roy's sensibility is to be sure, however modern, distinctly feminine in that she struggles to achieve a correlation between her intellectual and emotional responses rather than merely insisting that the correlation is there. As she is, after all, a woman, it seems

[13] Ellen Glasgow, *In This Our Life* (New York, 1941), p. 148. Page references to future quotations from this novel in Chap. 7 are given in parentheses or brackets after the quotations.

hardly fair to object as John Edward Hardy does[14]—on the basis of what one suspects is only masculine outrage at the very notion of feminine gallantry—that Roy's reaction is unrealistic, nay, unbelievable, particularly as his purpose, honest enough, however misguided, is to show that Miss Glasgow is not really a "realist."

But Roy's demonstrations of gallantry and misery (a combination impossible only for those who hold that one must enjoy the consequences of upholding one's principles, even as they become ironically a combination intensified in Roy's reactions by her guilt feelings over her misery in holding a gallantry) are surely authentically modern. They link her also to the Virginia Pendletons and Dorinda Oakleys. And her defiant as well as pathetic purchase of a red hat in order to show herself at least that she does not intend to allow her emotions to become martyrs to her principles, like Virginia's and Dorinda's surrenders to temptations to purchase blue dress material, indicates that she, like they and Ellen Glasgow, is determined that some joy must remain despite one's principles.

Roy's frenzied suffering, Asa insists, is not at all peculiar to those "bent on religion," for he never was. "All I felt was that I ought to do the best I could to keep things on the decent side. If you ask me why—well, honestly, I don't know" (148). The decent side, Asa realizes, is really what Roy is dedicated to, however strange its modern forms may seem to him; but even she is too eager to call her goal the search for happiness. And that worries him, for the young seem to justify any action as their right to happiness.

The mistake with them, Asa thought, and with the whole of their extraordinary place in time, was that they had never really broken through the tight shell of their egoism. The world without them existed merely as an extension of the confusion and thwarted longings of the world within. Even Craig, with his easy compassion and his earnest endeavors, was externalizing his own inner disorder. None of them, Asa mused, has a design for living; none of them has even a definition. It isn't that they see themselves in the terms of their age, but that they see their age only in wider terms of

[14] "Ellen Glasgow," *Hopkins Review*, V (Summer, 1952), 22–36.

themselves. Even Roy and Craig, who were superior in so many ways to the youth of his own period, had not yet found an escape from the general modern dilemma. No one among them had solved the intricate problem of how one may take one's pleasure and still have it [338].

Asa Timberlake scores for the "decent side" when he forces Stanley to admit her guilt in the automobile death; and he scores against Roy's indifference, the opposition of the others, and his own melting pity despite himself for a woebegone Stanley returned home for sympathy when her desires are defeated. True enough, his victory is undermined when neither the accused Parry Clay, an intelligent nearly-white Negro boy who aspires to be a lawyer, nor Craig Fleming, who is a lawyer, can control their emotional reactions to the travesty of justice. Parry, crushed and dispirited by a night in jail, loses hope and determination that he can ever break through to realize his ambition. Craig, quivering with solicitude and fear for Stanley, deserts Roy and flees the Timberlake house until concern for Stanley's fate drives him back.

Both Craig Fleming and young Parry, we are made to see, collapse under pressure because neither is equipped to fight for his commitment to fair play when the odds are against him. Their downfalls are intended to be as final as the suicide of Roy's husband, Peter Kingsmill, a talented young surgeon before his involvement with Stanley. Viewed collectively, these three young men represent the waste of aspiring young humanity in a patternless society. And the significance of their shared destruction seems enlarged because that destruction follows from a failure common to all three of them. It is tempting to point to Parry Clay's defeat as uniquely pitiable, following as it does from the now classic dilemma of one caught between two worlds dramatically colored black and white. But Craig and Peter, like Parry, are defeated by being caught between two worlds, and the color of the separate worlds is not the quality that is really significant for any of them. What is important is their failure to find emotional resources in their new society that might sustain them. These three young men are the reigning "intellectuals" of the novel, and, as intellectuals, most fully committed to the new society and cut off from the old. But Ellen Glasgow is not an intellectual; neither are Asa and Roy. And for Miss Glasgow, Asa, and Roy, Matthew Arnold's lament that he is a wanderer between a dead world and a world powerless to be born is not the last word to be said for the human condition, despite its appropriateness for Parry, Craig, and Peter, despite the rather too forced echoes of Arnold's mood she occasionally imposes on Asa's and Roy's verbal responses. In fact the final stand of Asa and Roy Timberlake is intended to answer rather than merely to echo Arnold's question from "Obermann Once More" that appears as the epigraph of the novel:

> Your creeds are dead, your rites are dead,
> Your social order too!
> Where tarries he, the Power who said:
> *See I make all things new?*

The Power that Ellen Glasgow has in mind is a very human power lying within the reach of all Asas and Roys; she shows them reaching for and grasping that power, if not quite making all things new.

Roy Timberlake chooses to rebel at Craig's desertion, but her defiant denunciation of the "rotten mess" that is life is at first so negative, so aimless that she, too, appears to be permanently lost. Running dramatically into the night and the rain, she feels only indifference at the thought of her father's inevitable desperate search for her: "He was, at the moment, only a part of it all. He was a part of the life that had hurt and betrayed her. He belonged to the world she had once loved, and now loved no longer; the world of solid institutions, of firm hypocrisy, of infirm human relationships" (440). Yet characteristically enough in Ellen Glasgow's work, another infirm human relationship restores Roy to her heritage. Through a strange, shadowy encounter with a physically scarred and spiritually maimed young Englishman who personifies "a modern malady, an individual fear of life which was seeking to lose itself in a collective fear of death,"[15] Roy rejects the modern malady for her tradition. Walking homeward in the windless dawn, she feels "as if she had overtaken time, and were walking into a new age and a new world" (461).

Miss Glasgow realized well enough the casual, amorphous quality of Roy's meeting with the young Englishman. Admitting that the scene might well seem to have no part in the book's "organic structure," she justified it simply by saying that she needed it for its "symbolic implications." And indeed she did, though the encounter is one that serves as negative illumination, perhaps chiefly of Ellen Glasgow's own reactions to the form of the "new" quest for certainty in life and literature. For her scarred and frightened young Britisher, dispossessed, disinherited by the past, yet determined to join the future to fight, for once, "what others are fighting," is her interpretation and condemnation of the modern hero of fact and fiction—a decent enough young man committed to following the wrong pattern. Here he is a young man to be pitied for his inverted idealism, and Roy's pity indicates that, for Ellen Glasgow, this young man is made of better stuff than his counterparts among the damned: the modern materialists and the "sensation-seekers" committed to violence for the sake of violence. He is no less surely damned. His design for living can lead only from a private to a communal hell on earth, and such a hell is not only wrong but evil.

The right pattern still possible, Miss Glasgow insists, in the new world and the new age is the one Roy returns to, the pattern of her father, Asa Timberlake. The design of that pattern in this novel is blurred, the pattern itself torn away and useless in spots; Asa himself acknowledges, and surely Roy believes the design often unsatisfactory, unpleasing to the senses, at once pretentious and inadequate. But if it is fading yet still it endures, promising if not victory, a vision which cannot be destroyed. Asa muses that even during

---

[15] *Certain Measure*, p. 256.

Roy's flight only he and Roy, who alone *In This Our Life* upheld both visions and patterns, remain unconquered. "Both had lost; yet both, he felt, would begin again, and would fight on toward an end which they could not see" (465). So when Roy returns, demanding, "Oh, but, Daddy, I want something to hold by! I want something good!"; Asa insists, "You will find what you are looking for. It is there, and you—if not I—will find it" (467).

"That this was a hopeless ending had not occurred to me," Miss Glasgow comments in *A Certain Measure* on Asa's answer as received by at least one critic. "Ironically, I had imagined that the book closed in the stern accents of our unconquerable hope. Was this because Asa's refusal to surrender seemed to me to be one of those rare defeats that are victories, and to restore, paradoxically, the demolished convention of the happy end?"[16]

Ellen Glasgow's sincere belief that her last novel ended on a note of "unconquerable hope" is not to be doubted; she even drafted a sequel treating of "Asa's hard-won freedom" called "Beyond Defeat." Her success in rendering the unconquerable hope is more difficult to establish, but the vision is there in Asa's last reflection:

> Youth, he told himself, has no finality. In seeking and in finding there is not ever an end, nor is there an end in seeking and not finding.
> Looking up at the closed sky, once again he had a vision of Kate and the harvested fields and the broad river. Still ahead, and within sight, but just out of reach, and always a little farther away, fading, but not ever disappearing, was freedom [467].

The burden, as always, is on the affirmation, and if the affirmation is only in the future, the future is very much present. Nor are Asa and Roy and Ellen Glasgow alone in their unconquerable hope. At least one other old man very like Asa Timberlake backs up his stand in fiction. Faulkner's Isaac McCaslin is a more dramatic and, I think, more convincing hero and visionary than Asa; he is made of the same stuff. The negative manner of his affirmation, played out to the accompaniment of a tragicomic parody of his denying, aspiring

[16] *Ibid.*, p. 257.

vision by his descendants is far bolder and broader. Yet his hope and his vision hold up, indeed are restored the more vividly for the greater strength of the paradoxes through which we see them. His silent cry of despair at the end of "Delta Autumn," "No wonder the ruined woods I used to know don't cry for retribution! . . . The people who have destroyed it will accomplish its revenge,"[17] overwhelms. But only for time present. What lasts is a sense of unfinished destinies, the promise of the ideal by which Isaac McCaslin endured. What lasts is Isaac McCaslin, pantsless, impotent, ridiculous on his hunter's cot realizing that Roth Edmund's bastard son is also descended from a colored McCaslin. And Isaac: "*Maybe in a thousand or two thousand years in America*, he thought. *But not now! Not now!*" Not now, but sometime. For the present, Isaac McCaslin, Asa and Roy Timberlake have no certainties. They can only stand firm for the dusty answers of their heritage. The Timberlakes and Ellen Glasgow have dedicated their souls in this our life to the faith that in the future (for there is a future) lies the new, paradoxical, and most Southern happy end.

[17] William Faulkner, *Go Down, Moses* (New York, 1942), p. 364.

THERE NEVER WAS A WAR THAT WAS NOT INWARD. — MARIANNE MOORE

But unlike Isaac McCaslin and her own fictional civilized souls, Ellen Glasgow remained to the end unwilling to trust the future to shape her dream as it saw fit. Herself in her seventies, bedridden, half-paralyzed by a series of heart attacks, she nonetheless completed three drafts of the unpublished novel "Beyond Defeat," the sequel to *In This Our Life*. "Beyond Defeat" is subtitled: "An Epilogue to an Era," and as an epilogue it fully vindicates its title and gives unique substance to the enduring qualities of Ellen Glasgow's American dream. For here in this last work, the characters actually keep house in a small Southern Eden. The Eden of "Beyond Defeat" is no brave new world, and it has only a handful of rather shabby, weary people in it, but it is a real garden, and the people are working hard to cultivate it and to harvest its fruits.

It is, of course, an American Eden. We recognize its national character partly by its unenclosed if isolated location amid the fields of an old plantation near the James River. We know this is an American Eden because the Edenites—Asa Timberlake; his daughter, Roy; her small, illegitimate son, Timothy; Craig Fleming, her husband-to-be; and Kate Oliver, the strong, kindly, shapeless middle-aged housemother are all such unremarkable people. Clearly the essentially dull, comparatively unterrible lives they have led and continue to lead stamp them as genuine native products. For if most of Asa's life has been divided between a miserable, mechanical existence as a tobacco factory laborer and a loveless marriage to a whining, genteel hypochondriac, he has always been decent, conscientious, and uncomplaining about it. If Roy has been deserted by her husband for her sister who drove him to suicide, once abandoned by Craig in favor of that same sister, and awarded an illegitimate child and a lonely, suffering existence in a distant city for one night's rash rebellion against her lot, none of these circumstances has sufficed to allow her to quit. Craig Fleming and Timothy, of course, are yet unformed by life. Craig has behind him only the temporary failures of his youthful idealism as a novice lawyer prepared to indoctrinate the world with justice. He is a neophyte lover unready to discriminate between love and pity, a neophyte would-be-dutiful World War II serviceman rejected for poor eyesight. Timothy has behind him only a little malnutrition and illegitimacy. As for Kate Oliver, she has had "twenty years of joy in life," and so is well endowed for her role as Earth Mother.

The point is that these people have earned their little portion of Eden, not least of all because they never stopped fighting or hoping for it. They are awarded their second chance at their homely second Eden because they work for it as our Horatio Alger heroes who relied on the American equivalent of God's grace descending—a bundle bestowed by a friendly millionaire—never did. And if there is anything "Southern" in spirit darkening the autumnal haze that lingers over the fields of Hunter's Fare, it is the common "heritage of failure" these persistent Utopians share.

I have stressed the past suffering surmounted by the characters in "Beyond Defeat" because the epilogue renders this suffering so undramatically, so much at a distance that we are often in danger of feeling that these people and Ellen Glasgow are just worn out, that they have settled for the sickly escapist reality of a rundown, overworked, undercultivated old plantation outside of Queenborough because this last horizon is level and it is quiet out there. Indeed there is much, perhaps too much, to support this feeling in the novel—in its heavy suggestion of burdens too long borne, its pervading sense of the blankness left by pain past and but dimly recollected, of the small world of Queenborough and the great

world of war thrust aside. It will not do, really, to remind ourselves
that "Beyond Defeat" is, after all, an epilogue, a coda, not especially
if the last word is that the best people have surrendered their bright,
lost visions in favor of the sort of contentment that springs from
resignation to the routines of life miscalled realities. It will not do
because although existential agonies tormenting Southerners remain
doubly unconvincing—generally traitorous, un-American sentiments, ill-fitting any people committed to what improvement comes
next, particularly alien pains for Ellen Glasgow's people whose
sorrows spring from the past, so many lives committed to existing
realities, bereft of visions, are so many deaths.

To be told as we have been told by our more skillful novelists of
manners that life in the best of families is, after all, largely a matter
of taking in the milk bottles and putting out the cat, reversing the
process smoothly, and declaring that we are happy quite often is
irritating enough, especially for its drop of truth. To be told by a
Southern idealist, however old, tired, and ill, that Asa Timberlake's
happiest hours are spent caring for his "good companions," the farm
horses, forces chiefly an uncomfortably farcical comparison with
Gulliver; to be told that Roy Timberlake's deepest concern in life is
to see her child bask in the infant ecstasy of a full stomach and a
sheltering roof reinforces both sadness and fury in finding Ellen
Glasgow's dreams so much debased, so far diminished. No matter
how dusty our certainties become, feeding horses and children must
not suffice for any American reality, let alone any American
dream.

Fortunately, happiness achieved through horses and children is
not what "Beyond Defeat" offers instead of dreams, despite Ellen
Glasgow's perverse pleasure in the reality of such happiness. What
"Beyond Defeat" does offer is something rare in any literature—a
glimpse of lives lived in the light of convincing compromises
between what Miss Glasgow calls "civilization and biology" or
"human beings and human nature." And if the compromises are
convincing chiefly because of what we have learned of the fate of
Ellen Glasgow's "civilized" characters throughout her literary

career, characters who stubbornly maintain their hopes and dreams in spite of biology, then biology, or human nature is at last accorded its full modern strength in "Beyond Defeat."

The Roy Timberlake who comes home again to Queenborough in this novel comes home because she is sick, suffering, penniless; she wants her father to shelter young Timothy while she recovers her health in the Adirondacks; in short, as Miss Glasgow makes us see, she wants to return to the pattern of her past, of her childhood, to heal her wounds. She is only twenty-six, and she has been brave and proud alone too long. She brings back from her futile attempt to escape the Queenborough where all those she loved deserted her expectations, a heightened sense of the sordid loneliness of life in an alien city. Roy has felt and still feels every moment of that bleak existence; not for her the gallant, go-it-alone spirit of Gabriella Carr, the fortuitous traditional miscarriage and new life consciously rejected for old obligations of Dorinda Oakley, the accepting, hopeful determination of Ada Fincastle to build a new world for her whole family. Instead Roy returns from an ugly and banal experience bearing the scars of her defeats and despairs.

What is more, she returns with her son to a house in which her homecoming is greeted with an ugliness and banality even more painful than that provided by the city's indifference to her plight. Her father, the center of her past and her faith in human beings, has finally left her mother to live at Hunter's Fare. Lavinia Timberlake, luxuriating in her invalid's state made comfortable by niggardly control over Uncle William's legacy, is finding her martyr's role as a deserted wife an added pleasure. Roy's reappearance annoys and alarms her, not least of all as a threat to her splendid isolation and her pocketbook. But, of course, most important, Lavinia's Queenborough standards are horrified by the existence of Timothy, Roy's living badge of shame; her concern is all for quickly dispatching Timothy to the most convenient orphan's home to the accompaniment of hastily circulated rumors of Roy's philanthrophy in accidently acquiring the foreign child of war victims. Lavinia intersperses her plans for Timothy's disposal with pleas for quiet and an acid insistence that Asa Timberlake and Kate Oliver are living in sin since no one is ever too old or too fat to create a scandal. Roy's Aunt Charlotte, like Lavinia well provided for by Uncle William's passing and wistfully anxious to preserve undisturbed her new-found comfort in a snug, modern apartment, Florida vacations, and romantic movies, offers Roy money.

Clearly Roy cannot come home again to the Queenborough world of her mother and her aunt, for if Charlotte's refusal to take Timothy because he would curb her small, long-deferred pleasures appears only natural self-indulgence, Lavinia's display of human nature is revealed as pernicious self-absorption. But Ellen Glasgow shows Lavinia's weaknesses at their worst as human weaknesses; it is the strength of the Queenborough standards she clings to, Queenborough "civilization" that destroys her humanity, permits her to view Timothy as an obtrusive object to be got rid of in haste, even as it is the lingering power of these standards over Charlotte that binds her to helpless accord with Lavinia.

Instead, Roy journeys to Hunter's Fare seeking to deliver her child to her father, to the one person from her past whose love has never failed her, no matter how much she feels his heritage has betrayed them both. She goes seeking help in desperation, but she brings with her a new strength and honesty which is met with a comparable new strength and honesty in her father and Craig Fleming. None of them is transformed in Eden. Indeed, their constant quivering, their terrible persisting vulnerability is at once their most endearing and convincing shared response to life. Roy, Craig, and Asa still feel and will continue to feel the pangs their past has provided them—the diminution of their ideals and dreams imposed on them by their double bondage to Queenborough civilization and their own human nature. But they have honestly gone beyond their defeats in the only way open to Ellen Glasgow's particular breed of hardy idealists and dreamers: through iron-willed determination to preserve the best of their tradition by facing the worst.

All three of them achieve their measure of victory by accepting their denials of "civilized" responsibility, their failures in "perfect" love. Over and over Roy explains her escape into the arms of the frightened, scarred Britisher, Timothy's unknown and self-fleeing father, as a wild, pitiful desire to hurt her father, to revenge herself on him, on Craig, on the dead Peter Kingsmill, all those whose love had failed her, and, above all, to shatter her father's pattern of life, the tradition she felt had destroyed her. She's only made a muddle of her life, she feels, failing herself, her father, and Craig, but she has come back to her "roots" with Timothy, still seeking the "taste of living," and beginning of happiness.

But Asa Timberlake, solicitous and tender toward his daughter as always, if startled despite himself by the presence of Timothy, is firm in his resolve not to return to the useless self-sacrifice of life with Lavinia, the pattern of obligations of his past that has meant the denial of his dream. Roy accepts Asa's refusal to give up his life at Hunter's Fare to care for Timothy almost joyfully. The refusal, of course, is deeply significant for both of them as a symbolic final breaking away from their past self-immolation; they are at last prepared to face the present fully aware of their need to place themselves in the center of any pattern they follow in the hope of giving substance to their dreams. Both the real and the symbolic consequences of this last recognition figure importantly in Miss Glasgow's final shaping of her American dream.

As is usual with Miss Glasgow's young men, Craig Fleming remains the weakest of her triumvirate of wounded Edenites. Roy accepts him as her hope for future happiness because she wants love and Craig, and Craig wants her and Timothy. We are never allowed to doubt the sincerity of his love and acceptance of both of them as necessary to his future happiness; nor are we allowed to doubt his feeling of having journeyed through hell to come to his present condition. But Roy is still allowed to reflect that Craig retains his old inspired fanatic gaze, and this characteristic Glasgow irreverence still seems to reflect on the relatively inferior quality of Craig's descent from paradise through hell to his present hopeful purgatory.

Yet the very strength of Craig Fleming's past, present, and future uncertainties serve in this novel to show that there is hope beyond defeat for those idealists in whom the vein of iron is comparatively weak and flawed. Craig's aimless past vacillation between his wishes for a world of perfect justice and his pity for Stanley Timberlake (banished by Miss Glasgow in this work to Hollywood and a rich, old husband) held him paralyzed; his present commitment to service in the armed forces is made to appear a rather dubious means of satisfying the universal urge to serve something larger than oneself, but he has nonetheless worked hard and usefully at Hunter's Fare to gain his limited goal of achieving the health necessary for service and, while he may well be killed or maimed in battle, if he returns it will be to Roy and Timothy, the family he wants. Meanwhile, Kate promises to shelter and provide for Timothy while Roy recovers her health, and Lavinia dies of a heart attack before Roy and Asa can be summoned to her bedside.

With Lavinia's death and Kate's life-force, Ellen Glasgow secures the present possibility of living their separate dreams of happiness beyond defeat for her last trio of dreamers. Lavinia's life personified the evil strength of Queenborough civilization, the life-denying pattern of the Southern tradition Asa, Roy, and Craig had to fight so hard, so long to begin their own lives. Lavinia's death seems a rather too sanguine symbol of the "end of an era," especially since it is the living destructive force of Lavinia both without and within themselves that Ellen Glasgow and her protagonists must continually battle for real victory. Yet even if Lavinia's death is symbolically contrived and convenient, it is the living Lavinia who actually succumbs to defeat in this novel. But not without Kate's help.

As a "life-force," the agent who makes rebirth possible for Miss Glasgow's last "misfits," Kate is the least "real" of all her characters in any of her works. She exists chiefly as a comforting presence, the preserver and restorer of these lives and this land, the guardian of present hopes and the promise of the future in a world stripped of certainties. But most important, as Miss Glasgow's final personification of the iron-veined shaper of Southern dreams, Kate is actually shapeless, strong, hardworking, kind, and capable of providing very practically for Timothy who is, of course, a real Southern infant as totally unconcerned as Kate is with any status—particularly his role as the heart of the future, the unknown. As the best of the old South and the hope of the new, Kate and Timothy are impossibly ordinary, garden-variety Americans. No one in "Beyond Defeat" is more cheering.

CONCLUSION

AND A MAN'S FOES SHALL BE THEY OF HIS OWN HOUSEHOLD. —
MATTHEW 10:36

In his review of Ellen Glasgow's autobiography, *The Woman Within* (1954), which he saw as "above all a story of a schism in a family," Alfred Kazin observed: "We do not get very much of this, which is the real note and the best in Southern writing anymore."[1] This note, which echoes the biblical quotation, might well serve as the keynote to all of Miss Glasgow's works. Her fictional foes, like her heroes, were chosen as representatives of those she knew and loved best in her life, and her ambitions for both foes and heroes were identical: she wanted them to conserve and to realize the Southern dream. Because she upheld the old ideals of honor, responsibility, and initiative through which the American dream, the Northern as well as the Southern version, was to become reality, she has always been considered even by critics as sympathetic as Kazin a writer who did not really revolt against anything. Surely this view of her achievement is one that confuses her steadfast commitment to the American dream and American dreamers with approval of Southern daydreamers of any age, confuses, in short, dedication to a goal with devotion to any means of achieving that goal.

After all, every revolutionary is committed to very similar goals. The American dream merely happens to be a special form of revolutionary goal, a bit more ambitious than most, the form most of us, and certainly Ellen Glasgow, like best. The really significant

[1] Alfred Kazin, "The Lost Rebel," *New Yorker*, XXX (October 30, 1954), 133.

consideration for any revolutionary, of course, is the way to the goal. Ellen Glasgow believed very deeply in the path to glory laid out by the Southern heritage despite its limitations, which she strove throughout her career to expose, despite the mockery made of that heritage by Southern fantasy, which she tried all her life to expunge. Her achievement is worthy at least of the observation that, if it is undeniable that the traditional revolutionary method is supposed to consist of discarding all established paths and building entirely new roads to glory, it may well be that the most arduous revolutionary undertaking is to straighten and broaden the old road to any dream. Allen Tate, in fact, insists on this interpretation of "revolution": "Reaction is the most radical of programs; it aims at cutting away the overgrowth and getting back to the roots. A forward-looking radicalism is a contradiction; it aims at rearranging the foliage."[2]

But despite the apparent identity between Ellen Glasgow's revolutionary technique and purpose and that of Tate and his fellow Agrarians, there remains and must remain a significant difference between her stand and theirs. This difference does not arise because Miss Glasgow refused to identify herself with the group or because she never condemned industrialism as wholeheartedly as did the Agrarians; there is good evidence within and without her novels that by the time they made their initial pronouncements, she was rather thoroughly and permanently disillusioned about the possibilities she had once seen in the South's industrial progress. But she had also by this time permanently rejected the possibility of realizing her vision through political leadership. The Agrarians had not. As Allen Tate remarked of the would-be revolutionary Agrarian: "Since he cannot bore from within, he has left the sole alternative of boring from without. This method is political, active, and, in the nature of the case, violent and revolutionary."[3] And if the Agrarians did not undertake to implement the revolution by running violently for public office, they did begin, in the aftermath of the original criticism of their doctrine, to defend themselves from the charges

[2] Allen Tate, "Remarks on the Southern Religion," in *I'll Take My Stand*, p. 175.   [3] *Ibid.*

that they wouldn't know what to do with a plow or a poor white if they learned to recognize one by extending their vision into a program, complete with a platform supported by recognized sociological and economic doctrines. Ellen Glasgow, on the contrary, from the time she wrote *Barren Ground* insisted on isolated heroes and heroines who did bore from within as her revolutionary leaders; their vision and hers was never to have a public platform through which it might be realized, however inflexible the private standards for realizing that vision.

Indeed, for all her rage for order, Miss Glasgow refused to allow the code she upheld to be implemented through any organized way of life, even that from which the code had been originally derived. Perhaps one should say *especially* that from which the code had been derived, since apart from her realization of the impossibility of returning to the old manner of life in the South, she was most aware of the imperfections of the way of life that had formulated the imperfect and imperfectly realized code her heroes were so constantly revising.

But this refusal to allow the code to be embodied anywhere outside individuals, to be realized in any way apart from quite isolated and disparate individual actions in a changing society makes for an important difficulty in Miss Glasgow's visionary world, namely: how is the code to be transmitted at all, let alone transmitted in any orderly and undistorted fashion? Resolutions of this difficulty have been proffered within and without fiction, though not, I think, answers sufficient for Miss Glasgow's world. As the Canadian Herbert Marshall McLuhan points out in his perceptive essay, "The Southern Quality,"[4] Southern novels such as *The Fathers, So Red the Rose, Night Rider,* and surely he might have included most of Ellen Glasgow's work, rely on much the same faith Yeats expressed when he remarked:

Considering that Mary Battle received our thoughts in sleep, though coarsened or turned to caricature, do not the thoughts of the scholar or hermit, though they speak no word, or something

[4] In *A Southern Vanguard*, ed. Allen Tate (New York, 1947), pp. 100–121.

of their shape and impulse, pass into the general mind? Does not the emotion of some woman of fashion, pass down although she speak no word, to Joan with her Pot, Jill with her Pail, and, it may be, with one knows not what nightmare melancholy to Tom the Fool?[5]

This last is, of course, the faith that illuminates Faulkner's *As I Lay Dying*, though the "passing down" realized in this novel, if still of nightmare quality, is comic rather than melancholy.

This faith is enough for most of us, even for idealists like Faulkner, but it is not really enough for Ellen Glasgow, whose heaven is to exclude no one. Her heaven needs, as I think the unconscious despair that broods over her final novels despite her determination for victory indicates, a sure and all inclusive path to salvation. It is this felt need that gives point to Elizabeth Monroe's observation about Ellen Glasgow's characters: "Their natural virtues rest on supernatural values which they cannot discern, and the fact that many of them retain their courage until the end is indeed remarkable."[6] Only from the viewpoint of Christian orthodoxy, of course, are Miss Glasgow's people unable to discern supernatural values; actually, their difficulty and Miss Glasgow's is that they cannot accept and cannot defend their values in terms of an orthodox religious framework. Their orthodox social framework has long since passed. Even if a heritage can survive indefinitely in memories, in blood, in dreams, the problem of how, in Miss Glasgow's sense, it may prevail in this world remains. Can a private heavenly heritage ever hope for the strength of a public heavenly institution? Both still await the Second Coming.

Meanwhile, we have Ellen Glasgow's novels to support her revolutionary faith in the possibility of broadening an old Southern path to glory into a durable public thoroughfare to heaven. The burden of carrying on her faith and her revolution rests with the people she created. But her people pose difficulties that appear to

[5] *The Autobiography of William Butler Yeats* (New York, 1953), p. 158.
[6] N. Elizabeth Monroe, "Ellen Glasgow: Ironist of Manners," in *Fifty Years of the American Novel: A Christian Appraisal,* ed. Harold C. Gardener, S.J. (New York, 1951), p. 65.

intensify the problem of communicating her dream, and these difficulties go even deeper than her solicitude for friends and foes alike. Richard H. Rovere once said, "It is often impossible to feel *for* Faulkner's characters, but it is almost always possible to feel *with* them."[7] Rather the opposite seems the case with Ellen Glasgow's characters. Admittedly, establishing rapport rather than identity with a novelist's people is the more common experience, and even in most instances the only desirable one. But the distinction here between the reactions to Faulkner's and Ellen Glasgow's characters is valuable because both treat the same subjects from very different angles of vision. Nor is the difference merely a matter of opposing techniques. Certainly it is not to be explained by any divergence in their purposes or commitments. If dedication to the ideal of an earthly paradise is romanticism, then both are romantics. If concentration on the perverse popularity of actual hells and purgatories is realism, then both are realists—though perhaps here Faulkner has the edge with the greater number of real hells.

Rovere complains that when he is reading Faulkner he always believes in the conduct of the characters, indeed feels with those characters, but often when he thinks later about a character, he is quite unable to believe in him, in his history or his motives as Faulkner has presented them. This division of a character against himself, "not only in desire which is intentional and the very meat of Faulkner's work, but in the chemistry of personality,"[8] Rovere concedes as proof of the greatness of the novelist's achievement. I would put the matter more baldly. Once you believe in one of Faulkner's characters, once you feel with him, Faulkner has got you. It is almost as though his characters were symbols of themselves; once you accept the symbol, you must face up to what it stands for; your secondhand protests are useless. With Ellen Glasgow's people this is not so, unfortunately. Her protagonists are all quite acceptably ordinary; always their immediate motives are commonplace and transparent; even when their problems seem a

---

[7] Introduction to William Faulkner's *Light in August* (New York, 1950), p. vi.
[8] *Ibid.*, pp. ix–x.

little odd, a bit silly, rather antiquated, you can as easily sympathize with them as you can with, say, Jane Austen's heroines. But just as you prepare to enjoy a dilemma with a comfortable and sensible solution, the vision explodes. You discover that every one of these protagonists has an exalted sense of mission, a common goal or vision which, however it is battered and punctured, he or she is expected to uphold. And in most cases to satisfy, right then, in the novel. Occasionally you cannot avoid the feeling expressed by Frederick McDowell in *Ellen Glasgow and the Ironic Art of Fiction* that "Miss Glasgow's struggling central characters succeed because they ought to, not because they convincingly master circumstances."[9]

In the same vein, Elizabeth Monroe has commented that Miss Glasgow's characters appear to have very little freedom of choice, that in effect the code decides for them.[10] This is too harsh a judgment, particularly of the later novels, where the old spend their time questioning the code and the young either criticizing or defying it. Nonetheless, one can see why Miss Monroe wants to deny real freedom of choice to Ellen Glasgow's protagonists, for their choice is always limited in two important ways. First of all, though they may reject or revise certain tenets of the prevailing code, they are never free to reject all codes; there must be a design for living that goes beyond the individual concerned to embrace the community. Second, it is the destiny of the strong to implement the code and of the weak to be dominated by it. For the Southern heaven also has its "elect," discernible neither by their piety nor their success but rather, for Ellen Glasgow, composed of those born with veins of iron. The iron-veined must lead the way to heaven, and the weak must follow. In this sense there is no freedom of choice. Or at least there ought to be none.

Perhaps the saddest thing about Ellen Glasgow's last novels is the prevailing sense, despite her efforts, that the weak are getting out of control, that salvation is more and more limited to a handful of iron-veined stalwarts who have lost the ability, and, even more formidable, the desire, to extend their influence over the community. One

[9] McDowell, p. 231.   [10] Monroe, *The Novel and Society*, p. 176.

has the feeling, intensified by Miss Glasgow's protests and denials, that there are too many Snopeses everywhere. Of course the vision that drives Miss Glasgow's iron-veined heroes and heroines, her "civilized" few, is a vision shared by Faulkner's idealists, his innocents, suicides, and intuitive idiots. But it is the vision that drives the Snopeses as well. It is no good blaming the Snopeses for littering and defacing the Southern Eden. But they do seem to be out of hand.

Ellen Glasgow's version of the enduring Southern dream cannot stand this disorder as well as Faulkner's can. This is not merely because Miss Glasgow is a woman who cannot abide a house that is not neat and tidy, although this may be true. Actually she shares with Faulkner the conviction, if not the creative vision, that despite bumbling stupidity, gross mistakes, cruelty and waste, through continual suffering and snail-paced enlightenment, man will prevail. What she cannot endure is the knowledge that without an enfolding design for living, many men will not survive. On this point Faulkner appears to have the new world, at least, on his side. Surely, Miss Glasgow has always had wisdom on hers.

Lamenting what she saw as the mounting surrender of order and design to violence and horror in our life and literature, she once declared:

Not the South alone, but the whole modern world, after its recent bold escape from superstition, is in fact trembling before its own shadow. We are trying to run away from our shadow under the delusion that we are running away from the past. But it is as useless to run away from what we call life. Wherever we go, we still carry life, and that root of life which is the past, in our tribal memories, in our nerves, in our arteries. All we can do is to deny or distort the shifting semblance we know as reality. And so the fantasy of abominations has stolen the proud stilts of the romantics. . . . Although the word Revolution is in the air, the true spirit is wanting. Instead we breathe in a suffocating sense of futility.[11]

Ellen Glasgow dedicated her literary career to preserving from futility the American dream and those who would realize it.

[11] "Heroes and Monsters," pp. 3–4.

BOOKS BY ELLEN GLASGOW

The Descendant. New York: Harper & Brothers, 1897.
Phases of an Inferior Planet. New York: Harper & Brothers, 1898.
The Voice of the People. New York: Doubleday, Page & Co., 1900.
The Battle-Ground. New York: Doubleday, Page & Co., 1902.
The Deliverance. New York: Doubleday, Page & Co., 1904.
The Wheel of Life. New York: Doubleday, Page & Co., 1906.
The Ancient Law. New York: Doubleday, Page & Co., 1908.
The Romance of a Plain Man. New York: The Macmillan Co., 1909.
The Miller of Old Church. Garden City: Doubleday, Page & Co., 1911.
Virginia. Garden City: Doubleday, Page & Co., 1913.
Life and Gabriella. Garden City: Doubleday, Page & Co., 1916.
The Builders. Garden City: Doubleday, Page & Co., 1919.
One Man in His Time. Garden City: Doubleday, Page & Co., 1922.
Barren Ground. Garden City: Doubleday, Page & Co., 1925.
The Romantic Comedians. Garden City: Doubleday, Page & Co., 1926.
They Stooped to Folly. Garden City: Doubleday, Doran & Co., 1929.
The Sheltered Life. Garden City: Doubleday, Doran & Co., 1932.
Vein of Iron. New York: Harcourt, Brace & Co., 1935.
In This Our Life. New York: Harcourt, Brace & Co., 1941.
A Certain Measure. New York: Harcourt, Brace & Co., 1943.
The Woman Within. New York: Harcourt, Brace & Co., 1954.
"Beyond Defeat." Manuscript on deposit at the Alderman Library,
   University of Virginia, Charlottesville.

SELECTED ESSAYS BY ELLEN GLASGOW

"Heroes and Monsters." *Saturday Review of Literature*, XII (May 4,
   1935), 3-4.

"This I Believe." *I Believe: The Personal Philosophies of Certain Eminent Men and Women of Our Time*, ed. Clifton Fadiman. New York, 1938, pp. 91–110.

"What I Believe." *Nation*, CXXXVI (April 12, 1933), 404–8.

REFERENCE WORKS AND CRITICAL MATERIAL

ADAMS, J. DONALD. "The Novels of Ellen Glasgow." New York *Times Book Review* (December 18, 1938), pp. 1, 14.

BAGBY, GEORGE WILLIAM. *The Old Virginia Gentleman and Other Sketches*. New York, 1910.

BECKER, ALLEN W. "Agrarianism as a Theme in Southern Literature: The Period 1865–1925." *Georgia Review*, XI (Summer, 1957), 150–54.

BRICKELL, HERSCHEL. "Miss Glasgow and Mr. Marquand." *Virginia Quarterly Review*, XVII (Summer, 1941), 405–17.

BUCK, PAUL H. *The Road to Reunion: 1865–1900*. Boston, 1937.

CABELL, JAMES BRANCH. *As I Remember It*. New York, 1955.

———. *Let Me Lie*. New York, 1930.

———. *Of Ellen Glasgow: An Inscribed Portrait*. New York, 1938.

———. *Some of Us*. New York, 1930.

CANBY, HENRY SEIDEL. "Ellen Glasgow: Ironic Tragedian." *Saturday Review of Literature*, XVIII (September 10, 1938), 3–4.

CASH, W. J. *The Mind of the South*. Garden City, 1954.

CLARK, EMILY, SARAH HAARDT, and STUART P. SHERMAN. *Critical Essays*. Garden City, 1929.

COUCH, W. T., ed. *Culture in the South*. Chapel Hill, 1934.

COULTER, E. MERTON. *The South during Reconstruction, 1865–1877. A History of the South*, VIII, ed. Wendell Holmes Stephenson and E. Merton Coulter. Baton Rouge, 1947.

COWLEY, MALCOLM. "A Promise Paid." *New Republic*, CXIII (December 10, 1954), 305.

DABNEY, VIRGINIUS. *Liberalism in the South.* Chapel Hill, 1932.

DAVIDSON, DONALD. *Southern Writers in the Modern World.* Atlanta, 1958.

EDEL, LEON. "Miss Glasgow's Private World." *New Republic*, CXXXI (November 15, 1954), 20–21.

EGLEY, WILLIAM. "Bibliography of Ellen Anderson Gholson Glasgow." *Bulletin of Bibliography*, XVII (September-December, 1940), 47–50.

EWING, MAJL. "The Civilized Uses of Irony: Ellen Glasgow." *University of Virginia Studies*, V (1951), 81–91.

FIELD, LOUISE MAUNSELL. *Ellen Glasgow: Novelist of the Old and the New South: An Appreciation.* Garden City, 1923.

FISHWICK, MARSHALL W. *Virginia: A New Look at the Old Dominion.* New York, 1959.

———. *The Virginia Tradition.* Washington, D.C., 1956.

GAINES, FRANCIS PENDLETON. *The Southern Plantation: A Study in the Development and Accuracy of a Tradition.* New York, 1925.

GEISMAR, MAXWELL. *Rebels and Ancestors.* Cambridge, Mass., 1953.

HAARDT, SARA. "Ellen Glasgow and the South." *Bookman*, LXIX (April 1929), 133–39.

HARDY, JOHN EDWARD. "Ellen Glasgow." *Hopkins Review*, V (Summer, 1952), 22–36. Reprinted in *Southern Renascence: The Literature of the Modern South*, ed. Louis D. Rubin, Jr., and Robert D. Jacobs. Baltimore, 1953, 236–50.

HOLMAN, C. HUGH. "Ellen Glasgow and the Southern Literary Tradition." *Virginia in History and Tradition*, ed. R. C. Simonini, Jr. Farmville, Va., 1958, 85–105.

HUBBELL, JAY B. *Virginia Life in Fiction.* Dallas, 1922.

KAZIN, ALFRED. "The Lost Rebel." *New Yorker.* XXX (October 30, 1954), 130–35.

———. *On Native Grounds.* Garden City, 1956.

KRUTCH, JOSEPH WOOD. "A Novelist's Faith." *Nation*, CLVII (October 16, 1943), 442–44.

LIVELY, ROBERT A. *Fiction Fights the Civil War*. Chapel Hill, 1957.

McDOWELL, FREDERICK P. W. "Ellen Glasgow and the Art of the Novel." *Philological Quarterly*, XXX (July 1951), 328–47.

——. *Ellen Glasgow and the Ironic Art of Fiction*. Madison, Wis., 1960.

McILWAINE, SHIELDS. *The Southern Poor-White from Lubberland to Tobacco Road*. Norman, Okla., 1939.

MANN, DORTHEA LAWRENCE. *Ellen Glasgow*. Garden City, 1927.

——. "Ellen Glasgow: Citizen of the World." *Bookman*, LXII (November 1926), 265–71.

MENCKEN, H. L. "A Southern Skeptic." *American Mercury* (August 1933), 504–6.

MIMS, EDWIN. *The Advancing South*. Garden City, 1926.

MOGER, ALLEN WESLEY. *The Rebuilding of the Old Dominion: A Study in Economic, Social, and Political Transition from 1880–1902*. Ann Arbor, 1940.

MONROE, N. ELIZABETH. "Ellen Glasgow: Ironist of Manners." *Fifty Years of the American Novel: A Christian Appraisal*, ed. Harold C. Gardiner, S.J. New York, 1951, 49–68.

——. *The Novel and Society*. Chapel Hill, 1941.

MOORE, VIRGINIA. *Virginia Is a State of Mind*. New York, 1943.

MURDOCK, KENNETH. "Folly and the Ironist." *Virginia Quarterly Review*, V (October 1929), 596–600.

ODUM, HOWARD W. *An American Epoch*. New York, 1930.

OVERTON, GRANT M. "Ellen Glasgow's Arrow." *Bookman*, LXI (May 1952), 291–96.

PAGE, THOMAS NELSON. *The Old Dominion: Her Making and Her Manners*. New York, 1908.

PERCY, WILLIAM ALEXANDER. *Lanterns on the Levee: Recollections of a Planter's Son*. New York, 1941.

PHILLIPS, ULRICH BONNELL. *Life and Labor in the Old South*. Boston, 1929.

QUESENBERY, W. D., JR. "Ellen Glasgow: A Critical Bibliography." *Bulletin of Bibliography*, XXII (May-August and September-December, 1959), 201–6, 230–36.

RANSOM, JOHN CROWE, et al. *I'll Take My Stand: The South and the Agrarian Tradition.* New York, 1951.

ROVERE, RICHARD H. "Introduction." *Light in August*, by William Faulkner. New York, 1950.

ROUSE, H. BLAIR. "Ellen Glasgow in Retrospect." *Emory University Quarterly*, VI (March 1950), 30–40.

——, ed. *Letters of Ellen Glasgow.* New York, 1958.

——. "Time and Place in Southern Fiction." *Hopkins Review*, VI (Fall, 1952), 37–61. Reprinted in *Southern Renascence: The Literature of the Modern South*, ed. Louis D. Rubin, Jr., and Robert D. Jacobs. Baltimore, 1953.

RUBIN, LOUIS D., JR. *No Place on Earth: Ellen Glasgow, James Branch Cabell and Richmond-in-Virginia.* Austin, Tex., 1959.

SAVAGE, HENERY, JR. *Seeds of Time.* New York, 1959.

SHERMAN, STUART P. "Ellen Glasgow: The Fighting Edge of Romance." New York *Herald Tribune Books*, I (April 19, 1925), 1–3. Reprinted in *Critical Woodcuts.* New York, 1926.

SIMKINS, FRANCIS BUTLER. *A History of the South.* New York, 1953.

TATE, ALLEN. *Man of Letters in the Modern World.* New York, 1955.

——, ed. *A Southern Vanguard.* New York, 1947.

TAYLOR, WILLIAM R. *Cavalier and Yankee: The Origins of the Old South as a Cultural Ideal.* New York, 1961.

THOMPSON, HOLLAND. *The New South.* New Haven, Conn., 1920.

WARREN, ROBERT PENN. *The Legacy of the Civil War.* New York, 1961.

WERTENBAKER, THOMAS JEFFERSON. *Patrician and Plebeian in Virginia.* Charlottesville, Va., 1910.

——. *The Planters of Colonial Virginia.* Princeton, N.J., 1922.

WILSON, JAMES SOUTHALL. "Ellen Glasgow: Ironic Idealist." *Virginia Quarterly Review*, XV (Winter, 1939), 121–26.

——. "Ellen Glasgow: 1941." *Virginia Quarterly Review*, XVII (Spring, 1941), 317–20.

——. "Ellen Glasgow's Novels." *Virginia Quarterly Review*, IX (October 1933), 595–600.

WOODWARD, C. VANN. *The Burden of Southern History*. Baton Rouge, 1960.

——. *Origins of the New South, 1877–1913. A History of the South*, IX, ed. Wendell Holmes Stephenson and E. Merton Coulter. Baton Rouge, 1951.

WPA IN VIRGINIA. *Virginia, A Guide to the Old Dominion*. New York 1940.

WRIGHT, LOUIS B. *The First Gentlemen of Virginia: Intellectual Qualities of the Early Colonial Ruling Class*. San Marino, Calif., 1940.

YOUNG, STARK. "Beautiful Apologia." *New Republic*, CIX (October 25, 1943), 588–91.

——. "Deep South Notes. VI: At Sheltered Valley." *New Republic*, LXXII (September 7, 1932), 100–102.

——. "Ellen Glasgow's New Book." *New Republic*, LXXXIV (September 11, 1935), 133.

——. *The Pavilion*. New York, 1951.

——. "Prefaces to Distinction." *New Republic*, LXXV (June 7, 1933), 101–2.

ELLEN GLASGOW'S AMERICAN DREAM

was composed, printed, and bound by
Kingsport Press, Inc., Kingsport, Tennessee.
The paper is Warren's Olde Style,
and the type is Janson.
Design is by Edward Foss.